KATE ROBERTS

THE ♥ OF FICTION

Reading for Character, Theme & Craft

Routledge
Taylor & Francis Group
NEW YORK AND LONDON
A Stenhouse Book

Designed cover image: Monica Ann Cohen

Published 2026
by Routledge
605 Third Avenue, New York, NY 10158

and by Routledge
4 Park Square, Milton Park, Abingdon, Oxon, OX14 4RN

Routledge is an imprint of the Taylor & Francis Group, an informa business

First published 2024 by Kate Roberts

ISBN: 9781041156888 (pbk)
ISBN: 9781003680741 (ebk)

DOI: 10.4324/9781003680741

Typeset in Sabon LT Pro
by KnowledgeWorks Global Ltd.

This book is dedicated to my sons' teachers. Your names are monuments in my heart.

Contents

Acknowledgments

This book has been a journey. Like every journey I've ever been on, internal or external, it has had both rough seas that had me clutching at the floorboards and miraculous breaks of light through the clouds.

The beams of light have always been other people...

...like the teachers I get to work with. I work in a lot of schools and have for decades now. One constant among these visits is the work that teachers do to help students learn, thrive, and engage, often among a sea of confusing change, conflicting ideas, and lack of resources. Every time I teach, I am humbled by the layers of consideration, the in-the-moment decisions, the tightrope walk between too much control and too much chaos, and how every decision you make tips the scale one way or the other. I honor the work that this profession demands of you, and I hope this book helps. Thank you. Particularly for this project, thank you to Melissa Bader, Kristen Hera, Derek Gould, Kathryn Gehrsitz, and Theresa Waters (who, incidentally, has had student work in every book I've written, a streak I hope to continue).

...like the students I encounter every day in schools. To this day I feel nervous before every lesson I teach. Standing in front of a room of students has always felt like the highest-stakes moments of my professional life. The work we do has always been about you—young people. The community we teach. The lives we affect, one way or another. Thank you to the students who took time and energy and ink and pen to try out these lessons and offer up their authentic in-the-moment work with us, so that we can see what students do as they approximate and grow under our care. Annika Morse, Miles Gruber, and Shea Paradis took on the herculean task of trying on each lesson in this book so we could publish what a sequence of work might look like. Thank you.

...like the people I've had the honor to work with on my past books. Tobey Antao, Brett Whitmarsh, Kim Cahill, the teams I had the pleasure of collaborating with at Heinemann, all offered their brilliance and labor to my random ideas and made books out of them. Amazing. And when life-lifed and the age of the pivot began, Monica Cohen, Holly Kim Price, and Lynne Costa deus ex-machinated the whole situation and saved the life of this book with their insights and talents. I'll never forget it. Thank you so much.

...like the educators who raised me, showed me that kids could read and write about their lives and interests, and that opening up to independence and choice and true coaching allows students to flourish in their humanity as they improve their skills. Time will show the deep value along with the weak spots of this work. It's been a beautiful process of discovery, and one I hope to continue for the rest of my career. I will never not be grateful for the experience I've had.

...like the people who keep showing up in my life. There is a reinvention in middle age offered to you, I think, if you're lucky. When Terry Thompson and I first met, there was a feeling that we would work together someday. How lovely that we both let that fact air out over time and life's tidal movements until the opportunity washed up on our shores. I am so happy to be working with you, to know you. And much has been written about friendship, and how the strength of your friendships in many ways determines the quality of your life as you age. I can tell the story of my life through the lens of my friendships, the ones that deepened me, carried me, ones I thought would last forever that didn't, ones that have stood strong through the rough seas. These last few years have offered newer friendships along with the old, blessed standbys: Amy, I could not have made it without you. Nawal, it has been a source of strength and support to be in this career (and life) parallel to each other. The Five Families: hopefully we won't need to enact our apocalyptic roles, but if we do, I'm glad it's you by our side. Abigail, Kate, Rachael, The Bowmans—you all bring light and insight and support to my days.

...and like my family. Maggie. Bo. Benji. There was a moment recently while traveling where the four of us faced a problem—nothing big, but there was struggle, and decisions to be made, urgently. Suddenly, each one of us clicked into our strengths, we intuitively understood each other and the situation, and we navigated the issue together wordlessly. It was the coolest feeling, and one of the best examples of what I love about family I can think of. Thank the universe for you people. I love you, always and forever.

Introduction

Coaching Students into More Powerful Independent Reading

Our students can get better at reading. More specifically, all students can get better at thinking about the texts they read. Even more precisely, students can get better at analyzing texts *on their own* so they can come to the conversation or the page or the activity with rich ideas ready to go.

Maybe this is obvious to you. As an idea, it does not seem that original, to be sure. Yet when I look at some of my classroom practices, and the classroom practices of others, it seems as though we have not quite, as a profession, figured out how to make this idea a systematized reality, particularly in middle and high school.

We are trying. We have good lessons and units created through backward design and standards we reach for and measurements we take. We have the knowledge and practice of building engagement and power and stamina for reading through choice. We have our own performance as teachers and the ways we work to connect to students and inspire our classes. We have equity practices that must take root in our schools to make sure that every student is heard, included, valued. We educators have lots of knowledge.

But when it comes to the practice of reading the books they've chosen or been assigned, often students wait to be told what to do—they don't feel ownership over the work and, as a result, don't find the work engaging, meaningful, or productive. We find students leaving our classes feeling like they can't—and don't want to—do the work we are inviting them to do, and this identity often sticks across the years for many students.

It doesn't have to be this way. *Kids can get better at reading books independently*. We can help all of our students understand and embrace what it means to be powerful readers, and we can help all of our students understand why it matters to be able to do so. Not just the kids who are already good at reading. Not just the kids in tracked honors classes. All kids.

Because kids want to be better at reading. Sure, there are students who don't like reading very much, and certainly many students would deny such a desire for improvement, but in my teaching experience I have never encountered a kid who didn't want to feel OK about the work they do. But they need a certain kind of help—a kind of help that supports their practice across texts, a help that fosters independence in all reading rather than mastery of only a single text.

Imagine for a moment that you ask your class, near the beginning of a fiction book they are reading, to tell you some of the themes that are being developed so far. I have asked this question infinite times to young people who have had trouble answering it on their own. No matter how many times they have been taught what theme is, how to identify themes, and what to do with them, there is often a baffled look.

The problem is that students have trouble performing or applying essential reading skills without plenty of reminders and support.

Wait, scratch that.

The kids are never the problem. They are the whole point.

The *real* problem is that I, *as the teacher, don't know what to do when my students have trouble performing or applying the essential reading skills that feed discussion, writing, reading, and engagement.*

Here is a typical way I used to respond when students had trouble with theme:

> **Me:** What themes are being developed in this book so far?
>
> **Them:** [*Blank stare*]
>
> **Me:** Let me rephrase that. What is this book really about?
>
> **Them:** Oh, it's about a guy who loves someone he shouldn't.
>
> **Me:** [*Leaning in earnestly*] Yes, but what is it *really* about?
>
> **Them:** [*Looking for an escape*] Uh . . .
>
> **Me:** Is it about love?
>
> **Them:** Yeah, sure, that's it.

In exchanges like this one, I do all of the work, and the student leaves feeling like what I am asking is vague and confusing and that somehow they didn't meet the mark. But it is not the kid who fails in these situations: they have told me exactly what they need—a way to figure out an emerging theme—and I have not given it to them. When students can't answer the question or perform the skill, they are telling us that they need something to help them do the work on their own.

That something is explicit, actionable, repeated practice and instruction in the skills of analyzing, inferring, and interpreting texts. That something might feel, in a snapshot, more like this:

> **Me:** We have been working on interpreting themes for a while now. How's that work going?
>
> **Them:** OK, I guess.
>
> **Me:** So, what themes are you finding so far?
>
> **Them:** [*Blank stare*]
>
> **Me:** Remember that one way to find a theme is to name a problem the character is facing and then put it in a word.
>
> **Them:** Oh, yeah. Well, there's a guy who loves someone he shouldn't.

Me: Classic. So, what word or phrase captures this problem?

Them: Like, *love*?

Me: Yes! That's it. What else?

Them: Um. Being a rebel? Or, like, doing what you are told?

Me: Fantastic. You got this. Your job is to keep looking for these themes that are emerging at the start of the book. Try to find . . . four or five? I'll check in with you and a few others who are doing the same work in a couple days. Nice job.

There are small but meaningful differences here. First, I know what to say when a student struggles. I have a strategy they can use to take a step forward. Also, there is a plan in place to work on the skill for a period of time—I indicate that we have been working on this and set up work for the future so that we can get some traction. In conversations like this one, students walk away feeling more like they have a foothold in the skill they need to work on. There is opportunity for growth.

All students need this opportunity. All students need to know that there is enough support there for them to grow and that our classrooms will be set up in ways that encourage, scaffold, and urge that movement.

Students want this opportunity. They want to feel confident and capable and comfortable in our classes. They want to be in on the conversation. They want to feel as though they have a place at the table in our classrooms.

In schools across the country there is great work being done teaching reading skills like inferring characterization, interpreting themes, and analyzing craft, and this great work takes many forms, but it is not sticking to kids as much as we would like. We are not creating, en masse, groups of students who are more powerful and independent in these (and other) core reading skills. We are not creating, en masse, groups of students who are more engaged and interested in reading when they leave us.

There's no single reason for this. Partly, it is because as readers are told to only read books that are quite challenging, their skill abilities naturally go down and they need supportive coaching. Partly, it is because we haven't quite figured out how to better transfer learning from year to year, or book to book. This means that sometimes it feels like we are starting from scratch when we discuss ideas or skills in books, and it means that students often come to us waiting to be told what to do. Partly, it is because—in many districts—the identity of teaching shifts dramatically from skills to content, and then we find ourselves not actually knowing how to coach into skills when students struggle, so they continue to struggle. Partly, it is because when students do learn reading skills explicitly, we do not ask them to work in ways that create automaticity. We've all seen what it looks like when kids don't own their reading: students who are not quite sure how to go about unpacking a scene they are reading or teenagers waiting for the teacher to tell them exactly what to think about on a given page. At the same time, we've all heard muttering in the faculty lounge from colleagues who are frustrated with what their kids "can't do." All of these frustrations come partly from the same point: despite our best efforts, many kids have not been given the tools to do the work better—independently, without our constant guidance and instruction.

Whatever you believe about teaching middle and high school readers, one point of the work is that the kids get fundamentally and demonstrably better at reading things without us. For our teaching to truly impact students, *all* students, we need to collectively understand how to teach some core reading skills with depth and breadth, regardless of the text, the student, or the teacher.

How This Book Works

This book is an examination of three widely taught skills in middle and high school—thinking about (inferring) character, interpreting themes, and analyzing craft (or literary technique or voice or style, whichever term your community uses). It offers some answers to this question: How can we help coach our students toward more powerful, independent practice when they read?

One answer, and the main focus of this book, is to have at the ready strategies for each of these skills. Strategies are the actionable, replicable ways that we can repeatedly practice a skill or habit. I offer strategies that are organized by when readers most commonly use them: before they begin reading, as they begin the book, when they're in the middle of the book, and when they're at the end. While you should not use this structure strictly, as many of the strategies can work across a text, for many of the skills we use when we read, much of the work is about knowing where we are in the book and which strategy will get us the most out of our reading.

There are probably more strategies here than you would teach your whole class. Reserve some for individual conferences and small group work. You might love some of these strategies, but you will most likely think of replacements. That's great. This book is not *the* answer to teaching these skills. It is an iteration of what it might feel like to improve a skill by using strategies repeatedly over time and texts.

So, for three reading skills—inferring characterization, interpreting themes, and analyzing craft—I lay out strategies we can coach students to practice across time and texts. Each strategy has two parts: In "Thinking About the Strategy" I reflect on how this strategy works in text and life, and in "Teaching the Strategy" I share a sample lesson for you to try, improve on, or thoughtfully reject in service of another.

Thinking About the Stategy

To be honest, I've rarely seen a kid get excited when told, "One way to interpret themes is to analyze the critical scenes for an issue, unpacking the subtle ideas that are building toward the end." The language of reading strategies doesn't often connect, doesn't help people to feel their power, doesn't help kids understand why we are teaching this stuff. It's the human connection that matters.

Often, we hope students feel connected to texts: *I love this book, so I want to know more about how to read this book*. But there is another way we can connect to the work of reading—by knowing that what we do when we read is also what we do in our very human lives. The strategies included here are not just good ones to employ when you are trying to get a B in my class. They are ways of seeing—ways of living—that can shift and enrich your life.

To this end, for each strategy, I attempt to model the kinds of conversations I think we should be having with kids about the reading work we do. Real conversations around what it means to know someone, what we learn in our lives, how we express ourselves to each other. Each reflection tries to answer this question: Why does reading fiction matter? The strategies here are not things that only readers do. They are also ways we all can think about and see our life. Without a sense of that connection, that reason, that passion, our strategy teaching can become dry and clinical.

Also threaded throughout these reflections are models that show how I used these strategies with two novels I was reading at the time: *Aristotle and Dante Discover the Secrets of the Universe*, by Benjamin Alire Sáenz, and *The Namesake*, by Jhumpa Lahiri. I chose these books because they capture the main target ages for the strategies I am teaching here: middle and high school aged kids. I also chose

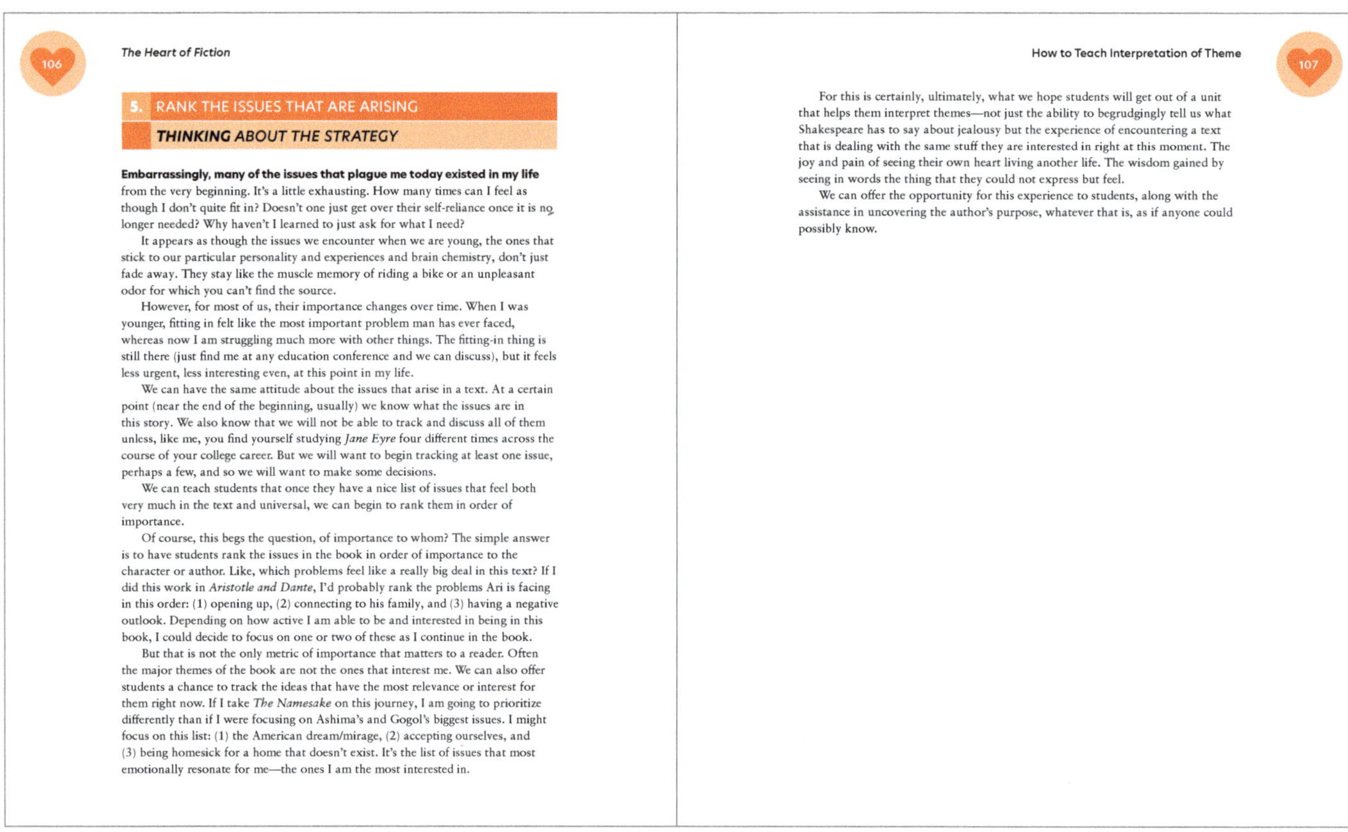

106 *The Heart of Fiction*

5. RANK THE ISSUES THAT ARE ARISING

***THINKING** ABOUT THE STRATEGY*

Embarrassingly, many of the issues that plague me today existed in my life from the very beginning. It's a little exhausting. How many times can I feel as though I don't quite fit in? Doesn't one just get over their self-reliance once it is no longer needed? Why haven't I learned to just ask for what I need?

It appears as though the issues we encounter when we are young, the ones that stick to our particular personality and experiences and brain chemistry, don't just fade away. They stay like the muscle memory of riding a bike or an unpleasant odor for which you can't find the source.

However, for most of us, their importance changes over time. When I was younger, fitting in felt like the most important problem man has ever faced, whereas now I am struggling much more with other things. The fitting-in thing is still there (just find me at any education conference and we can discuss), but it feels less urgent, less interesting even, at this point in my life.

We can have the same attitude about the issues that arise in a text. At a certain point (near the end of the beginning, usually) we know what the issues are in this story. We also know that we will not be able to track and discuss all of them unless, like me, you find yourself studying *Jane Eyre* four different times across the course of your college career. But we will want to begin tracking at least one issue, perhaps a few, and so we will want to make some decisions.

We can teach students that once they have a nice list of issues that feel both very much in the text and universal, we can begin to rank them in order of importance.

Of course, this begs the question, of importance to whom? The simple answer is to have students rank the issues in the book in order of importance to the character or author. Like, which problems feel like a really big deal in this text? If I did this work in *Aristotle and Dante*, I'd probably rank the problems Ari is facing in this order: (1) opening up, (2) connecting to his family, and (3) having a negative outlook. Depending on how active I am able to be and interested in being in this book, I could decide to focus on one or two of these as I continue in the book.

But that is not the only metric of importance that matters to a reader. Often the major themes of the book are not the ones that interest me. We can also offer students a chance to track the ideas that have the most relevance or interest for them right now. If I take *The Namesake* on this journey, I am going to prioritize differently than if I were focusing on Ashima's and Gogol's biggest issues. I might focus on this list: (1) the American dream/mirage, (2) accepting ourselves, and (3) being homesick for a home that doesn't exist. It's the list of issues that most emotionally resonate for me—the ones I am the most interested in.

How to Teach Interpretation of Theme 107

For this is certainly, ultimately, what we hope students will get out of a unit that helps them interpret themes—not just the ability to begrudgingly tell us what Shakespeare has to say about jealousy but the experience of encountering a text that is dealing with the same stuff they are interested in right at this moment. The joy and pain of seeing their own heart living another life. The wisdom gained by seeing in words the thing that they could not express but feel.

We can offer the opportunity for this experience to students, along with the assistance in uncovering the author's purpose, whatever that is, as if anyone could possibly know.

FIGURE I.1: *Sample Essay*

them because I was reading both of these books for the first time, and wanted to model a somewhat authentic reading experience with these lessons, as our students will. If you have not read these novels, I believe the examples will still make sense, however I also can't recommend these titles enough, so if you are looking for the next text for your book club . . . .

It's my hope that these essays also help us remember the power in teaching young people who are developing their ideas about the world. Sure, in the books they read, but also, more importantly, in the lives they lead. Take these essays as you will. I loved writing them, and I hope you will love coming up with your own connections to share with your students.

Teaching the Strategy

After each reflection is a step-by-step outline for teaching the lesson and samples of student work. This is offered as *one* way things could go in a classroom—since there is no best way. I have endless empathy for the workload of teaching. Countless times I found myself wanting to adopt something I heard at a PD session only to realize that I just didn't have time to revise and rework and create a new lesson plan. These strategies are ways I have found success; I bet you can make them better.

You can use this book as a way to shape a unit and plan curriculum or as a grab-and-go resource when you are in need of a good lesson for an important skill. The former is, I think, more powerful for students. But I also remember well the feeling of being overwhelmed and not sure what to teach next period, and I hope this book helps you in those situations as well.

I hope these strategies will help you, but without the work outlined in the rest of this chapter they will not, in my opinion, do enough. Strategies don't teach students. They are important ingredients, but teaching is much more layered. This is why, as Donalyn Miller reminds us, "Pinterest is not pedagogy" (2015, 101). If our goal is growth for all of our students, then we must work to create conditions that support and encourage all students to grow as readers.

In addition, each lesson has one or two graphic organizers or visual guides for that lesson. They are online resources you can download from kateandmaggie.com/the-heart-of-fiction-resources. You will see—from the student work included and my own models—that I tend not to use them. I prefer to have students develop reading notebooks where they have more agency in how their notes look. At the same time, as discussed earlier, I know well the need for materials you can grab and use, and so I offer them to you.

Scan this code for online resources.

How Do We Help All Students Grow as Readers?

Before we think about specific lessons or strategies to help kids meaningfully and effectively practice reading, let's take a wider view. Strategies alone will not teach students to become more independent readers. When I first started teaching, I remember how attached I was to the idea that if only I had the right lesson, the best handout, the most clearly laid out assignment, things would go well. This attachment made it difficult for me to focus on professional development that didn't help me get through the week. I craved concrete things to do, not big ideas to consider.

The truth is that I needed both. I did need strategies and lessons to help me keep the class focused and working on something good while I figured out the bigger issues. But I also desperately needed to focus on the ideas, structures, and philosophies that would govern my classroom. So, while this book mostly offers the strategies that might help us all become more proficient and engaged with the teaching of reading in middle and high school, let's take a moment and think about what conditions we may need to set up in our teaching for this concrete work to stick and for our students to truly grow into themselves as readers.

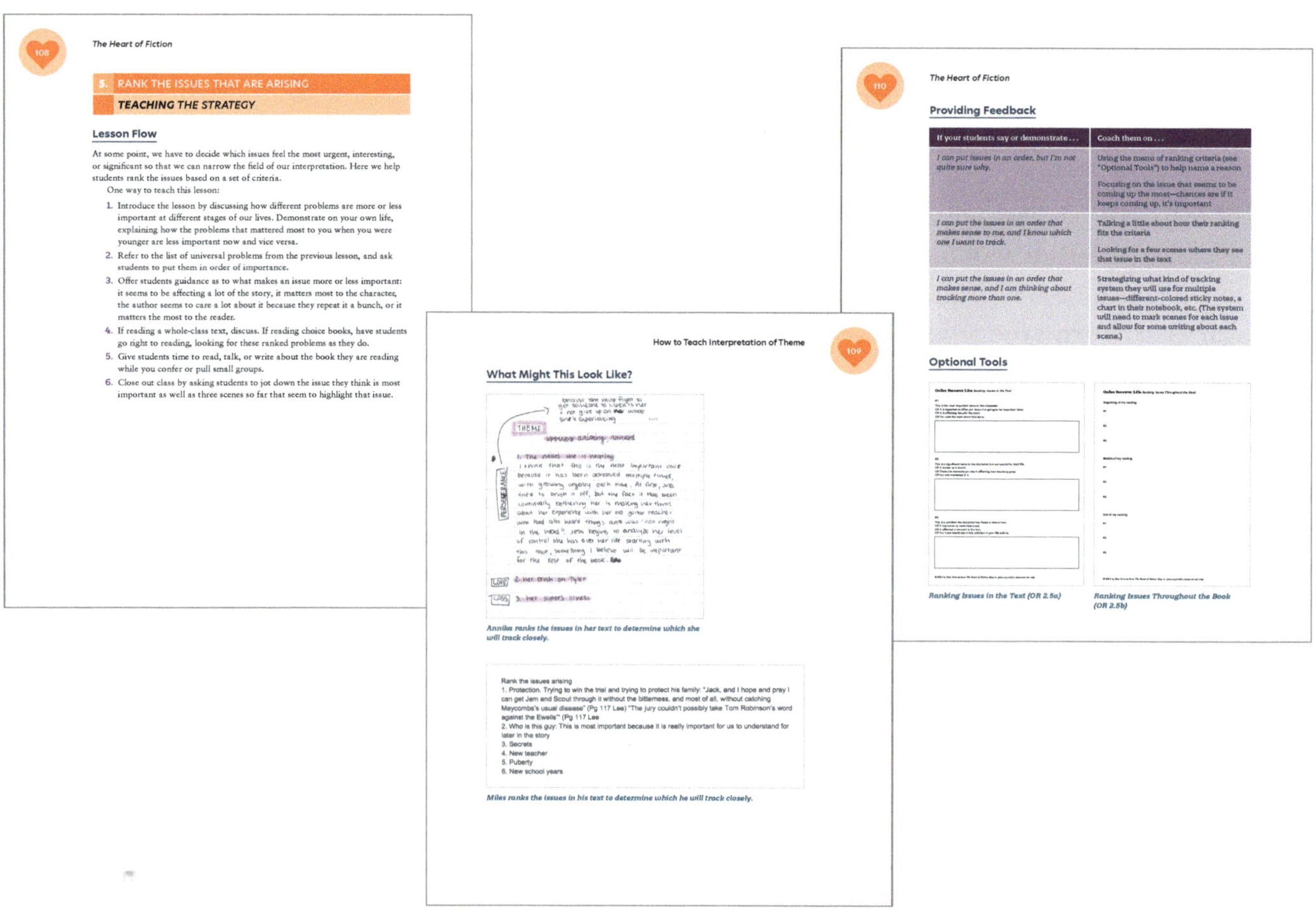

FIGURE I.2: *Sample Lesson*

First Condition for Growth: *Prioritize Focus and Depth in Your Units*

There can be a jerky quality to the way we teach skills. My own classes felt this way sometimes. One day we would look at internal conflict in characters. The next day we would pivot to thinking about motifs and symbolism. The following day, theme. Perhaps this is an exaggeration; maybe you spend a couple of days on each reading skill. But the result is the same: students don't get better at analyzing text.

Instead, could we look at our curriculum and for each unit ask, "Out of all of this good stuff, what do I want to teach versus what I want to cover?" This distinction becomes central to our work as teachers, and the answer of course depends on our kids. To begin this process, list out all of the reading skills that a unit suggests students should master, and then really look at your students, and ask yourself, "Which of these skills do I think they need to master *first?*"

Perhaps you can answer that question because you have been listening to your students deeply (something that many remind us is critical in order for learning to thrive). Perhaps you will answer that question based on a vertical translation of your district curriculum. Perhaps you will assess how well your students know how to perform these skills to direct your teaching. However you get there, it's important that our units develop a clear and attainable goal. If they don't, our students come into our classrooms unsure of what is about to happen, of what they will be asked to do, and of the direction the class is taking, and this, by definition, creates a relationship of dependence. The students need to wait for the teacher to tell them what to do.

Instead, when we focus on a skill as one of the pillars of a unit, and we learn to teach that skill deeply, our students develop an understanding of what their job is in the class. They understand what they will be expected to work on and learn and how they will be assessed. They develop a confidence in participating in class because they have a foothold in the content.

A while back, I worked with teachers to revise the curriculum to make sure we had solid foundations in place. We took their *Romeo and Juliet* unit first. We stacked binders and professional texts on the tables, and we opened up all of the various curricular documents. It was a lot of material. Every time there was a lesson that most teachers used we jotted it down. Then we tried to name the skill suggested. Our list wound up looking like the one in Figure I.3.

We paused and reviewed the list. There was lots of good and necessary stuff there. But we had to be honest with ourselves: Was this a list of the skills we expected every kid to get fundamentally better at? Or was it simply a list of stuff we *did*? Both have their merits, but

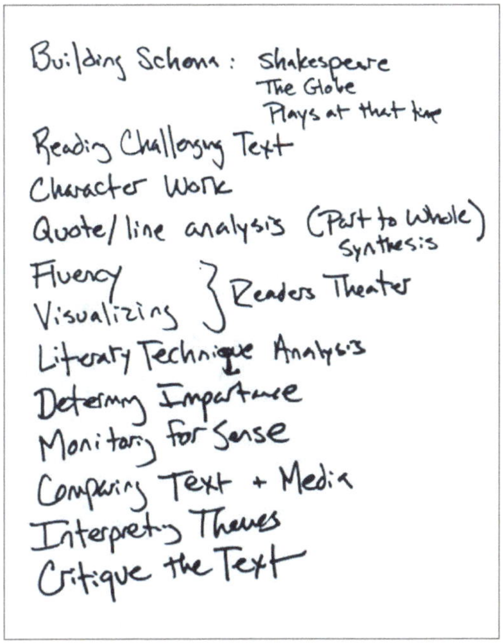

FIGURE I.3: *Listing skills from a unit*

we create confusion when we lump them together. Often, we conflate all of the things we do with the things we teach deeply.

So, we create these long lists of skills that require real work to master, and we put them out into the world as if to say the kids will have mastered all these things. Then we spend a day or two on each skill, and we put up elaborate hoops for students to jump through that explicitly ask them to do the work of the day. And then we move on. The process leaves us exhausted and frustrated: planning for this level of complexity is draining, and trying to coax our students through the intricate unit plans we've created is often more so. Worse, students often have not learned to do this work independently, and they have not improved in their abilities in the thing itself, yet the unit presents the list of skills as if we have taught it.

Instead, we can choose what we will focus on deeply. In our *Romeo and Juliet* unit, we chose to focus on reading challenging texts and making character inferences. These were the skills that we felt the students needed growth in *first* (see Figure I.4).

For this unit, the goal would be that the students in this class get fundamentally better at reading texts that felt challenging and at analyzing the characters in a text. Not just in *Romeo and Juliet*, but every time they read from now on. We would assess their needs around these skills multiple times, and we would differentiate instruction to make sure that every kid got what they needed. And we would put our teaching souls into this work, being sure to try different angles, strategies, and styles for teaching these skills so that every kid is invited into the

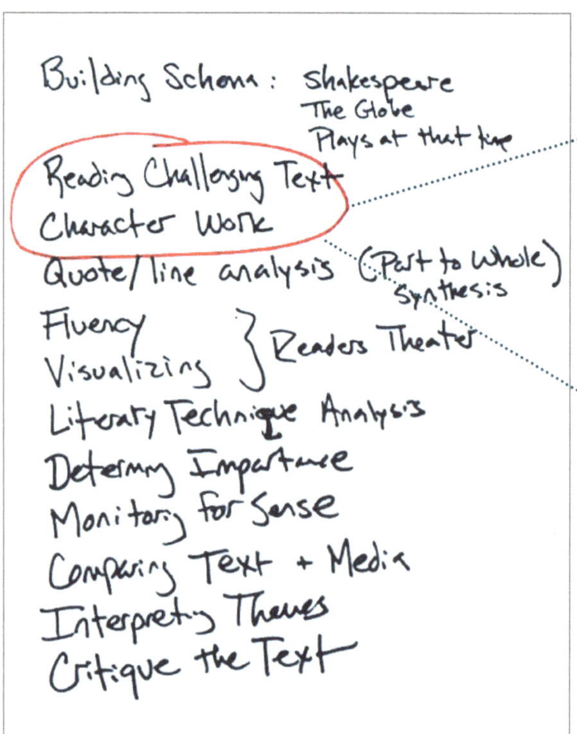

FIGURE I.4: *Choosing a skills focus for a unit*

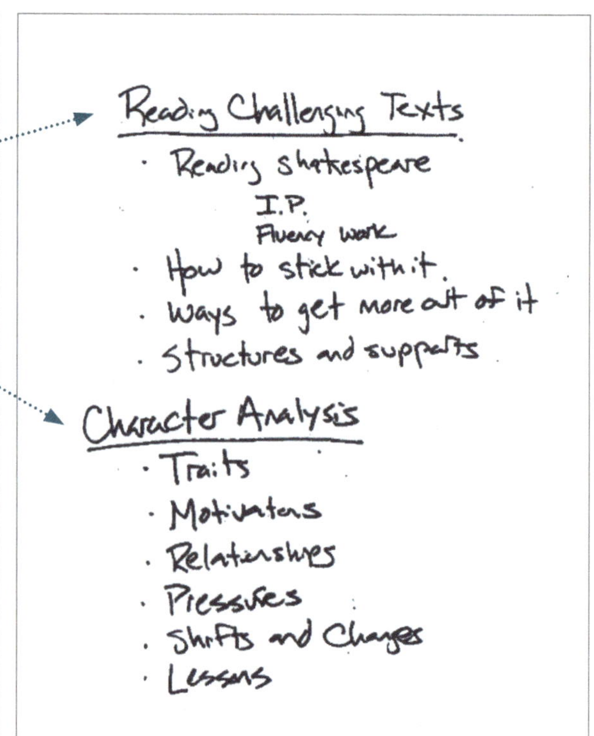

FIGURE I.5: *Identifying strategies to support the unit's skills*

club. It is not that we wouldn't discuss the themes in this text, but we would not address themes deeply and repeatedly—that would be a focus skill for another unit.

After all, each of these skills takes time and practice to master. Our units then turn from long lists of disparate skills to a focused study of a few (see Figure I.5).

By focusing our units, we allow our students a grip so that they may begin to climb more on their own. Without such a focus, we find many students grabbing at air, scrambling to perform each skill well enough to cling to the wall before we move on to the next thing we ask them to do. Students want to do well; they want to feel as though they are successful, on the right track. They want to see approval in the eyes of the adults around them. When we focus in and get the fundamentals down, we help students feel more like they are on a team and less like they are lost in the woods.

Second Condition for Growth: *Practice the Skills Yourself*

The next thing we need to do as we prepare to teach and coach kids is make sure we are pretty good at performing these skills ourselves. This isn't so that we can wow students with our aptitude for text analysis; it's so that we recall what it feels like to apply these skills as we read a variety of texts *the first time*. How well are we able to analyze characters in a text we haven't read before? What does it look like for us when we try to think about what themes are being developed in the first few chapters of a fresh, tough text? Do we have clarity around what we mean when we say "voice" or "technique" or "craft"? What happens when we try to discuss our ideas?

The best—and, honestly, most fun—way to check in on these things is to get together with colleagues and have some book discussions. Pick some texts—a YA or middle-grade book, a classic that will prove challenging for adults, a comfortable contemporary text. Then read at least a little of them and discuss chapters and scenes through the lens of each skill. Practice. Remember what it feels like to infer, analyze, and interpret before you begin coaching your kids to do it.

As you do this work, be aware of the hierarchies in the room. Some of your colleagues will be just brilliant. That's fun! I love it when I am with someone better than me at thinking about books—it gets me excited and impressed and, well, just happy. But sometimes, when I am leading this work with adults, the people who are just awe-inspiringly good at this stuff will do their thing and it winds up silencing everyone else. Have you noticed that too? Someone says something so brilliant that I just stay quiet because what the heck am I going to say after that? Just because someone shares a clever insight in a discussion, it doesn't mean that they are a smarter, a more cultured, or an all-around better person, but it can feel that way to the others in the room. Pay attention if this happens, because the same thing happens in our classrooms.

The kids who are *already* really good at reading and analyzing texts show themselves right away. Everyone knows who they are. You know who they are.

That's fine. It's also fine that you delight in their abilities and enjoy having them in your classroom.

But be careful. Because just like in the PD sessions where the teacher who has read all the things can inadvertently silence their colleagues, when we as teachers smile brightly at the kid who already gets it and dim a bit when the rest of the class slogs along trying to get there, we send a powerful message: *I like kids who are already great at this.*

We need to be absolutely sure that we are not falling into the trap of enjoying the kids who have a natural aptitude born of talent (and often privilege) and feeling a little less excited about the rest.

If you are wondering if this preferential attitude is present in your school or your practice, just examine the language that you hear at school when discussing your readers. Do you have tracked classes? How do you and your colleagues talk about those classes? How do you feel about one class versus the other? If your classes are heterogeneously mixed, does your school community use language like *low*, *struggling*, and *highfliers*?

It's natural to be pleased with students who are already good at what we teach just like it is natural to be thrilled if you have some talented players on your baseball team. But it is imperative that we reset ourselves continually to understand that while the kids who already know stuff are great and deserve our attention and mentorship, our actual job is to make sure every kid gets fundamentally better at the work we take them through than they were when they came to us.

When we practice a skill ourselves, we can start to explore exactly how these skills are difficult or easy for us and others. It expands our empathy as our students begin the work.

Third Condition for Growth: *Coach Students Toward Purposeful Practice*

Reading is an ability similar, I think, to playing a sport. You need lots of practice in different situations for both, and most need great coaching if they are to become great, no matter their natural abilities.

There are of course times when our readers need a professor. They need someone to offer up insights and questions that delve into the heart of a specific text. They need to see someone who is really great at this stuff do their thing in front of them. It is inspiring, it is a model, it is important.

But simply being the professor will never help all of your readers be great themselves. For that, they need you to coach them.

Imagine you are coaching a sport, say, baseball. You have a team full of kids with the same diversity of ability and interest for playing baseball as you do in your classroom now for reading. You wouldn't imagine that they were done learning the skills and the foundations of baseball, would you? You wouldn't say to your team, "Hey, we are done practicing because you have learned baseball, and so now we will just play games and you will also go watch games. I expect all of you to reach the World Series by the end of the season." No. You, like every coach in the world, would consistently focus on the fundamentals, while challenging your players with increasingly difficult opponents. You would think about your team, who they were, what they brought to the table, what *they* needed. And then you would create time to practice these things, sometimes all together, sometimes individually or in groups.

To do this, to be a great coach, you need to know the skills of baseball deeply. It helps if you are also a decent player, but this work isn't about your own ability on the field; it's about how you can help your players improve their performance. After all, it's not true that the best athletes all go into coaching. The best coaches know how to *coach*, not necessarily play.

Yesterday my son and I were throwing a baseball back and forth. He got a mitt recently and we were breaking it in. He was throwing wildly and not catching anything and getting frustrated. I kept saying the one thing I knew to say when dealing with sports: "Keep your eye on the ball."

But this was not working for him. In fact, he stopped at one moment, threw down the mitt, and yelled, "My eye is on the ball and I keep missing!"

I asked him to give me a moment. I told him I was going to talk through what I did to throw the ball where I wanted it to go. As I did, I said, "So I guess what I do is really picture in my mind the ball going right where I want it to go. It sounds silly, but it's like I imagine it in my mind's eye; instead of *thinking* about how to do it, I see myself having done it." And just like that, it worked. His face lit up. He tried it again and his aim was so true I didn't even have to move my hands a centimeter to catch it. We did the same thing with catching and—bam—he was better at it.

My son needs a coach, not a great ballplayer.

In teaching, though, it is so tempting to rest on our own abilities as readers in trying to help kids understand a text. After all, many of us spent years in college English classes fine-tuning those abilities. Instead, we can focus on coaching our students to become the better readers we know they can be.

Fourth Condition for Growth: *Teach Strategies to Help All Kids Practice the Skill Work*

The next step is to be sure you have many strategies that can help students better practice a certain level of a skill on their own.

As a teacher, a critical turning point for me was when I realized that when my students weren't sure how to do the thing I was asking (when they defaulted to retelling or shut down or acted out or missed the mark), they were asking me for a *strategy*. Of course, what they would have said they *wanted* was for me to help them with the answer in that moment, but what they needed, what their inner reader was begging for, was a strategy that they could use anytime someone asked them to do this work.

Let's go back to our sports analogy for a moment: When I was tossing the ball with my son, and he was struggling, I first repeated the instructions to him. I then guided his arm with mine so he could feel the way he should throw. But these didn't help him. He needed a key to unlock the door to that level of sport he was working on. He needed the strategy of "athletes work on their aim by picturing the ball going where they want it to go in their mind's eye." That was the key that worked.

But what is a strategy exactly?

A strategy is *the how*. If the skill is *the what*, and the progression (or rubric or standard) shows us *at what level*, strategies are little things that we can do to chip away at that level of work. "Keep your eye on the ball" is a strategy. "Picture the ball going into the mitt" is another, and it's the one that worked with my son.

That's the thing about strategies—when teaching a skill, I have a sense of the strategies that tend to work for most. But I know that all students won't fit on grids or lists or pacing charts. I will need more strategies available to me than I can teach if I want to truly know how to teach a skill well and flexibly.

If we shift to reading, and thinking about character analysis, say there is a student who is trying to work on thinking about character motivation. But when they practice, their work sounds pretty literal, or obvious—Romeo is motivated by love, Katniss wants to win the Hunger Games, Starr wants justice for her friend.

Before I knew strategies, I would fumble in this situation quite a bit. Either I would accept their rough-draft idea as good enough, which didn't feel right, or I would pose vague questions with strange emphasis on certain words:

> "But what *really* motivates them?"
>
> "Say *more* about that."
>
> "Go *deeper*."

Really, *more*, and *deeper* are not strategies. They are signals to kids that they did not answer right and we don't know how to help them. Instead, we can be ready to teach students actionable steps they can take when trying for something new. In the case of character motivation, maybe I could say something like this:

> "OK, now when you work on motivation, try to ask what they want from other people."
>
> "Sometimes it helps to ask yourself, *Why is this character the way they are? What motivated them to be [fill in the blank]?*"
>
> "Motivation has some categories you can always think through. Let me teach you: you could think about motivation for self, others, the world, their personalities."

These strategies give kids a foothold in the work they are trying to do and help us to coach rather than model or assign all of the time. Certainly, out of all of the conditions outlined in this chapter, this is the one that you will find the most support for in this book, particularly around the reading skills of inferring character, interpreting theme, and analyzing craft.

Fifth Condition for Growth: *Offer Repetitive Practice*

OK. So let's say that we have waved a magic wand and magically put into place all I have presented in this chapter so far. Your units have focus; you are ready to coach into the practice of the skills you are focusing on. And yet this is all the work that I am doing as the teacher. What about the work kids need to do?

To foster growth, we need to set up repetitive practice. Without rich repetition, it feels like we're saying to kids, "Can you do it? No? Oh well, we are moving on." Or, "Oh, let me help hoist you over that wall and then let's move on. Yeah, you didn't really learn to do it yourself, but we've got to keep going."

For growth to occur, we must instill useful and authentic repetitive practice throughout our units. Students need to know what their job is when they read; they need a clear set of options for what that job might entail, and those options need to be strategies, not skills or big ways to respond. This might feel restrictive, commanding, closed. But I don't think it has to be. In fact, I think that sometimes being told thoughtful things to do can be a relief, particularly for students who are already carrying a heavy mental or emotional load into our classrooms.

Repeated practice allows for growth. It allows for confidence to bloom, for comfort and a willingness to try, for moments of "I get it!" That is, as long as the repeated practice is interesting and generative. Drill and grill could be seen as an example of repeated practice, but it has the very opposite energy and effect from what we are, I believe, working toward. For growth, confidence, comfort, and willingness, the repetitive practice we set up must be open yet focused, clear yet complex, finite yet generative.

It might sometimes seem as though not *all* kids need repetition. That students who fit into the conventions of school easily, who enjoy English class and are good at it won't need this kind of practice. And I can see why we might think this. I have taught groups of students who, if you asked them a question, would strive to answer it, and they would take your breath away with their insight and humanity. They would perform, and generally they would do well.

Yet it is often these same kids who are riddled with anxiety about what the assignment is, who have been taught that grades are everything but that the grading system is in the hands of the teacher and that grades equal measuring up to standards you hope you understand. They fulfill the assignments but are scared to go in a direction that is not laid out for them with rubrics and assignments.

The students who come to us knowing school and having some talent for reading need this repetition not so much because they need the footholds of the strategies to function but more because they need to know that this work we are doing can and should become ingrained. They should know, someday, that when reading a chapter, they can follow multiple replicable pathways to insight and that by working these pathways on their own they can come to class, come to their paper, come to the assignment ready to go. They should know that they do not need to wait for or be limited by a teacher's question, a specific assignment. They have the ability to dig in and read deeply, and we should be fostering a repetitive practice that makes this work automatic and freeing and more enjoyable.

At the same time, our students who do not identify in these ways, who do not feel like readers yet, who don't quite get it the first time, who may not want to do any of this, really, need this repetition as well. They need to feel the success of figuring out how this reading stuff works without always needing help from the teacher or a graphic organizer that does the conceptual work for them. They need to feel the thrill of trying a new way of seeing a scene and having a new thought about a book on their own that feels smart. And interesting to think about. And new, at least for them.

So if repetition is important, what is it that students should repeat exactly?

In order for students to get into the flow of repetitive practice, they will need a consistent assignment when they read. If we have students listen to new directions every day and try to synthesize those directions into their work, we create inefficiency in service of variety. Instead, think about the everydayness of reading and thinking and annotating. What should students do in your class every day when they read, or every time they pick up a book at home, that will allow them to practice the work of the unit without being a laborious, boring task that strips reading of joy and falsifies what it means to make meaning of the text?

I set the stage for this work by letting students know that I expect that every time they read, they will jot down between two and four ideas they are having about the text. I don't care whether they do those jots at the end of their reading or as they read. They do not, at this stage, need to give me text evidence to support their thinking, although they should jot down the page the idea relates to in order to make it easier to refer back.

Then, as I teach strategies, I create a class chart listing them. I number them as well. So, if you are using this book and you are working on character, your list by day five of the unit might look like this:

How to Analyze Characters

12. Read with a pen in hand.
13. Evaluate relationships.
14. List out problems.
15. Look for causes and effects.
16. Notice shifts and changes.

I direct students to choose from this list when they are jotting down their thinking, and I ask them to number each jot with the strategy they used so that we can look at the kind of work they are trying on as they read. Of course, they can also jot about the things that strike them in a text—their own authentic responses—but it's the numbered jots that I focus on here as part of practicing particular skills.

Once this routine is in place, I am able to do all sorts of things as the teacher. I can go to a student at any time and ask them how their work is going, and they should have something to show me that I can respond to that fits the work of our unit. Because the jots are numbered, I can refer to strategies quickly and nimbly. I can talk to students about which strategies they tried and why. I can give kids credit for keeping up with the work each day, and I can ask them to choose some to show me when I want to take a deeper look.

I assign other work that creates nuance or variety or text-specific engagement, but it is my belief that if we want good reading *practice* to occur in our classrooms, then we need to be clear about what that practice should look like.

Sixth Condition for Growth: *Provide Repetition Across Texts*

So, to take stock: We choose a skill or so to root our work in a unit. We learn how to coach into that skill. We set up structures and conditions for students to repeatedly practice that skill as they read with coaching from us. In my experience there is another condition that we should think through: transfer. How will kids carry this work across multiple texts?

This may take a second to think through, particularly if you are used to centering the work on one main novel per unit or quarter. But the general idea is this: students benefit from seeing how these skills differ and stay the same across a wide variety of texts. Classics. YA novels. Short stories. Movies and TV shows. In a dream scenario we get to move across tons of texts, practicing our analytical and interpretive moves as we do, continually adapting and playing around with how these skills work and what they can offer us when employed. Of course, in reality we don't often have endless time and resources.

But there are ways to get at the essence of this idea—that it will help everyone to try the skill practice again in another book—regardless of how your class is set up.

Perhaps we think about the marking period as having three phases: a whole-class text we read together where I introduce and support the skills and strategies and tools we will use, a book club or independent reading phase where students choose another text to read while practicing the same skill work with greater independence, and then a writing unit or project unit. (If you've read my book *A Novel Approach*, this might sound familiar to you.)

Or perhaps you will use a short text as a model, and across the entire unit students will pick texts to read and practice on, either in clubs, in partnerships, or on their own. Either way, students will benefit from seeing that the theme work we do does not apply just to *Of Mice and Men*.

How you create these conditions and solve the problems that arise as you do is of course up to you. I don't argue here for one particular way or solution. I do argue, however, that these are the problems we need to solve. Your way will be better than mine because it will be yours.

Independence Is the Goal

There is a skill I am trying to learn. I've dabbled in it across the decades. There have been times when I was forced to use this skill on demand; there have been other times I could kind of choose whether I wanted to use it or not. Now, though, I really want to learn it. I want to be better at it, without reminders or disasters or coddling.

I am learning how to take care of myself.

While it is humbling to me that I don't know how to do this on my own very well yet, there it is, and I am taking it on. I have a few teachers, friends, mentors, people in my life, even Facebook friends who are helping me. Because my goal is to truly learn how to do this thing better, there are some things my teachers are helping me avoid, such as these:

1. Beating up on myself for not being great right away
2. Thinking about growth as linear—as constant progress
3. Dismissing the work I am doing as not important

And they encourage and remind and coach me to

1. Take things in baby steps—one move at a time
2. Celebrate every small step forward
3. Remember why I am working on this—setting the goal that matters

It has occurred to me, as I've worked on this in my life, that this is also a feeling we'd like to create in our classrooms if we want all students to become independent readers. After all, until now the way I have handled this skill of self-care is to wait for someone to remind me to do it. Just like our students, I waited until my wife would say, "You need to take a break." And then I would either comply or rebel. What I was not doing was taking the work seriously as a goal *for myself.*

I cannot force anyone to internalize a goal. But I can set up the conditions for these goals to take root. I can create units and practice pedagogy that allow for and urge all students to become more independent readers and thinkers. In my experience, when this work gains traction, one by one students begin to see success, and they begin to feel more confident, more able to take risks in their thinking, more engaged in the work we are doing.

A piece of this puzzle is knowing, deeply, the strategies that will help students take the next step in their practice. Without them, the work remains vague, and vagueness is an enemy of growth. When our intentions are vague, when what we expect from students is cloudy, when they are not sure how to try, we suggest somehow that reading work is a magical talent that some people have and some people do not.

Instead, by setting up the conditions like the ones outlined in this chapter and then feeding them with the strategies in the rest of this book, we can help make what used to be vague clear.

CHAPTER ONE

How to Teach Character Analysis

What It Means to Analyze Characters

Right before my dad died, I went on a road trip to visit him. It was the last time I saw him. On our last day together, I realized I hadn't helped him with as much as I'd meant to. I started frantically boxing up some of his old books, cleaning his living room shelves, hammering wildly at a leaning bookshelf, trying to finish before I had to leave. Dad watched me for a bit and then said, "Kiddo, you are so hard on yourself." He was right of course. But how had he seen that from the way I packed books in a box?

My dad was able to see so much in the pause of a finger, the hesitation of a reach, the bead of sweat on a brow. He had seen my anxiety in tiny gestures, in my tone of voice, even in my body language. He was able to see so much about me in such little moments.

The way my dad read me is the way we want our students to read the characters in the books they read. Whether it is in the whole-class novel we read together, the book club book they read with classmates, or a choice book they have selected, we hope that students read the characters with a sense that every gesture matters and every word is a window into who they are and what they have to show us about our own experience.

I want them to do this because it matters. Certainly, it matters in books. It is difficult to get into literature if our read of the characters depicted within it is shallow. A long time ago, as a student teacher, I set a class up to read novels in book clubs. They did it completely independently. I didn't know how to teach yet, so they just read the books without me. That's all I thought independent reading was at the time—just reading alone. At the end, a group of boys who read *Night*, by Elie Wiesel, came to a conclusion about Elie. "He was a bad man," they said. See, they had read the scene where Elie had been forced to leave his father behind. "We would never do that," they said. And so, their analysis of Elie Wiesel was shockingly off. It turns out that analyzing people in stories is a skill that needs to be taught.

At the same time, I very much want my students to come to their own conclusions about the characters in the books they read. If I am too controlling around the experience my students have of the fictional people they encounter, I close them off to discovery, insight, and their own view of the world. Like the teacher who recently told his eighth graders that they were wrong to think that Atticus Finch was not a hero. Whether that statement makes you cringe or cheer, the kids in that room had a theory backed up by text evidence and literary criticism, but the teacher, like so many of us, like myself, had such strong ideas of who the characters were in the books he taught that he refused to budge.

What I dream of are classrooms where students can analyze characters independently but rigorously. Classes where students know how to think about, relate to, and critique portrayals of humanity on their own.

It matters. It matters that they can do it well but also, and more importantly, without me. Like in the sample notebook page in Figure 1.1, where KT takes her own route in thinking about a character in a book she is reading, working to uncover interesting ideas, like the confusion we all face sometimes when trying to get free—how to do it in ways that are healthy versus destructive.

It matters, too, that our students are able to do this work in the world. Of course, they are already doing it. They might even be better than us at analyzing the small moves a person makes and considering what larger ideas those moves suggest about the people around them. Our students have theories about their parents and caregivers, their friends, their crushes, and most certainly us. And yet I believe we can help them become even more powerful observers of the people they know, love, are afraid of, respect, and desire. We can nurture their abilities to observe closely, to consider, to theorize, and to keep learning about people in their lives. It's what we do when we read. And it's what we do when we live our lives with our eyes wide open.

On that last day with my father, I read him every bit as much as he read me. I saw how the coughs that shook his body got deeper during that last visit. I saw how his oxygen tube was dark brown from the cigarette smoke he still insisted on breathing in and out every minute he was awake. I saw how he couldn't quite walk to the kitchen without grabbing a chair for balance. I saw how he had only steak, frozen bean salad, and beer in the fridge. I saw these things and I was able to analyze them: this might be the last time I see him.

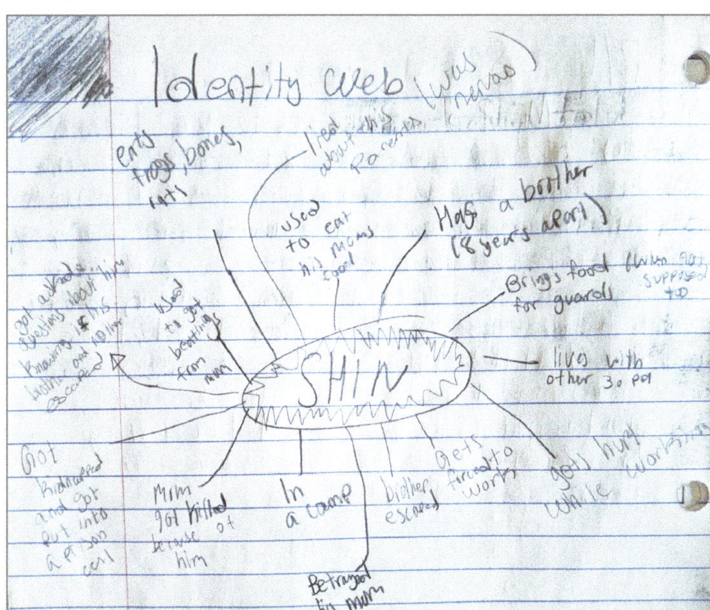

FIGURE 1.1: *This student works to find a tapestry of significant details about a character in the book they are reading.*

When my friends came to pick me up that last day, I knew I was saying goodbye to my dad for the last time.

And because I knew how to read people, to read my dad, I soaked up every single detail of that last day. It's not up for analysis though. Those details live in my heart, just like the best moments with our most beloved characters do.

How Character Analysis Works

Before I go into how thinking about characters in texts works, I need to pause and reflect a little on what I mean by "works." The dream is not that students follow my lead all of the time, though certainly this will be a side to our learning relationship. No, what I care the most about is what students are able to do independently, without my help. So when I discuss how character analysis works, what I really mean is, how do students do this work on their own, generally, without the constant guidance of a teacher? How do kids come to class ready to say things about the characters in the books we read without me setting the stage or feeling as though I need to pull ideas out of them like teeth from a stubborn jaw? How does every student in my class—yes, even that one—get significantly better at thinking about and noticing and mulling over the characters they encounter in the books they pick up in my class, in every class, on their own? For that matter, how can this work we are doing bleed into their other texts—the movies they watch, the YouTube and TikTok videos they consume, and the narrative video games they play? And while we are dreaming big, how can this study of character analysis help all of us become just a little bit better at thinking about the people in our lives, our heroes, our nemeses, ourselves?

So, the focus of this book is not how to make kids do good character work in that one book we are all reading. Text-directed questions, teacher-led discussions, engaging activities—these can all help us understand Ari and Dante (*Aristotle and Dante Discover the Secrets of the Universe*) and Gogol and Ashima (*The Namesake*). The focus of this book is instead on how we can widen our lens to the work that all readers tend to do in pretty much all books and how to then tie that general work into the specifics and power of a particular text.

So, let's begin. Or, more accurately, let's begin where we need to begin: before the beginning.

BEFORE YOU START READING

In this section, we'll discuss the following strategies:

4. Know What to Expect

Giving students a bit of guidance, vision, and structure to help them set up a few simple notebook pages can create a road map for the kind of thinking you will invite them to do as they read.

5. Build Your Schema

When we help students build the context of the novel they are reading and give them a refresher on the details of the time and place of the text, they can pause and gather some information and background before they start.

When I start a book, I tend to do some prep work first. The prep depends on my purpose for reading. If I am reading for pleasure, I try to be sure to have things that make me comfortable: chair, coffee, light. I also have a pen ready and my phone in case I want to take notes and look stuff up. If I am reading to learn, I have my notebook ready and I begin to set up pages. I also know I'll need context as I read, so I am ready to do some research as I get a sense of the setting. It is tough to just dive into a book cold. Unless the world of the story acts as a mirror to my own (as Rudine Sims Bishop [1990] teaches us books can do), some knowledge of the context, the time, and the place will help me a great deal. Unless I have an incredible memory, not having a place to store my thinking will weaken my reading, my retention, and my experience as I read.

Prepping before we read, though, can be an unnatural feeling for our students. In their years at school, they may have learned to wait to be told the info they need, to be given the graphic organizers they will grapple with. We hope that the habits of preparing to read will become ingrained. If that is the goal, it helps to teach these habits explicitly, to show kids that they can get themselves ready to read, whether it's for my class, their future college courses, or in the course of their own literary lives.

1. KNOW WHAT TO EXPECT

THINKING ABOUT THE STRATEGY

I am the worst at picking books to read these days. I pick up a novel and check out the title, the back of the book, the first page and . . . meh. It's not that I don't love to read or that I don't think that the book is good. Instead, a weird ennui settles over me as I scan the overview of the world I hold in my hands. I've seen this all before, I think to myself. I know how this will go, I grumble internally.

I'm wrong, usually, of course. But there is this feeling, this annoying sense that I know how most books go.

I'd like to bottle this feeling I have and offer it in small doses to kids as they begin a book.

Don't misunderstand me—I don't want to see young readers feel bored before they begin (goodness knows, many of them already do without my weird magic dosing idea). But I would like for students to know, as they hold a book that they have not yet opened, that they know some things about this book already and that there is information they can find out before they begin that will help them enter the word of the story with much less struggle. That most if not all fiction contains a character with many traits, who is going to have relationships and problems that are complicated and intertwined, and all of these things will change and they will learn something. That our job as readers is to pay attention to all that stuff and to open ourselves enough to be moved by the things we are moved by and to critique what falls flat.

So maybe they could get themselves set up for this work ahead of time?

Before we start a book for school, we can set our notebooks up with pages ready to hold our thinking along the predictable lines of character. We might have a few pages ready for different characters, so that we can keep track of the various traits and motivations that we encounter. A page for keeping track of the matrix of problems that a character will face that they—and we—will learn from. A change tracker, particularly one that helps students focus on moments—lines—where the change begins. A list of lessons learned or not grasped by the end of the book. These note pages will be ready for kids as they read and will serve as reminders of the work they should be doing as they read a book in depth.

Figures 1.2 a–d are examples from my reading of *Aristotle and Dante Discover the Secrets of the Universe*, which I use as a model for students as I am teaching.

In addition, students might look for articles that can help them begin to lay the groundwork for the context of the novel. As I got ready to read *The Namesake*, by Jhumpa Lahiri, I read an interview by the author, a few essays on the experiences of children of immigrants, and a piece about Bengali culture. While these texts by no means gave me a definitive understanding of the setting and context of *The Namesake*, they helped prepare me to learn from Lahiri and her characters.

I lean toward self-made notebook pages rather than photocopied templates and graphic organizers. Certainly in some ways it would be easier to hand the kids worksheets to fill in and a folder to keep them in until they are due, or to lean into the digital world and put it all online. But I encourage you to resist this inclination if you can for a few reasons.

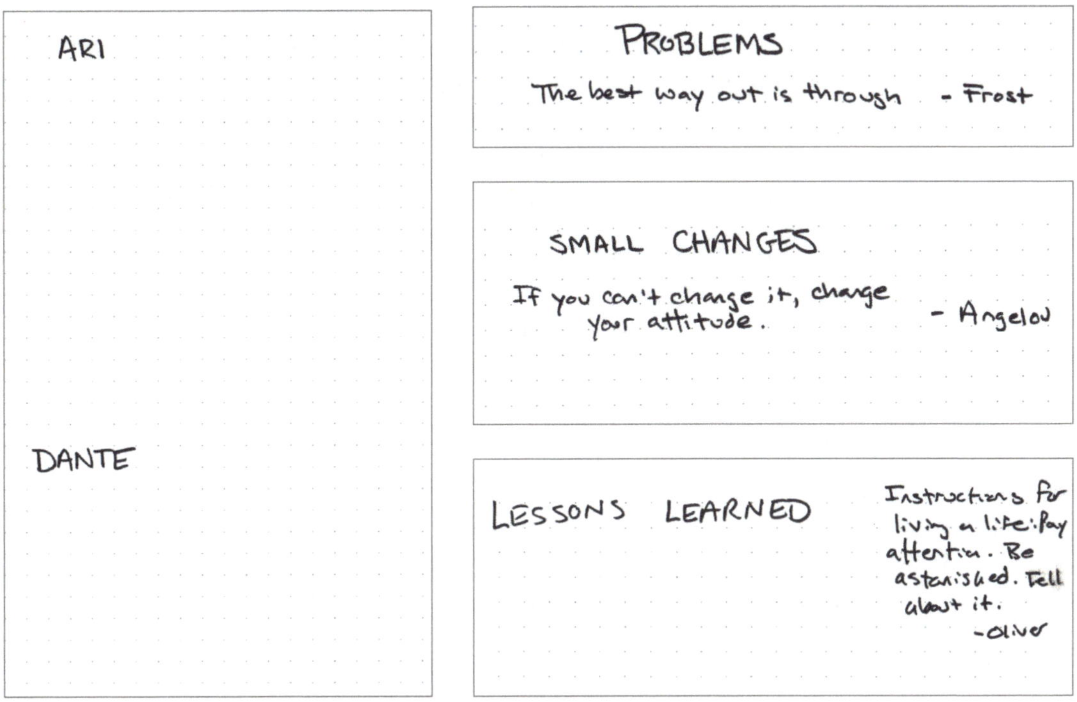

FIGURES 1.2 a–d: *Setting up a reading notebook for character work*

Why No Worksheets?

1. They can be less engaging. While worksheets do make things easier for the teacher and the student, because they make things easier, they also sometimes take some of the energy out of the room. While this is not always true, we want to be on the lookout for places where we can make our work feel authentic.
2. They are inflexible. The fact is that I want kids to explore their own ways of taking notes and tracking ideas in the books they read. Every time I show students an example and then have them invent their own offshoot, I am impressed by many of the results. The fact is that students often come up with methods that work better for them.
3. They are loose. And that means they are hard to keep. Sure kids can use a Trapper Keeper (who remembers?) or a folder or staple them or whatever. Of course, it can all be on the computer. But a notebook just keeps things tighter and treats our students' thinking like something to keep.

At the same time, if the make-or-break issue for you is the convenience of a worksheet, by all means give your kids a template. It's not the end of the world. That is why I offer a graphic organizer for each lesson. I don't want to use them myself, and I encourage you not to, but we all need to get through the day productively, and sometimes a box and lines and instructions help us do that.

> *A great discussion of the difference between a template and a worksheet can be found on Jennifer Gonzales' (2018) fabulous* Cult of Pedagogy *blog post "Frickin' Packets," in which she explores the nuances around this issue, such as "what distinguishes a 'busy-work' worksheet from something that delivers real value, why teaching with worksheets is usually not the best choice for learning, the reasons teachers default to worksheet teaching, and what other learning experiences would be better for our students."*

1. KNOW WHAT TO EXPECT

TEACHING THE STRATEGY

Lesson Flow

Giving students a bit of guidance, vision, and structure to help them set up a few simple notebook pages can create a road map for the kind of thinking you will invite them to do as they read.

One way to teach this lesson:

1. Introduce the lesson with a time from your life when you needed to set yourself up to do good work (writing a video game tutorial, planning a party, creating a packing list for a big trip).
2. Explain that it will help students as readers to have some pages set up in their notebooks ready to capture certain kinds of thinking about characters. Show a list of options and a few examples (see Figures 1.2a–d for a few of my models).
3. Encourage kids to be creative: the format of the page and even the type of page they want to create can match their own goals and interests.
4. Time how long it takes the class to make one page (give about two minutes), and then have them share with a partner.
5. Give time for the class to set up the rest of their notebook pages (approximately ten minutes).
6. As the class works, offer models to kids who are stuck and encourage focus and speed.
7. Share any pages that show clarity or creativity.

Providing Feedback

If your students say or demonstrate . . .	Coach them on . . .
I need some more time, but I am able to create the pages I was shown.	Speeding up and letting go of perfection around handwriting, straight lines, or spelling
I can quickly and efficiently complete the task, mirroring the examples the teacher gave me.	Playing around with the format and content of each page, or try inventing a page from scratch
I consider the kind of work that I would find meaningful or demanding and create or modify notebook pages that will capture this thinking.	Trying out new kinds of notebook pages or making a page for something not mentioned in class

Optional Tools

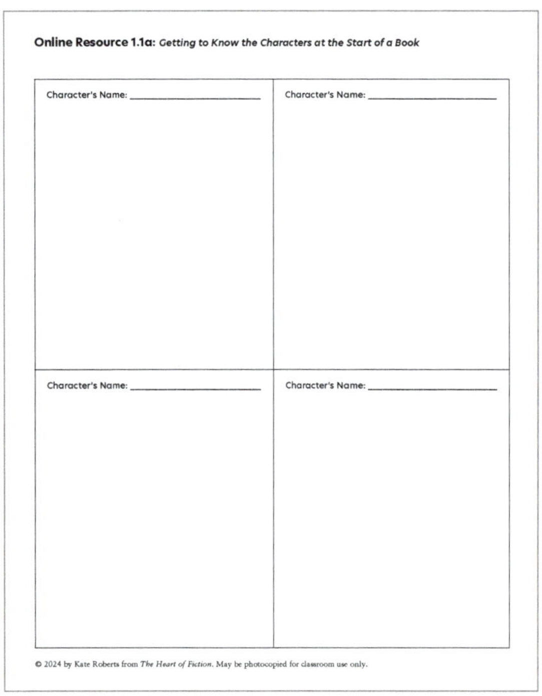

Online Resource 1.1a: *Getting to Know the Characters at the Start of a Book*

Character's Name: ______________	Character's Name: ______________
Character's Name: ______________	Character's Name: ______________

Getting to Know the Characters at the Start of the Book (OR 1.1a)

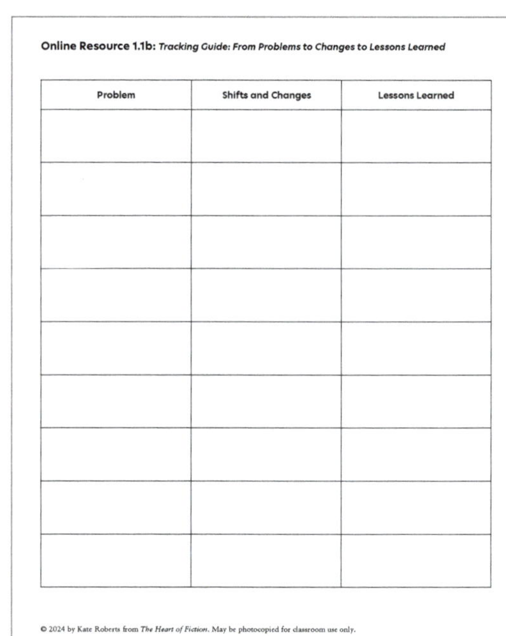

Online Resource 1.1b: *Tracking Guide: From Problems to Changes to Lessons Learned*

Problem	Shifts and Changes	Lessons Learned

Tracking Guide: From Problems to Changes to Lessons Learned (OR 1.1b)

2. BUILD YOUR SCHEMA

THINKING ABOUT THE STRATEGY

When I travel, before I enter the town or city, I do what you probably do too: I take out my phone. "Best Restaurants in Denver," "Things to Do in Kansas City," "Diners in Upstate New York." I want to get a lay of the land before I start charging into a new place, looking for food.

The same is true in books. Before we turn the first page and dive into the story, it makes sense to get to know the time and place we are about to enter. You know this. Chances are you do this with your students. But if you are like the majority, you may be giving students the background information yourself, spoon-feeding them each photo and fact to make sure they know what they need to know. While this makes sense—we can't deeply understand *Just Mercy* if we do not at least loosely understand racism in the criminal justice system before we start reading—it gets problematic when we teach our kids that they always need us to build background knowledge.

I believe that one question we need to ask is this: When exactly do we teach our students to build their own schema for a book they are about to read? For the content of the context is surely important. As E. D. Hirsch (2020) and his legacy of educators have insisted, without content knowledge, reading can become inefficient and unnecessarily difficult. But it can't possibly be sustainable for us to have to give kids all of the knowledge they need, can it? It's not sustainable or ideal, as we want to also foster curiosity and interest, which is a personal thing. Instead, let's focus on teaching students that there is some work they should do before they read to be sure they have a sense of the world they are stepping into.

Take the notes I took, for example, before reading *Aristotle and Dante Discover the Secrets of the Universe* (see Figure 1.3) and the articles I found to help me begin to understand the world of *The Namesake*. In not that long a time, I was able to build a sense (by reading the back of the book and searching the internet, letting keywords and hyperlinks guide me) of the setting, context, and ideas I was about to encounter in the novels before I read, and I didn't need anyone else's PowerPoint to do it. Our kids, with their digital prowess and visual aptitude, often prove themselves to be far better and faster at this schema building than we are. Let them do this work themselves.

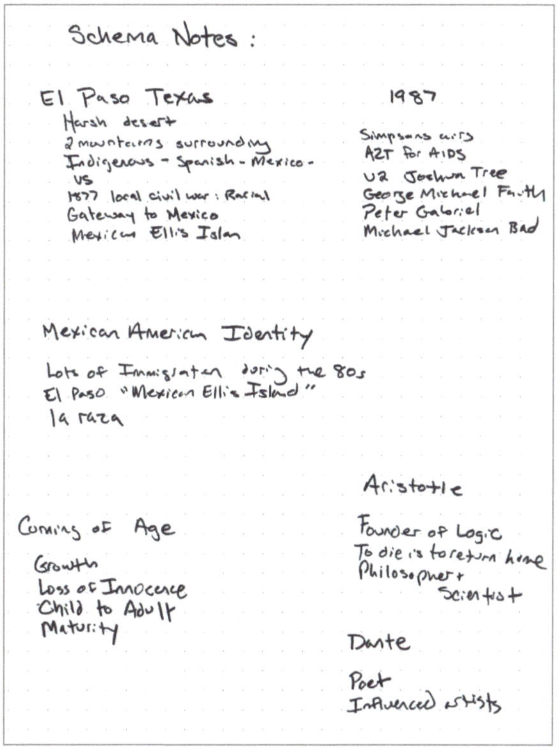

FIGURE 1.3: *Notes from building schema work*

2. BUILD YOUR SCHEMA

TEACHING THE STRATEGY

Lesson Flow

When we help students build the context of the novel they are reading and give them a refresher on the details of the time and place of the text, they can pause and gather some information and background before they start.

One way to teach this lesson:

1. Students will need devices or laptops to use during this lesson. Begin by stating the obvious fact that we don't always need someone else to give us information anymore. When we start a novel, we can do some informal research on our devices or laptops to build a text set that can help us understand where and when the book takes place.
2. Make sure each student knows the time and place of the novel. (If doing a whole-class novel, this is easier of course. When they are reading different books that they have chosen on their own or in book clubs, they can look at the back of the book, scan the first chapter, or check the internet.)
3. Offer students a list of the kinds of texts they will be looking for: photos, videos, summary articles, infographics, songs. Students may need help crafting search terms. If so, give a few examples ("songs of the 1940s," for example, or an image search using the term "civil rights").
4. Give students less time than you think you should to find a selection of texts from or about the time period. The urgency is important. Setting a timer for ten minutes and asking kids to find at least five good texts creates the energy you want for this lesson.
5. After the time is up, give students about twenty minutes to read through the texts they have found, taking notes on a T-chart with the headings "I Notice" and "I Think" as they do. Create a quick model ahead of time.

What Might This Look Like?

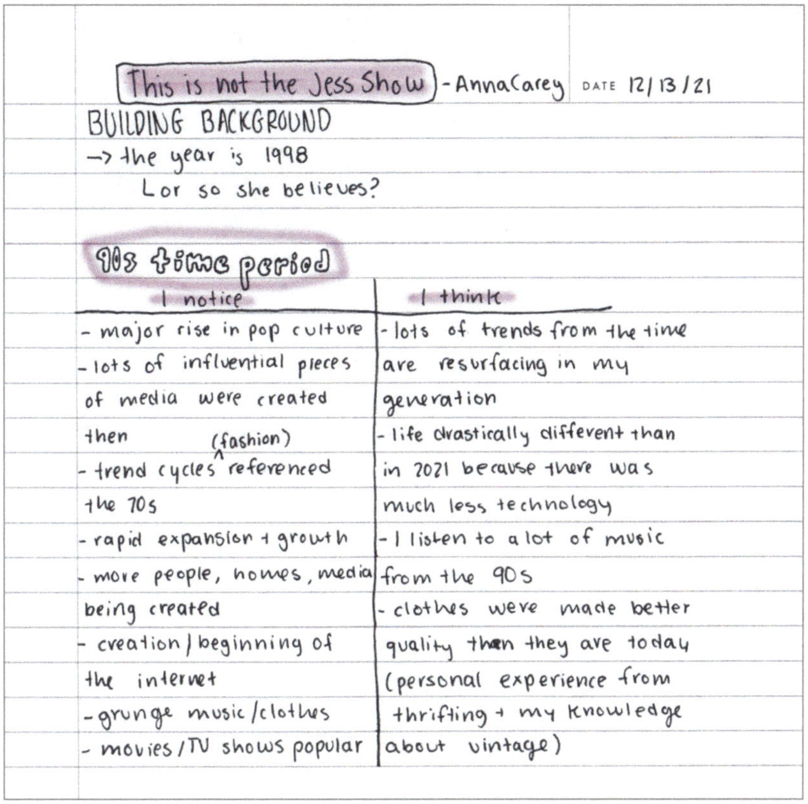

This is not the Jess Show - AnnaCarey DATE 12/13/21

BUILDING BACKGROUND

-> the year is 1998

L or so she believes?

90s time period

I notice	I think
- major rise in pop culture	- lots of trends from the time
- lots of influential pieces	are resurfacing in my
of media were created	generation
then	- life drastically different than
- trend cycles (fashion) referenced	in 2021 because there was
the 70s	much less technology
- rapid expansion + growth	- I listen to a lot of music
- more people, homes, media	from the 90s
being created	- clothes were made better
- creation / beginning of	quality than they are today
the internet	(personal experience from
- grunge music / clothes	thrifting + my knowledge
- movies / TV shows popular	about vintage)

Here Annika discovers information—and questions—she has about where the book takes place before she starts reading.

Shay collects photos and facts to help them build some prior knowledge.

Providing Feedback

If your students say or demonstrate . . .	Coach them on . . .
I am able to find information across media that gives me a sense of the setting.	Thinking about which information might be significant to the book Reading a bit about the book first to help decide which information might be most important
I am able to select significant information across media about the setting and context of the text. I can name what feels like the most important information I've learned.	Tagging their notes with what the information makes them think about or question Ranking the info they found in order of expected importance
I am able to collect impressions and ideas based on my research. I have a sense based on this, the title, and the back of the book of what ideas from the setting are likely to influence the characters I am about to read.	Anticipating some themes or details that might show up in the text they are about to read

Optional Tools

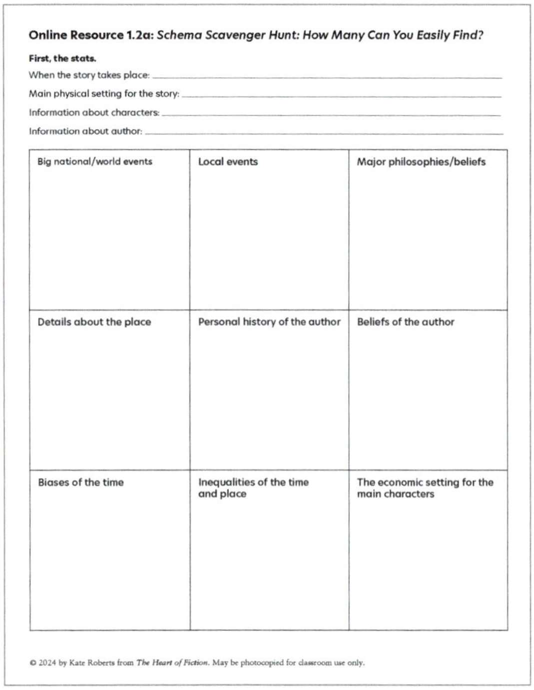

Online Resource 1.2a: *Schema Scavenger Hunt: How Many Can You Easily Find?*

First, the stats.

When the story takes place: ____________

Main physical setting for the story: ____________

Information about characters: ____________

Information about author: ____________

Big national/world events	Local events	Major philosophies/beliefs
Details about the place	Personal history of the author	Beliefs of the author
Biases of the time	Inequalities of the time and place	The economic setting for the main characters

Schema Scavenger Hunt: How Many Can You Easily Find? (OR 1.2a)

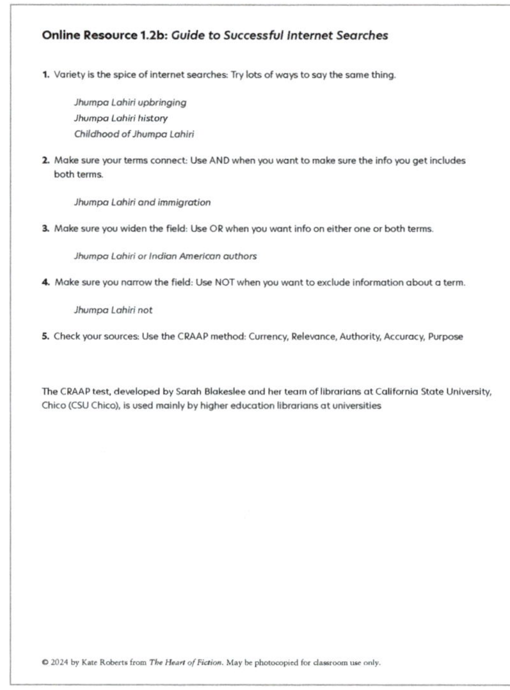

Online Resource 1.2b: *Guide to Successful Internet Searches*

1. Variety is the spice of internet searches: Try lots of ways to say the same thing.

   Jhumpa Lahiri upbringing
   Jhumpa Lahiri history
   Childhood of Jhumpa Lahiri

2. Make sure your terms connect: Use AND when you want to make sure the info you get includes both terms.

   Jhumpa Lahiri and immigration

3. Make sure you widen the field: Use OR when you want info on either one or both terms.

   Jhumpa Lahiri or Indian American authors

4. Make sure you narrow the field: Use NOT when you want to exclude information about a term.

   Jhumpa Lahiri not

5. Check your sources: Use the CRAAP method: Currency, Relevance, Authority, Accuracy, Purpose

The CRAAP test, developed by Sarah Blakeslee and her team of librarians at California State University, Chico (CSU Chico), is used mainly by higher education librarians at universities

Guide to Successful Internet Searches (OR 1.2b)

AS THE BOOK BEGINS

In this section, we'll discuss the following strategies:

3. Read with a Pen in Hand

By encouraging students to challenge themselves to add more thoughts per page, you can teach your class to sift through texts more thoughtfully.

4. Track Relationships and Problems

Teach students how to go deeper in their analysis of relationships in the text and move beyond naming the big, obvious obstacles the character faces.

5. Notice What Else Stands Out

This is a good lesson to teach when you start feeling anxious that you are spending too much time on character work at the expense of the other elements of the text that beg for attention, particularly when you know that your class has been taught a bunch about theme or literary techniques.

If our goal is to deeply understand the characters in a text, there is no time when we will work harder than at the beginning of the story. This is a similar feeling to real life, because when we are first invested in getting to know someone, we pay close and constant attention to the kind of person they are, the flavor of their humor, what they believe and enjoy and avoid. When I began my first year of teaching, for instance, I paid close attention to my new principal, taking stock of gestures, inflections, and turns of phrase to try to figure out both what kind of boss he would be and how he thought I was doing. I was not right, necessarily, for certainly he was more complex than I first made him out to be, and the picture was in no way complete. But we spend real energy uncovering the traits, flaws, likes, and peccadillos of the people we need to get to know. At the start of a book, if we are invested, the characters are people we need to know if the book is going to have the impact it can. Teaching students how to roll up their sleeves at the start of a novel and get to work will pay off impressively as the narrative rolls out.

3. READ WITH A PEN IN HAND

THINKING ABOUT THE STRATEGY

At the start of a novel, an engaged reader's mind is practically on fire with thinking about the people in the pages. The novelist is offering us countless clues as to what sort of person the character is. What do they worry about? How do they react to their environment, to others, to events? What do all of these things show us about their personalities? What layers of traits and flaws cause them happiness and ease, and which cause discomfort and conflict? In the first few chapters of a book, the ideas should be flying off each page until we get a pretty good sense of who we are dealing with in this story.

By contrast, we know what can happen when we ask readers to analyze characters they're not invested in: they reach for the biggest box to put each character in. They say, "This character is brave and this other one is mean," and they have barely a thought for the minor characters in the background.

We want to teach our students that as you begin a novel, you can take on the attitude of an archeologist, sifting through the text for clues, for discoveries, for inferences, for guesses. We want to teach students to have their notebook out, ready to be filled with their thinking about the characters as they read each line, paragraph, page. In fact, we want to suggest that it is almost unthinkable that we would read a page of a book without having one thought or another about the characters, particularly at the start.

For example, as I began both *The Namesake* and *Aristotle and Dante*, I made sure to capture as much thinking as I could on the characters' respective pages. I knew that these introductions were going to be packed with hints as to their personalities, and I knew that if I put the work in to understand them now, the thinking I would do later would come much, much easier to me. (See Figures 1.4 and 1.5.)

There is healthy debate around how much and when students should write about their reading as they read. Colleagues I respect feel, rightly, that when we ask kids to do too much writing about their books, we destroy the engagement and flow that we want them to experience as they read. And there is truth to this. If I have to stop every few minutes and write down my thinking, I could indeed lose steam, particularly if I do not already love to read. At the same time, if I read without writing down my thinking, I just don't think as deeply as I do when I jot down my best ideas as I take in the text. And so I am a proponent of asking readers to annotate their thinking in some way as they read a book.

That being said, I don't really care how they do it. For me, it helped to stop as I was reading these books. I paused every paragraph or so and considered if a new idea had been offered about these people. Sometimes the answer was no—my previous ideas were simply confirmed or deepened. But this allowed me to pick up a bunch of smaller, more nuanced ideas about the characters than I would have if I had waited until the end of my reading to take notes. And yet for some readers this stopping and starting will just not work. The interruption of their reading will exact too great a cost to the flow of their reading. For these readers, it makes sense to read, then double back and go page by page, looking for the ideas they want to capture.

Another reason why writing about reading can become soulless drudgery for students is that the writing itself can be, in fact, soulless. If you don't teach me not to, when I read a scene where the character is crying, I will write, "She is sad." While this is true, it is not the kind of idea that will lead me to greater understanding of the characters or the text or myself. In fact, sometimes the things that students write down barely feel like ideas at all; they are the tiniest leaps of inference: crying equals sadness. Instead, we want to teach and model for students that the whole point of writing about reading is to try to push yourself to have a new idea every time you put pen to paper. These notes are not about recording; they are about discovering. While not every student will take you up on this invitation, some of the lessons and tools we will discuss later on in this chapter will help remind and encourage students to take a risk in their thinking, to push and see what they might uncover with a little effort. When this happens, writing about reading is more about creativity and less about drudgery.

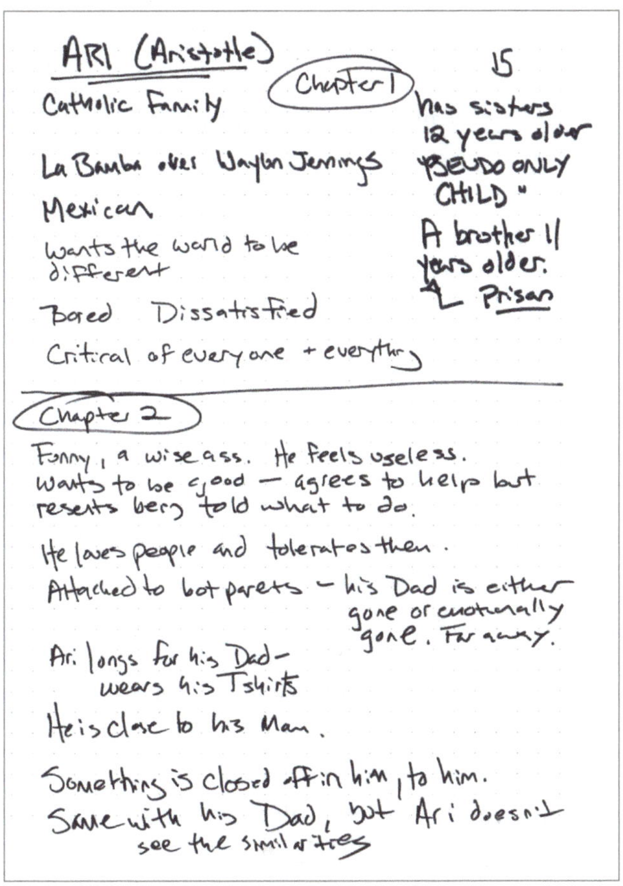
ARI (Aristotle) Chapter 1 15
Catholic Family
La Bamba over Waylon Jennings
Mexican
wants the world to be different
Bored Dissatisfied
Critical of everyone + everything
has sisters 12 years older
"PSEUDO ONLY CHILD"
A brother 11 years older. Prison
Chapter 2
Funny, a wise ass. He feels useless.
Wants to be good — agrees to help but resents being told what to do.
He loves people and tolerates them.
Attached to both parents – his Dad is either gone or emotionally gone. Far away.
Ari longs for his Dad – wears his T-shirts
He is close to his Mom.
Something is closed off in him, to him.
Same with his Dad, but Ari doesn't see the similarities

FIGURE 1.4: *Model notebook pages at the start of* Aristotle and Dante

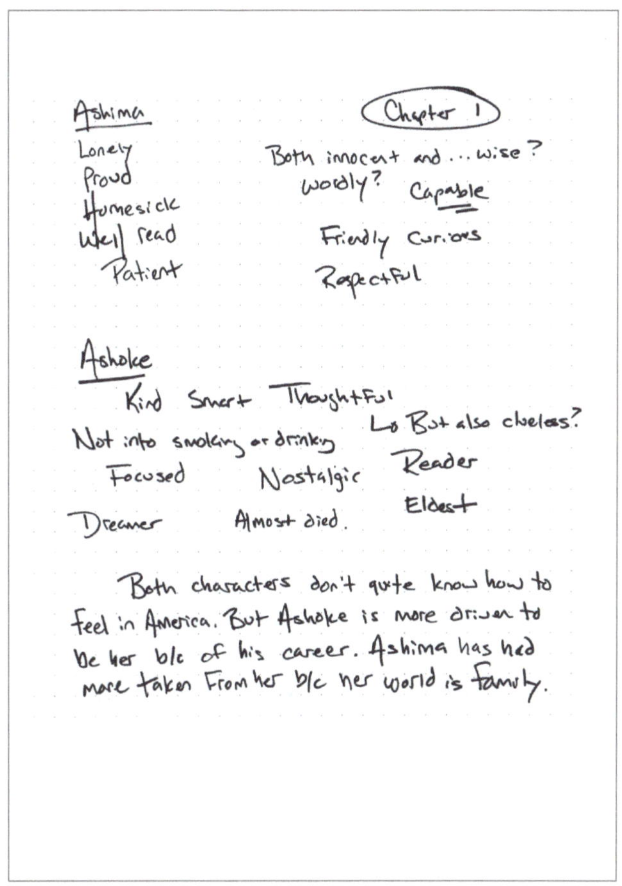
Ashima Chapter 1
Lonely
Proud
Homesick
Well read
Patient
Both innocent and ... wise? worldly?
Capable
Friendly Curious
Respectful
Ashoke
Kind Smart Thoughtful
Not into smoking or drinking
But also clueless?
Focused Nostalgic Reader
Dreamer Almost died. Eldest
Both characters don't quite know how to feel in America. But Ashoke is more driven to be here b/c of his career. Ashima has had more taken from her b/c her world is family.

FIGURE 1.5: *Model notebook pages at the start of* The Namesake

3. READ WITH A PEN IN HAND

TEACHING THE STRATEGY

Lesson Flow

By encouraging students to challenge themselves to add more thoughts per page, you can teach your class to sift through texts more thoughtfully.

One way to teach this lesson:

1. Introduce the lesson by making a comparison to getting to know someone well—how at the beginning of that experience, we notice everything about them. (I like to talk about falling in love and how each tiny gesture seems to mean something, but of course the same could be said of meeting a good friend or an enjoyable nemesis.)
2. Name the task: we will be reading each page of our books looking for something new to add to our understanding of the character, even if it is just a word to the kind of person they are, even if it is us trying to describe something that is hard to describe.
3. Take a page of a common text (a whole-class novel or a story you read aloud earlier in the year). Model how you can stop after each line or couple of lines and have a thought about the character (see my models in Figures 1.4 and 1.5 for some examples).
4. Be sure to model and name explicitly the following: not all of your ideas are amazing; you work to be specific with your language, particularly about emotions and traits; and you strive to describe ways of being that you don't have the exact words for ("He's the kind of guy who walks into a room announcing his presence" works as well as the word gregarious).
5. Have students practice as you read aloud another page of the common text. They can do this out loud, or you can stop every few lines and have students talk to a partner. If you hear students struggling to infer, choosing simple words like sad or brave, or repeating themselves, make a mental note to work on this skill with them in a small group.
6. Come together and list a bunch of the thoughts the class had and collectively notice how much thinking can come from one page.
7. Set students up to do similar work in the beginning of their book: tell them to read with their notebook open to the pages for the characters in the scene, writing down tons of thoughts about them in the initial chapters. Be sure to highlight that this intensive note-taking is really necessary only at the start; perhaps students set a goal of how many pages or chapters it makes sense to work on. Send them off to read and write while you confer and coach into small groups.

What Might This Look Like?

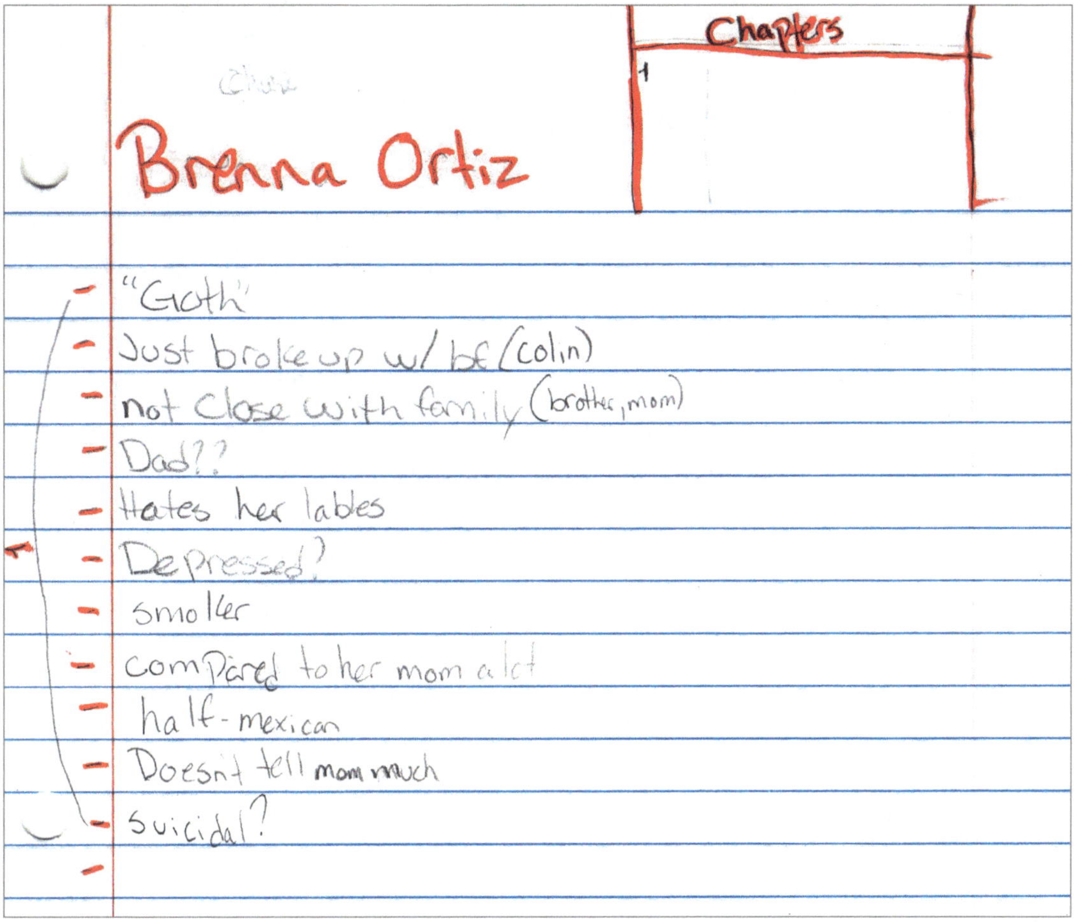
Chapters
1
Brenna Ortiz
- "Goth"
- Just broke up w/ bf (colin)
- not Close with family (brother, mom)
- Dad??
- Hates her lables
- Depressed?
- smoker
- compared to her mom a lot
- half-mexican
- Doesn't tell mom much
- Suicidal?

Shay starts out strong, capturing what they notice about the kind of person this character is.

Providing Feedback

If your students say or demonstrate . . .	Coach them on . . .
When I think about characters, I tend to name the emotions they are feeling.	Choosing precise language to describe emotions Thinking about how the way a character feels in a particular situation gives clues about who the character is—what kind of person feels this way in this situation?
When I think about characters, I list out layers of traits and I strive to describe complex traits that I may not have the words for.	Asking what is making characters the way they are Looking for ways that characters don't make sense or are contradictory
When I think about characters, I think about what caused them to be this way, what they want out of life and from others, and what makes them complex or contradictory characters.	Doing this work on smaller bits of text: micro actions, fleeting thoughts, lines of dialogue

Optional Tools

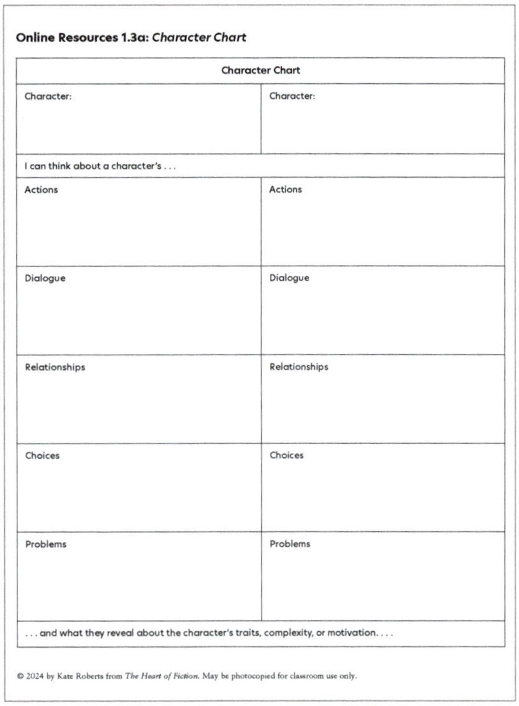

Online Resources 1.3a: *Character Chart*

Character Chart	
Character:	Character:
I can think about a character's . . .	
Actions	Actions
Dialogue	Dialogue
Relationships	Relationships
Choices	Choices
Problems	Problems
. . . and what they reveal about the character's traits, complexity, or motivation. . . .	

© 2024 by Kate Roberts from *The Heart of Fiction*. May be photocopied for classroom use only.

Character Chart (OR 1.3a)

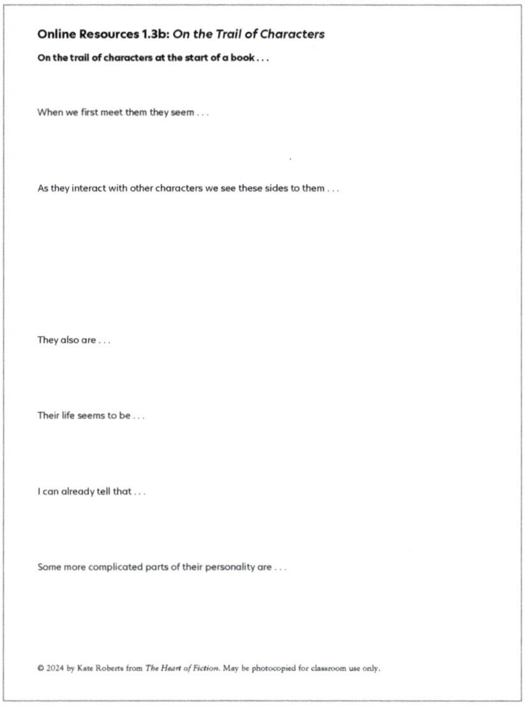

Online Resources 1.3b: *On the Trail of Characters*

On the trail of characters at the start of a book . . .

When we first meet them they seem . . .

As they interact with other characters we see these sides to them . . .

They also are . . .

Their life seems to be . . .

I can already tell that . . .

Some more complicated parts of their personality are . . .

© 2024 by Kate Roberts from *The Heart of Fiction*. May be photocopied for classroom use only.

On the Trail of Characters at the Start of a Book (OR 1.3b)

4. TRACK RELATIONSHIPS AND PROBLEMS

THINKING ABOUT THE STRATEGY

I have a few traits that are pretty obvious to people as they get to know me. I am earnest, I am funny (sometimes with too much sarcasm), and I can be passive and cynical if I don't watch out. These are just ways that I am, regardless of what is happening around me. And yet I don't exist in a vacuum. Depending on who I am with, and what is happening to me, my traits bloom or recede, become assets or flaws. When an unchecked crush of daily stress and responsibilities is upon me, my laziness disappears but my sarcasm becomes biting. When I am with new people that I hope will like me, my earnestness can be a little too much. It's as if my character traits are dials on a control board that situations and people can turn up or down. My relationships and problems affect who I am in a given moment.

As a book begins, we get a pretty good sense of the baseline of relationships and problems that will help and hinder our main characters. We see which relationships are supportive, nurturing, and fun and we see the ones that feel more destructive, limiting, or harsh. We see which relationships feel real and which are dreams—the unrequited fantasies (not all romantic) where we project what we want onto others instead of what is. We see the distant parents, the long-lost friends. This is what matters most in our lives and is often what will have the most impact on characters in books—the people we know. We want to teach students at the start of the novel to always get a sense of the web of people that influence the characters they are most interested in, to keep track of who is who and the effect they are having on each other.

Like I did in my model notebooks, students can begin to examine the relationships that are unfolding as they get to know the characters in books (see Figure 1.6 for one example).

They also will need to pay attention to the problems in the beginning of the books they read. Like relationships, most problems in books are at least hinted at early on (though more may be revealed). And while many students may view the problems in a text in broad strokes, we will want to push our students to think of conflict in deeper, more nuanced ways than self, others, or society.

If you look at the parts of my life that could have been novelized (not now, since my life is currently often a beautiful yet monotonous tapestry of work, chores, parenting kids, and scrolling), the problems I faced were like fractals: they reflected and built on each other, creating matrices that influenced my choices, enhanced or sublimated traits, forged or strained relationships.

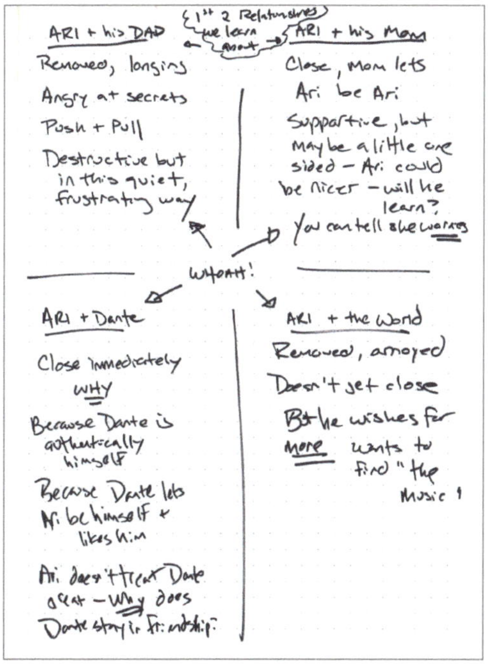

FIGURE 1.6: *Model page tracking the relationships in Aristotle and Dante*

There were the big, obvious problems: my struggle to nurture healthy love, a propensity for self-destruction, countless experiences of homophobia. These problems demanded a resolution and took my attention; they wreaked havoc on my life in obvious ways. But they were also fed and complicated by the layers of subterranean problems I faced: insecurities, a childhood that taught me to be absurdly self-reliant, deep financial insecurity, a vague existential dread.

When we begin a novel, we want our understanding of the problems a character is dealing with to have this breadth and intimacy. Most of us get a feeling for these things as we read, but it may take a little more thinking to name specifics. Just as it took me time to actually articulate the list of problems in my twenties that I wrote earlier, it might take some time to get the layers of difficulties a character seems to be experiencing into words. Yet it will help us immeasurably as we dive into the further sections of a book if we take the time to do so, since these difficulties will most likely shape and shade the arc that is to come.

You will notice that in both instances—tracking relationships and problems—I am going through a process of categorization as I work. I take the relationships in the book and look for the categories of "supportive," "destructive," "dreams," and so on (and then work to say how they are that way). For problems, I uncover the personality issues and the love, family, work, and friendship issues. The problems that arise from inequalities or the big three of race, gender, and class. Certainly I look at the setting for problems caused by time and place. This categorization helps me find more than I could if I simply kept asking myself what other problems I could find. (See Figures 1.7 and 1.8.)

Spending some time at the beginning of a book uncovering the things that will push and pull, motivate and demoralize our characters will help mightily as the mechanisms of plot speed up and we are asked to follow along.

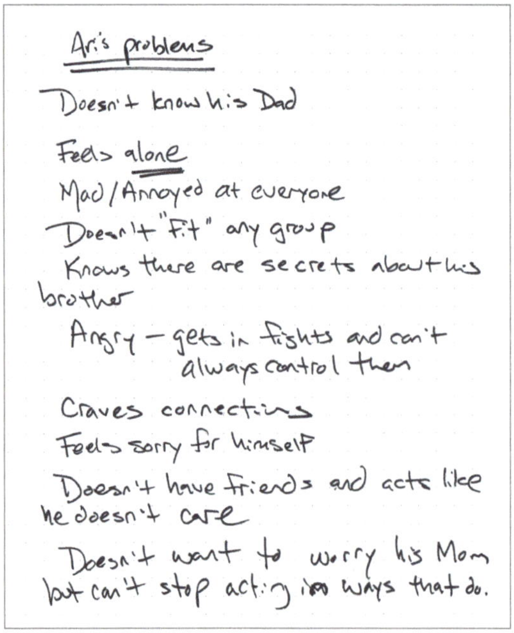

FIGURE 1.7: *Model of problems list at the start of* Aristotle and Dante

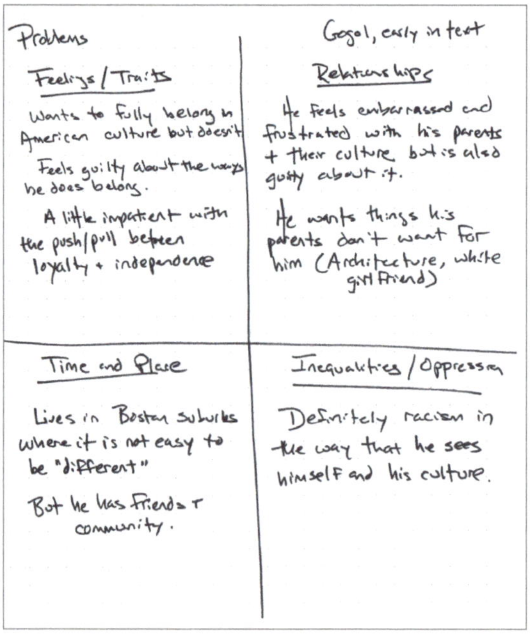

FIGURE 1.8: *Model of problems list at the start of* Aristotle and Dante

4. TRACK RELATIONSHIPS AND PROBLEMS

TEACHING THE STRATEGY

Lesson Flow

Teach students how to go deeper in their analysis of relationships in the text and move beyond naming the big, obvious obstacles the character faces.

One way to teach this lesson:

1. Talk about a time when you stayed on the surface about your life with someone that was a missed opportunity (that person you wanted to be friends with but never pursued, the family member who passed before you got to ask them those questions about their life or yours).
2. Point out that the relationships and problems in our books will stay that vague for us unless we do the work to put words to what we are sensing. It's about finding the layers. I'm not wrong to say a relationship in a book is "good"; it's just that there is more to it than that. Same with problems. Sure, the problem in the book is kind of obvious at first—it's the big thing happening, like war. But there are other hidden problems that affect the text, and we can pay attention to those more sneaky issues too.
3. Show the Relationship Continuum and the Problem Matrix (Online Resources 1.4a and 1.4b) or a graphic organizer of your own to help students track relationships and problems as they read. Share that in any given scene, one of these is probably taking center stage. The author is either developing a relationship or probing a problem.
4. Read aloud a scene from a common text. Have students talk to a partner about which is taking center stage here—relationships or problems. Vote as a class.
5. Whichever the class chooses, refer to the chart and have students either discuss or write out their thinking that digs under the surface. Share as a class.
6. If there's time, repeat with another scene that centers the other frame (relationships or problems). If there isn't time, consider repeating the next day for that frame, as repeated practice will only help your class become more independent.
7. Set students up to read with these two things in mind. Show your reading notebook and how you could set up your page to collect your thinking across relationships and problems as you end sections or chapters.

What Might This Look Like?

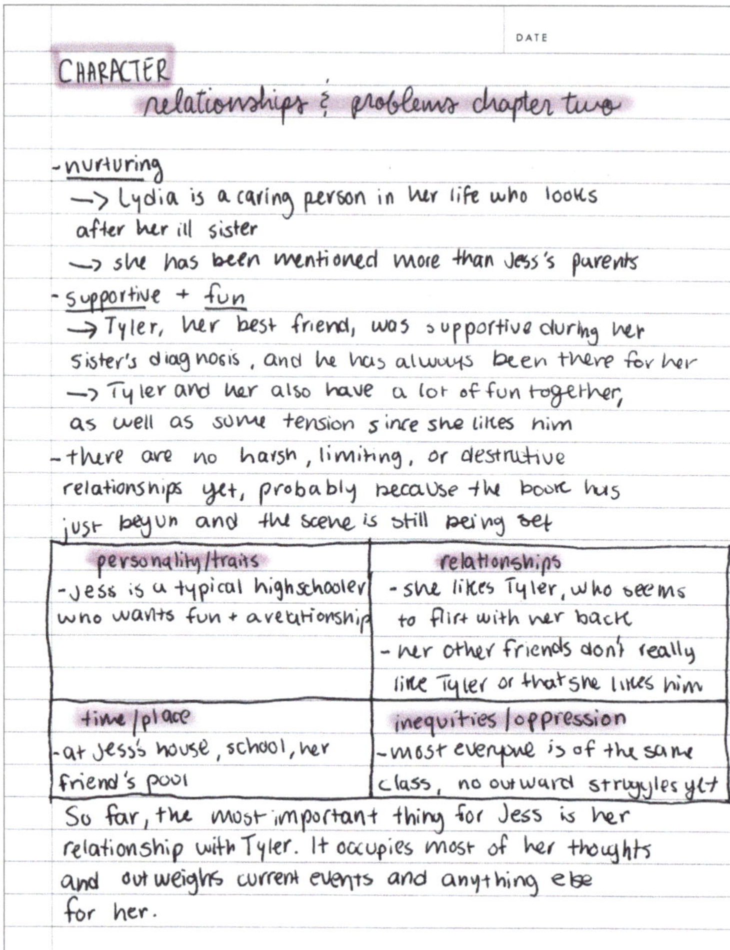

DATE

CHARACTER

relationships & problems chapter two

- nurturing
  - → Lydia is a caring person in her life who looks after her ill sister
  - → she has been mentioned more than Jess's parents
- supportive + fun
  - → Tyler, her best friend, was supportive during her sister's diagnosis, and he has always been there for her
  - → Tyler and her also have a lot of fun together, as well as some tension since she likes him
- there are no harsh, limiting, or destructive relationships yet, probably because the book has just begun and the scene is still being set

personality/traits	relationships
- Jess is a typical highschooler who wants fun + a relationship	- she likes Tyler, who seems to flirt with her back - her other friends don't really like Tyler or that she likes him
time/place	**inequities/oppression**
- at Jess's house, school, her friend's pool	- most everyone is of the same class, no outward struggles yet

So far, the most important thing for Jess is her relationship with Tyler. It occupies most of her thoughts and outweighs current events and anything else for her.

Annika takes some time to reflect on the relationships and problems in her book.

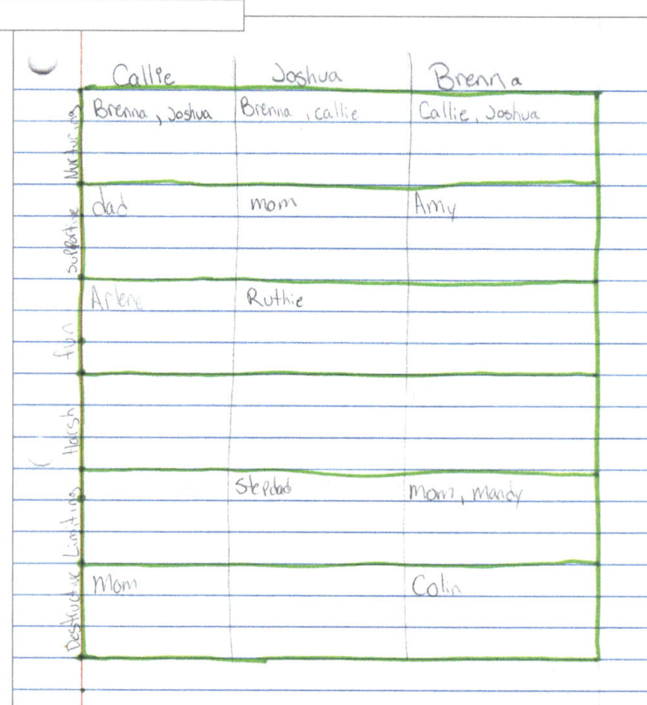

	Callie	Joshua	Brenna
Nurturing	Brenna, Joshua	Brenna, Callie	Callie, Joshua
Supportive	dad	mom	Amy
fun	Arlene	Ruthie	
Harsh			
Limiting		Stepdad	Mom, Mandy
Destructive	Mom		Colin

Shay sets up a continuum to examine relationships.

Providing Feedback

If your students say or demonstrate . . .	Coach them on . . .
When I think about relationships and problems, I tend to name the emotions they cause or one big trait that describes them.	Choosing precise language to describe emotions
When I think about relationships and problems, I list out layers of traits and I strive to describe complex traits that I may not have the words for.	Asking what is making relationships and problems the way they are Looking for ways that relationships and problems don't make sense or are contradictory
When I think about relationships and problems, I think about what caused them to be this way and what makes them complex or contradictory.	Doing this work on smaller bits of text: micro actions, fleeting thoughts, lines of dialogue

Optional Tools

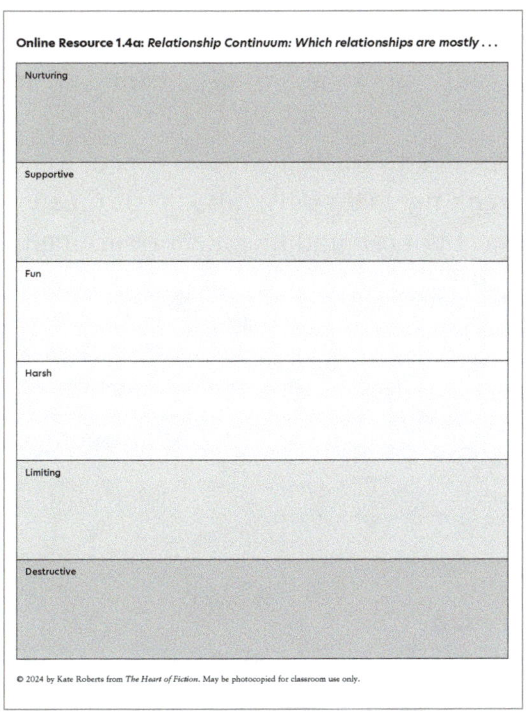

Online Resource 1.4a: *Relationship Continuum: Which relationships are mostly . . .*

Nurturing
Supportive
Fun
Harsh
Limiting
Destructive

Relationship Continuum (OR 1.4a)

Online Resource 1.4b: *Problem Matrix*

Personality/Traits	Relationships
Time and Place	Inequities/Oppression

Problem Matrix (OR 1.4b)

5. NOTICE WHAT ELSE STANDS OUT

THINKING ABOUT THE STRATEGY

While I believe it is important to clarify for kids what their primary work should be in the books they read, it would be foolish to think that kids will think only about characters in *The Namesake*, or *Aristotle and Dante*, or *The Great Gatsby*, or *Kindred*. So yes, it might be true that in this unit students are focusing mostly on character, but certainly we want to teach them to pay attention to the other stuff the novel is offering them as well.

What that other stuff is will depend on a lot of things, however. First, it might depend on what they have been taught before. Like, if your eighth graders had a unit focusing on interpreting themes last year, they certainly could begin to look for themes arising now. If you taught your sophomores the power of imagery, then they should certainly keep noticing it (and how it basically lays out a major theme of the text) in the first scene in *Of Mice and Men*.

This may require a little front-loading, of course. You might need to remind students of what they have learned (which often feels like the yawning abyss of teaching). And yet if students set up their notebooks to track something that they know is important and that has helped them think powerfully in the books they have read in the past, you will find that as they primarily think about characters, other elements will pop in their heads from time to time, creating great opportunities for synthesis.

In my reading of *Aristotle and Dante*, I decided to track themes as I read. In *The Namesake*, I looked for craft. These weren't my main jobs, but I spent time in the beginning of each novel jotting down what I noticed and then kept returning to these pages as I read. (See Figures 1.9 and 1.10.)

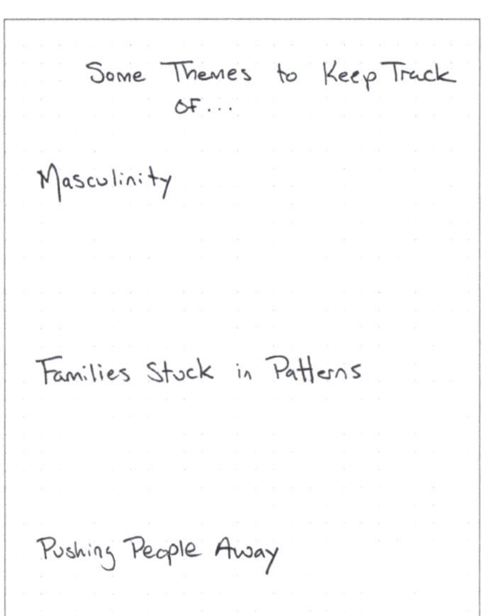

FIGURE 1.9: *Things that stuck out at the beginning of* Aristotle and Dante

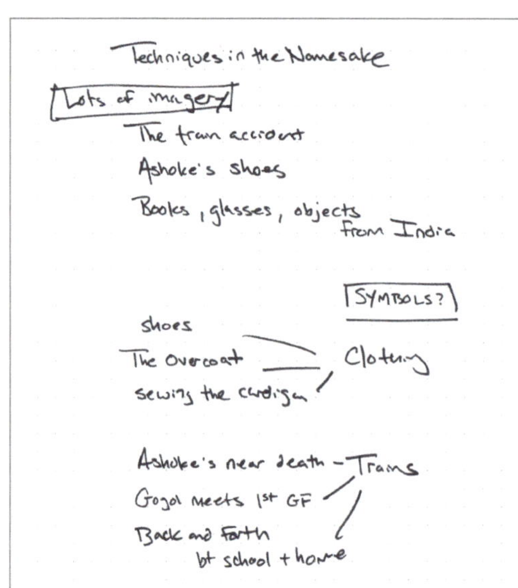

FIGURE 1.10: *Things that stuck out at the beginning of* The Namesake

5. NOTICE WHAT ELSE STANDS OUT

TEACHING THE STRATEGY

Lesson Flow

This is a good lesson to teach when you start feeling anxious that you are spending too much time on character work at the expense of the other elements of the text that beg for attention, particularly when you know that your class has been taught a bunch about theme or literary techniques.

One way to teach this lesson:

1. Project or hand out a short text that is rife with literary technique, something like Sandra Cisneros' "My Name" from *The House on Mango Street* (2004). Read the passage aloud to your class and have a discussion about the characters in similar ways to show how you have been working so far (their traits and relationships and problems, for instance, if you are following this book). Then step back and point out that it would be strange to think only about the characters in a text that has such a rich voice.
2. Have students pull out lines they notice from the text, lines that stick out because they are beautiful or interesting. Ask students to think a bit about how those lines might connect to the thinking you just did about the characters. Don't worry if their answers aren't super sophisticated. This lesson is touching on what kids are able to do independently, but you are not teaching craft right now; you are just revisiting.
3. Have students consider the book or text they are working on independently. What feels like something they should be noticing? Is it literary technique or voice? Is it the strong theme or social issue that is coming through in the pages?
4. Have students set up their reading notebooks so that they are ready to notice and think as they read. Show examples like mine in the earlier section or the student samples that follow.
5. This is a good time for students to take stock of how their work is going. At this point students have three jobs to do as each section or chapter ends: revisit their traits list, add to or name new relationship dynamics and problems that are being introduced, and now notice other stuff that demands attention. Have students reflect on which work feels the most vital and the most interesting to them, so that they can set some priorities for what they will spend more time on. Then, send them off to read and work independently or in partnerships as you confer and pull small groups.

What Might This Look Like?

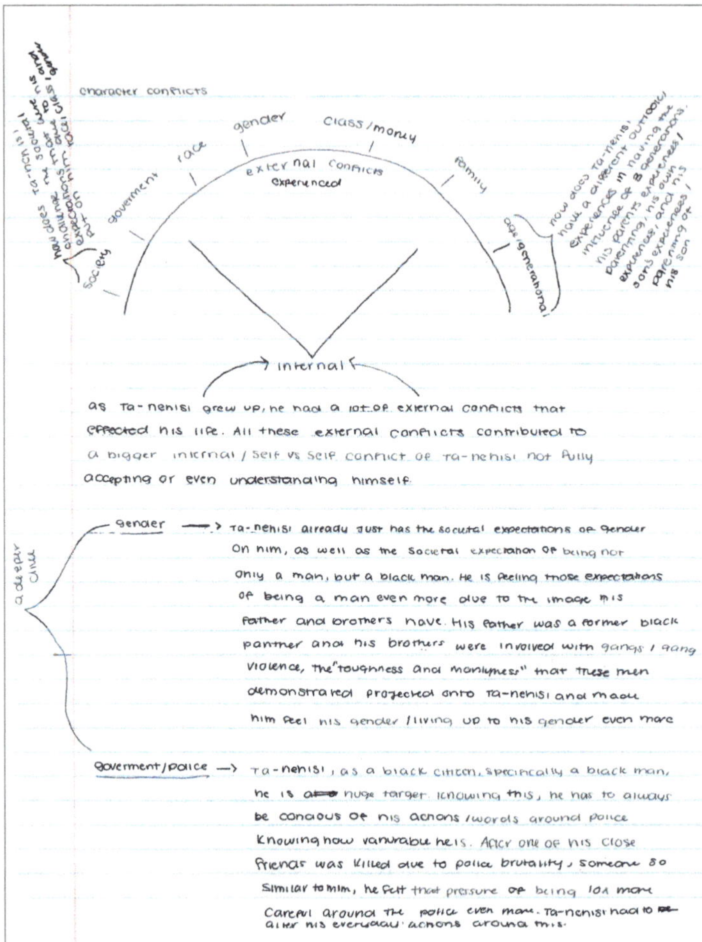

as Ta-nehisi grew up, he had a lot of external conflicts that effected his life. All these external conflicts contributed to a bigger internal / self vs self conflict of Ta-nehisi not fully accepting or even understanding himself.

a deeper dive

gender → Ta-nehisi already just has the societal expectations of gender on him, as well as the societal expectation of being not only a man, but a black man. He is feeling those expectations of being a man even more due to the image his father and brothers have. His father was a former black panther and his brothers were involved with gangs / gang violence, the "toughness and manlyness" that these men demonstrated projected onto Ta-nehisi and made him feel his gender / living up to his gender even more

government/police → Ta-nehisi, as a black citizen, specifically a black man, he is a huge target. knowing this, he has to always be concious of his actions / words around police knowing how vunrable he is. After one of his close friends was killed due to police brutality, someone so similar to him, he felt that pressure of being 10x more careful around the police even more. Ta-nehisi had to alter his everyday actions around this.

A student explores the connections between character, conflict, and theme.

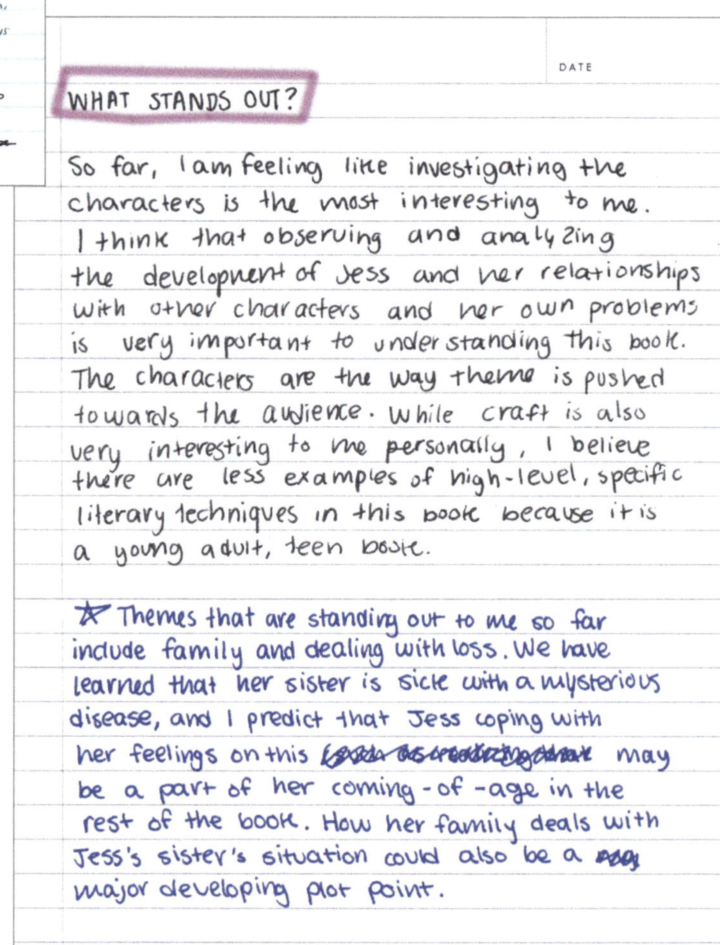

DATE

WHAT STANDS OUT?

So far, I am feeling like investigating the characters is the most interesting to me. I think that observing and analyzing the development of Jess and her relationships with other characters and her own problems is very important to understanding this book. The characters are the way theme is pushed towards the audience. While craft is also very interesting to me personally, I believe there are less examples of high-level, specific literary techniques in this book because it is a young adult, teen book.

☆ Themes that are standing out to me so far include family and dealing with loss. We have learned that her sister is sick with a mysterious disease, and I predict that Jess coping with her feelings on this may be a part of her coming-of-age in the rest of the book. How her family deals with Jess's sister's situation could also be a major developing plot point.

Annika pauses in the text to see what other elements she can connect to her character analysis.

Providing Feedback

If your students say or demonstrate . . .	Coach them on . . .
I am able to name literary techniques or themes that are arising from the text.	Considering what the author might be trying to show about that theme or with that technique
I am able to name techniques or themes and think a little about why the author might be introducing these elements.	Anticipating where the author might be going with this theme or what they might be hinting at with that technique
I am able to name techniques or themes and theorize, using what I know about how books go, where this is going to lead.	Looking for patterns of theme or technique across the text, as well as exceptions

Optional Tools

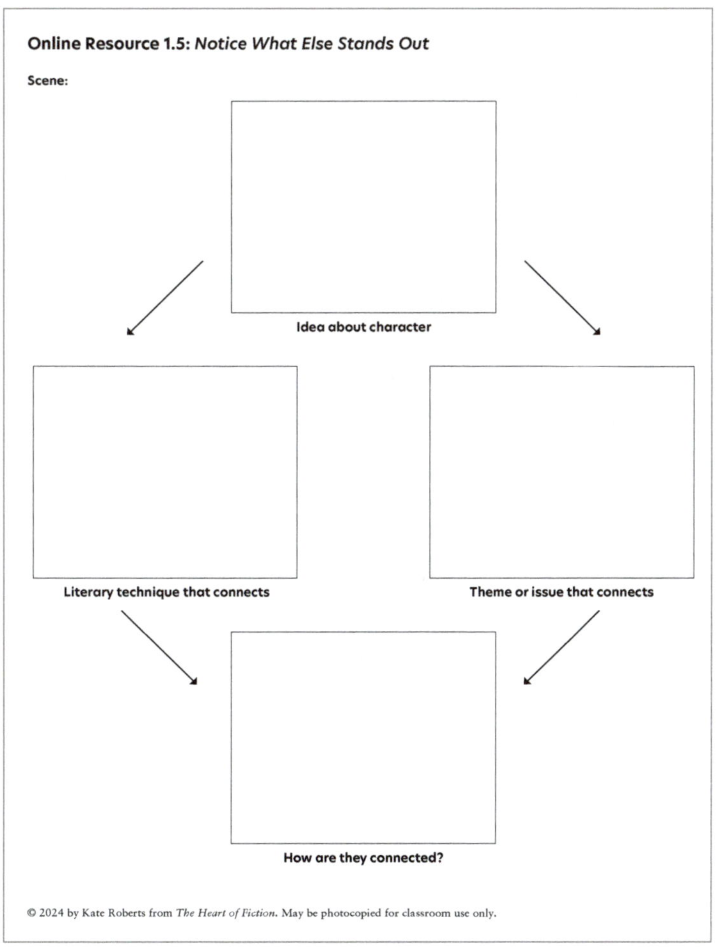

Online Resource 1.5: *Notice What Else Stands Out*

Scene:

Idea about character

Literary technique that connects

Theme or issue that connects

How are they connected?

Notice What Else Stands Out (OR 1.5)

IN THE MIDDLE OF THE BOOK

In this section, we'll discuss the following strategies:

6. Unpack Causes and Anticipate Effects

This lesson can help students discover depths of understanding for the characters they are reading when they find themselves staying at the surface. In it, we press Pause and look backward for causes and forward for effects at a critical moment in the text.

7. Become Attuned to Shifts and Changes

By the time you get to the middle of a book, it is a good idea to notice how things are starting to shift, helping students zero in on the smaller, more subtle moments of change.

8. Sink into Empathy and Compassion

Help students develop their ability to understand people's experiences and grapple with the significant differences between them.

If we have done good character work from the start, as we find ourselves in the midst of the novel, we'll begin to reap rewards. We know the characters well. The way they respond to things clicks and makes sense; their relationships feel familiar, as do the difficulties they face. There is a temptation sometimes to rush through the text: as we read the middle chapters our inner voice has a Seinfeldian refrain: Yada yada yada. I get it.

Yet the center of a text is the place where we deepen our connection and understanding of the character. It's not the first date; it's couples counseling. There is glue here; there is intimacy. The middle is where we form our true bonds.

It is also where we see the author take risks, offer minor characters and tangents, and throw in weird stuff that we should figure out how to deal with. They have done the work of laying the foundation, and soon they will need to forge a resolution, but here, in the middle, they can play a bit. There is room.

So while often our reading work from the beginning can really get some traction here, and perhaps we can read a bit faster, it will also help us immeasurably to pause and analyze the parts of characterization that tend to live in the eye of the novel.

6. UNPACK CAUSES AND ANTICIPATE EFFECTS

THINKING ABOUT THE STRATEGY

There is a moment for most of us where we learn to be a bit more self-aware than we were in our youth. Of course, when that happens varies. I did not have a deep and healthy sense of who I was and how I affected those around me until my early thirties. Hopefully you found that wisdom earlier. Perhaps you were born with it.

This awareness helps me now to live fully in my life. To integrate parts of myself, my story, and my circumstances. For example: I can be difficult to communicate with sometimes. I tend to want to be right; I tend to try to outargue; I try to fix things too quickly. When I was younger and heard this critique from others, I rejected it—I thrust the information away, feeling it was their fault. Now I am learning to take this trait and unpack why I am like that. I think about what tends to trigger this response in me. Ultimately I had to unpack the causes of this trait: the historical origins as well as the immediate catalysts.

The middle of a book is a good time to consider the causes for the character's various traits, problems, and circumstances. OK, cool, this character pushes people away. But why are they like that? And what situations bring it out in them? After the beginning of a text, we should know a lot about how the characters are, and now we can explore why.

Similarly, as we become more self-aware, we are able to predict the effects of our actions. I know now that when I feel that rising sense of "I'm right," that blush of indignation, if I act on those feelings I will not only intensify the argument I am having with someone but also foster bad feelings that can fester over time.

This is where living a self-aware life and being a wide-awake reader differ, however. In my life what I do with this information is change. (Hopefully.) I have worked hard in the course of my relationships to listen more. Of course this comes back to me, too, and the end effect when I am able to live better is that I feel loved more deeply, more connected to those I care about.

In books we can't make the characters change, and of course if they did become self-aware at the first sign of trouble, our novels would be quite short and boring to read. When we read with an awareness of how the character will affect others, we live in a state of anticipation. We watch Ari snub another advance of friendship and think, "Ah, Ari, this is just going to make you angrier, buddy." We become psychics within the world of the story, making predictions of how this is all going to shake out based on all we know about the characters so far. (See my examples in Figures 1.11 and 1.12.)

Of course, our predictions might be wrong, but living in the state of anticipation and theorizing means that as we move through the text, we have formed a backboard of ideas for the scenes to hit against. We read and confirm our expectations, or we meet moments that surprise us and cause us to rethink our understanding.

Help your students find places to pause in the text. Then teach them that in these places, they almost have to mentally rewind the text to look for causes and fast-forward to predict effects. As we move toward the end of the book, this work will help students do a great deal of analysis work on the text and themselves that they won't be able to do as well if they have not been wide-awake, self-aware readers.

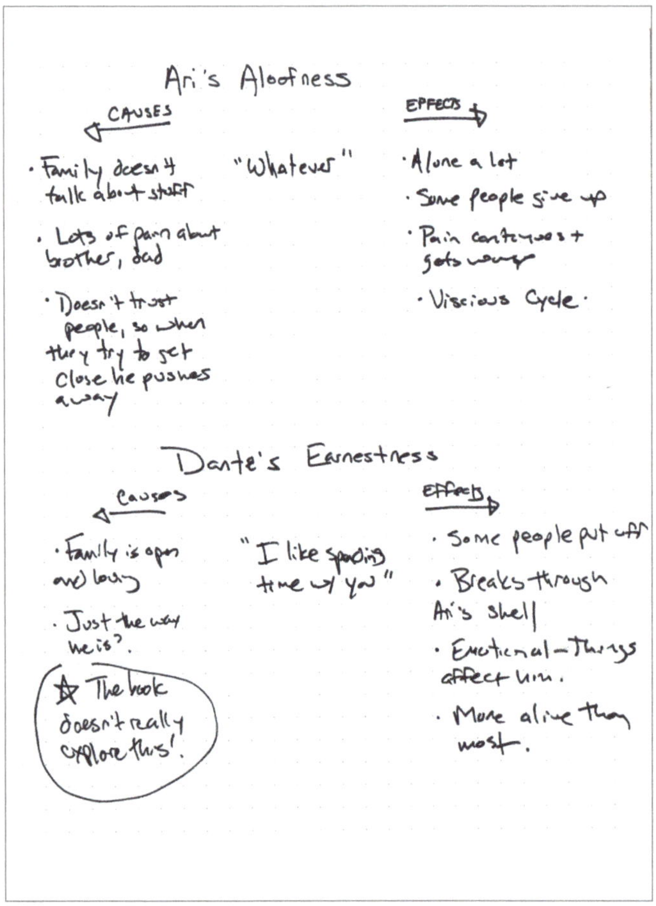

FIGURE 1.11: *Model notes on causes and effects of character traits*

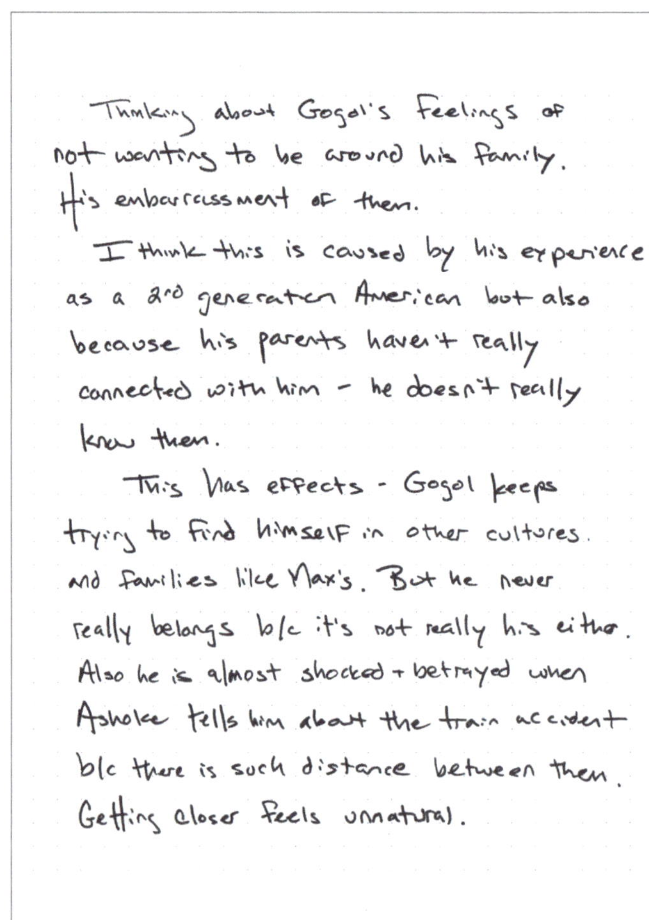

Thinking about Gogol's feelings of not wanting to be around his family. His embarrassment of them.

I think this is caused by his experience as a 2nd generation American but also because his parents haven't really connected with him – he doesn't really know them.

This has effects - Gogol keeps trying to find himself in other cultures and families like Max's. But he never really belongs b/c it's not really his either. Also he is almost shocked + betrayed when Ashoke tells him about the train accident b/c there is such distance between them. Getting closer feels unnatural.

FIGURE 1.12: *Model notes on causes and effects of character traits*

6. UNPACK CAUSES AND ANTICIPATE EFFECTS

TEACHING THE STRATEGY

Lesson Flow

This lesson can help students discover depths of understanding for the characters they are reading when they find themselves staying at the surface. We can teach students to press Pause and look backward for causes and forward for effects at a critical moment in the text.

One way to teach this lesson:

1. Take a critical moment in popular culture your kids know about and talk about how there are these moments in texts where you need to hit Pause. And when you do, you need to rewind and fast-forward in your mind: Rewind to think, Wait, do I understand what led this person to this moment in time? And fast-forward to consider all of the ramifications of the choice they have made.
2. Have students pick a moment in their book that merits this kind of consideration. Tell them it is usually when the character has made a choice or when they are acting in ways that are hard to understand.
3. Show students a way of thinking about cause and effect in writing. You might use the following graphic organizers (see "Optional Tools"), but certainly students could and might prefer to just jot in their notebook.
4. Model how you use this way of thinking in a class text: name a moment and think through all of the causes and all of the effects from this one moment. Have students work on their own books independently or with partners or clubs if they are reading the same book.

What Might This Look Like?

Shay unpacks a moment in the text for its causes and effects.

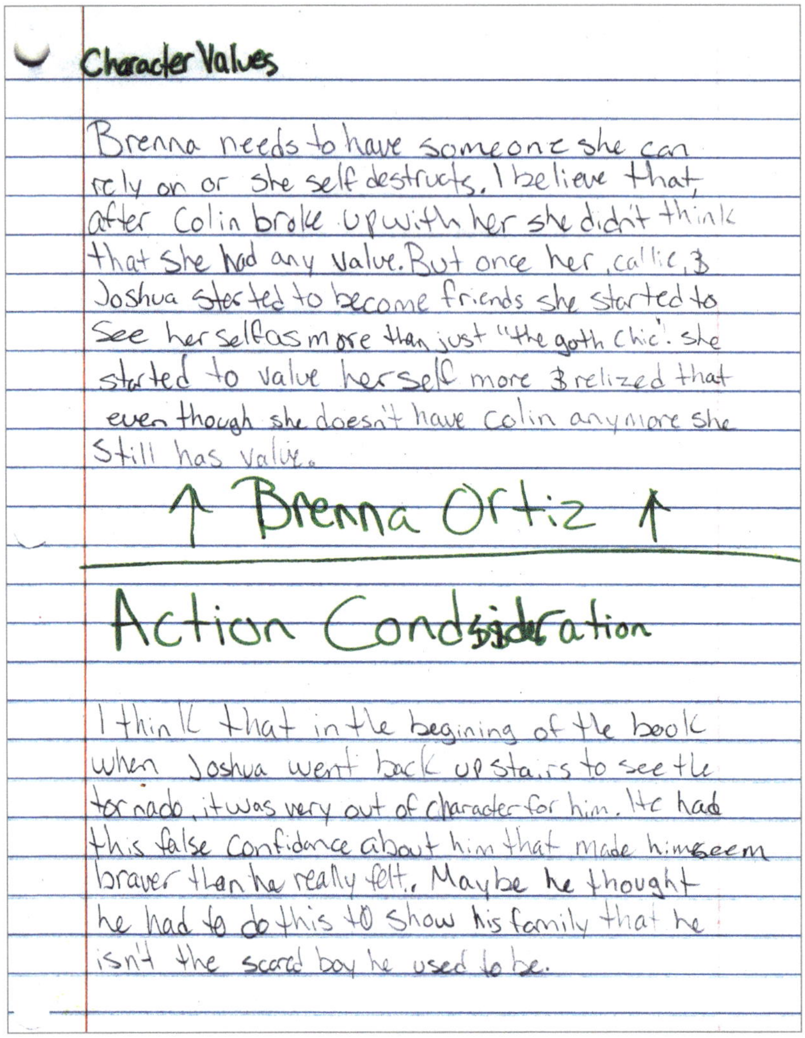

Character Values

Brenna needs to have someone she can rely on or she self destructs. I believe that, after Colin broke up with her she didn't think that she had any value. But once her, callie, & Joshua started to become friends she started to see herself as more than just "the goth chic". she started to value herself more & relized that even though she doesn't have colin anymore she still has value.

↑ Brenna Ortiz ↑

Action Condsideration

I think that in the begining of the book when Joshua went back upstairs to see the tornado, it was very out of character for him. He had this false confidance about him that made him seem braver than he really felt. Maybe he thought he had to do this to show his family that he isn't the scared boy he used to be.

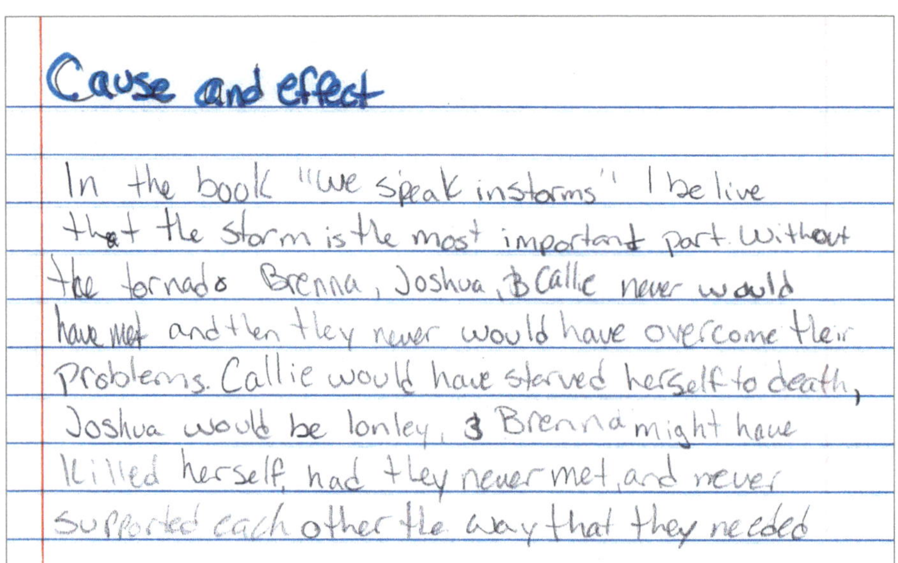

Cause and effect

In the book "We speak instorms" I belive that the storm is the most important part. Without the tornado Brenna, Joshua, & Callie never would have met and then they never would have overcome their problems. Callie would have starved herself to death, Joshua would be lonley, & Brenna might have killed herself, had they never met, and never supported each other the way that they needed

Providing Feedback

If your students say or demonstrate . . .	Coach them on . . .
I can name the events that led to this moment and the events that might follow.	Asking what this event might cause the character to feel or how they might act afterward Asking how the feelings or traits of the character led them to this moment
I can think about how emotions or traits led to and will come from this moment.	Thinking about how a character's motivations led them to certain events and how events might cause a motivation as well
I can consider how what characters want affects their choices and how the complexity of their lives motivates them to act this way. I can forecast how this moment will affect the way that characters see the world, the choices they make, and the relationships they have.	Doing this work on less obvious events, smaller moments, or events that don't necessarily fit the major narrative

Optional Tools

Online Resource 1.6a: *Rewind and Fast Forward to Uncover Causes and Effects*

1. What is it that you want to analyze? Character trait? Event? Motivation? A problem?

START: What you are analyzing.

REWIND - what are the causes?

FAST FORWARD - what are the effects?

Rewind and Fast-Forward to Uncover Causes and Effects (OR 1.6a)

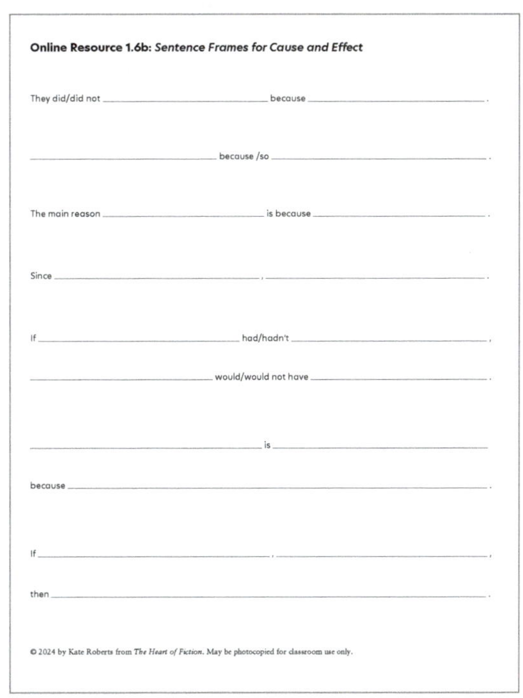
Online Resource 1.6b: *Sentence Frames for Cause and Effect*

They did/did not ____ because ____.

____ because /so ____.

The main reason ____ is because ____.

Since ____, ____.

If ____ had/hadn't ____,

____ would/would not have ____.

____ is ____

because ____.

If ____, ____,

then ____.

Sentence Frames for Cause and Effect (OR 1.6b)

7. BECOME ATTUNED TO SHIFTS AND CHANGES

THINKING ABOUT THE STRATEGY

Change is constant, and change is hard. Life doesn't like to let us get dusty on a shelf. It shakes us up and forces us to confront the eternal choice: change or die. Maybe not literally in most cases. No, in most cases when we don't change, we just . . . calcify. We stop growing, since growing, of course, means transforming.

As much as change is constant, it is also so very slow sometimes. Growing up, I watched He-Man and the Masters of the Universe and my favorite part of each episode was the moment when Prince Adam held up his power sword and transformed right before our eyes into the titular hero. As much as I wish my own transformations could have been so sudden and complete, they rarely were. Instead, change was gradual. Glacial, more often than not.

When students read for change, they often look for the big metamorphosis. And this is good. When we are engaged readers, we stand up, call out, or cry when Ari kisses Dante. When Gogol realizes his deep connection to his culture, his family. When Romeo dies. Yes, those are very important moments of change. But they did not come out of nowhere. As we teach students to study characters, we need to teach them to look for the little moments, the tiny shifts. The expression on a character's face as they react to something with a slight new awareness. The fleeting thought that you barely register as you read but then think, Wait a second, that's different. Yes, Ari kissing Dante is a big change, but before that he starts working a job and hanging out with kids in a new way. Before that he holds his tongue when he wants to say something snarky. Before that he asks his dad a question. These little shifts all lead to the big ones.

When we look for changes like these while reading, we read for more detail, and with more thoughtfulness, than if we just waited for the big reveal at the end of the novel.

7. BECOME ATTUNED TO SHIFTS AND CHANGES

TEACHING THE STRATEGY

Lesson Flow

By the time you get to the middle of a book, it is a good idea to notice how things are starting to shift, helping students zero in on the smaller, more subtle moments of change.

One way to teach this lesson:

1. Tell students that today they will be playing a game or entering a debate (whichever phrase will help them lean in more). The rules of the game are this: students and their team (anyone else who is reading the same book as them) will list out three ways a character is starting to change. Set kids up into teams and have them list their moments of change.
2. Next, for each moment of change, students will look for the exact line that first shows that change happening. The point is to quote a line or phrase, a word or even a punctuation mark that the reader feels is the moment the shift begins. Model this work on one change in a common text. Have students do this work independently.
3. In timed sessions, students will compare their moments of change with those of their teammates and argue why theirs is the true moment when the shift began. You might refer to the Shifts and Changes Bingo Card in the "Optional Tools" section.
4. Coach students to try this work more authentically as they read, pausing at the end of each chapter or section in the middle of the book to notice moments of shifts and changes.

What Might This Look Like?

CHARACTER
the changes - mid of book

1. - page 89, Jess starts to distrust everyone else in her life, and suspect things aren't as they seem

ex. • "I still felt so separate from them, even now. They were supposed to be my best friends, but lately everything was off."

[her friends always change the subject to what THEY want]

~~causes~~
- Jess is hearing strange noises others deny are there
- she feels like she's not in control of her own life, and relates to her old guitar teacher who others say went crazy
- her friends aren't supportive of her and Tyler, and are pushing her to date Patrick Kramer
- her sister got really sick with zero warning
- Jess is also convinced something happened to her dog, but her parents, friends, and Tyler brush it off

~~affects~~
- she will probably start to drift more from her friend group
- there will be a plot twist soon... what are these events leading up to?
- Jess may get closer to Tyler if she can't trust anyone else, or another newer character
- these changes may contribute to her desire to get out of her town, possibly for college

Annika dives deep into the text to think through all of the changes the character is starting to undergo.

2. "I tried to back away but I knocked against the sink. There was nowhere to go. I couldn't believe I'd ever kissed him. That I'd ever *liked* him." Page 113
- This moment of change is really important because it signifies the switch in the main focus of the book – going from sterotypical 'boy troubles' as the biggest issue to something much more complicated and scary (the reality that her life is a TV show and everyone around her is acting).

3. "... I was also acutely aware that we were back on camera, back to everyone watching us ... All the memories were rewriting themselves, taking on new meaning." Page 119
- This moment is the first time we see Jess fully start to grapple with the complete switch that has just happened in her reality. She starts to look back on her past and analyze her present under a completely new lens – that none of it is as it seems.
- Also, this moment opens up a new question/conflict to the audience: What will Jess do in this situation? Will she attempt to get out, and how will she do so?

I've learned so far is that Kaz Brekker usually never loses his cool. He is usually the picture of calm and collected. "He was afraid for you." "Kaz isn't afraid of anything" "you should have seen his face when he brought you to me." And before this (long story short) he actively "tortured" the guy that hurt Inej then killed him. Like wow, a bit much but whatever. There are probably better examples I could've used but the book has this going on throughout the entire thing. Again I wish I could explain this better but I'm not sure how to put it all into words. All I can say is that I love and hate this at the same time, Kaz and Inej need to just sit down and talk. This book is amazing

Here, a student unpacks a shift they see in a character in the book they are reading.

Providing Feedback

If your students say or demonstrate . . .	Coach them on . . .
I notice the change in the way a character acts or reacts to events or people in the text.	Looking to see if there is also a change in how the character feels about something or if their personality starts to change
I notice a change in the character's traits and emotions.	Noticing when the character sees something differently, when their opinion or worldview shifts, or when they think in a different way
I notice a change in the way a character thinks or sees the world or a shift in their motivation and dreams.	Doing this work on smaller, more subtle shifts and changes

Optional Tools

Online Resource 1.7a: ***Shifts and Changes Bingo Card***

They did something they would not have done before.	**Their reaction to an event is slightly out of character.**	**They see someone in a new light.**
A new piece of information is learned.	**They have a conversation that changes the way they see something.**	**They start to struggle with something that wasn't a problem before.**
They ask a new question about themselves, others, or life.	**The tone of the writing shifts around a character.**	**A new character is introduced.**

Shifts and Changes Bingo Card (OR 1.7a)

Online Resource 1.7b: ***Tracking Change Across a Novel***

In the beginning the character is . . .

But then . . .

And so . . .

Which then . . .

Except . . .

All of which leads to . . .

Tracking Change Across a Novel (OR 1.7b)

8. SINK INTO EMPATHY AND COMPASSION

THINKING ABOUT THE STRATEGY

We can think of empathy as being the ability to put ourselves in another person's shoes—to feel what they feel. Empathy can take time to develop. Certainly there are people we understand immediately, people we just get. But for most of the rest of the population, it takes a little work.

I think this is primarily because people just don't behave the way they are supposed to—or, at least, the way we think they're supposed to. A friend recently suffered a great loss and instead of being sad and quiet and introspective, she was pissed and kept cracking bitingly sarcastic jokes that made me uncomfortable. In that discomfort I had to decide: Am I going to work to understand and give space to the way she is acting, or am I going to go away? Almost always the work is worth it (unless there is true harm being enacted of course).

The work of empathy is more than putting yourself in another's shoes. If I really want to empathize, I need to do more than this—I need to think about how they feel, not how I would feel. Why are they acting that way? What do they really want? Really mean? Really need? As Aeriale Johnson (2020) points out in her *School Library Journal* article "Teaching Compassion—Not Empathy—and Critical Reading," empathy sometimes does not feel like enough because it does not lead to critique—or action.

Characters in books are sometimes easier to understand than people in the wild. The author gives us insight into what's happening in characters' heads and hearts, and because they are plotted out, they are missing the entropy of humanity. And yet it's still work to get them in ways that will pay off in our analysis and in the wisdom we gain from reading. When we help our students work toward empathy as they read, we can first help them understand the position they find themselves in: as Rudine Sims Bishop (1990) teaches us, books can act as mirrors, windows, or sliding glass doors. They can reflect our experience, becoming a mirror. Or they can allow us entry into another's world and perspective, opening as sliding glass doors. They can also remain windows: a removed experience of simply looking into another's space. To begin creating sliding glass doors, we first must name how much of this text is familiar to us and how much we have to learn. We can think of the text as being an absolute reflection, a distorted reflection (think fun house mirror), or a view (and hopefully an entrance) into an unfamiliar world or experience.

Where we need to work the hardest is when we are having trouble understanding a character—their responses or choices or way of being in the world. When this happens, it helps to start with what is familiar, to name first what it is that we can relate to. We can then name the differences between us, both in circumstances and in intensity of those circumstances. Living in this gap, to empathize we must build bridges with questions and connections like "Why would someone . . . ?" and "What they really want is . . . ," and "I've acted like that before because . . . ." As I read about Ari, I struggled to understand his desire to push everyone away. It felt repetitive and, quite honestly, annoying. I wrote out some thoughts, trying to build bridges into his experience (see Figure 1.13).

With Gogol I did the same, but I hit a challenge. I found myself trying to overrelate with him. I was doing this by saying things like, "Well, one time, I had this experience, and it's sort of the same." But I had to pause. Because our experiences were not the same at all. As humans, yes, we have experienced similar emotions. But our circumstances were very different. I realized I needed to do a little more research on the world and culture and beliefs that Gogol was coming from. My writing took a turn into deeper understanding, as you can see in Figure 1.14.

When we truly live in empathy, we know that there is almost always another layer of understanding to reach. We know this in our lives: I am consistently understanding my wife of thirteen years better and hope for many more years of this deepening. Our relationships with characters are often much briefer than this, but we can still choose to dive into the deep end and get out of the wading pool of empathy.

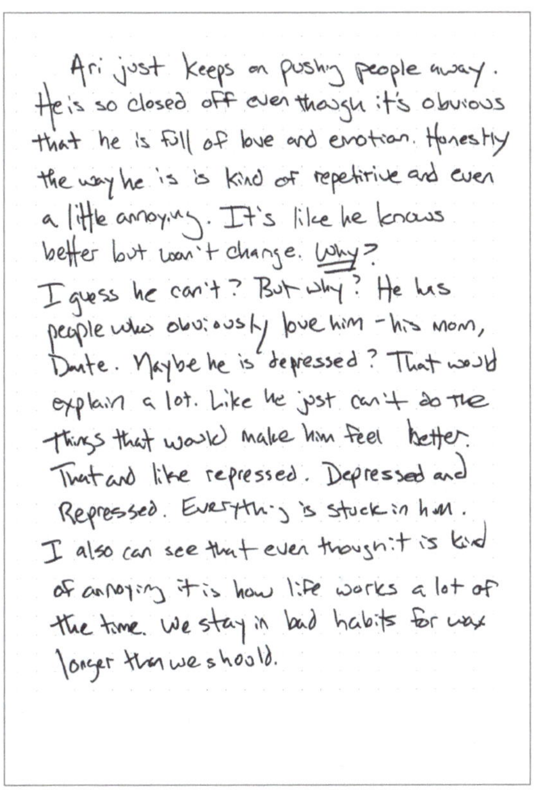

Ari just keeps on pushing people away. He is so closed off even though it's obvious that he is full of love and emotion. Honestly the way he is is kind of repetitive and even a little annoying. It's like he knows better but won't change. Why?
I guess he can't? But why? He has people who obviously love him - his mom, Dante. Maybe he is depressed? That would explain a lot. Like he just can't do the things that would make him feel better. That and like repressed. Depressed and Repressed. Everything is stuck in him.
I also can see that even though it is kind of annoying it is how life works a lot of the time. We stay in bad habits for way longer than we should.

FIGURE 1.13: *Model of writing long to build empathy*

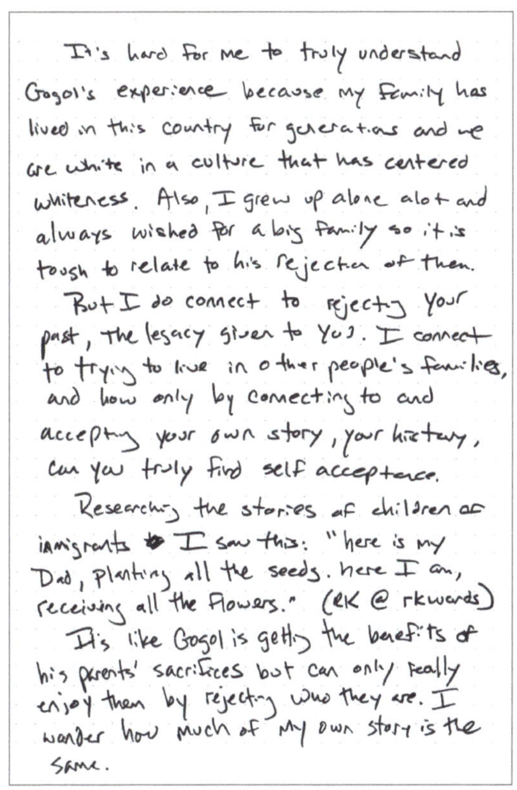

It's hard for me to truly understand Gogol's experience because my family has lived in this country for generations and we are white in a culture that has centered whiteness. Also, I grew up alone alot and always wished for a big family so it is tough to relate to his rejection of them.

But I do connect to rejecting your past, the legacy given to you. I connect to trying to live in other people's families, and how only by connecting to and accepting your own story, your history, can you truly find self acceptance.

Researching the stories of children of immigrants I saw this: "here is my Dad, planting all the seeds. here I am, receiving all the flowers." (RK @ rkwords)

It's like Gogol is getting the benefits of his parents' sacrifices but can only really enjoy them by rejecting who they are. I wonder how much of my own story is the same.

FIGURE 1.14: *Working to fill in gaps of understanding through research and relating*

8. SINK INTO EMPATHY AND COMPASSION

TEACHING THE STRATEGY

Lesson Flow

Help students develop their ability to understand people's experiences and grapple with the significant differences between them.

One way to teach this lesson:

1. First coach students to gauge how closely they relate to the characters in the text. Take a scene from a common text and annotate in the margins which parts of the text feel exactly like your experience, which feel similar but with important differences, and which moments make you feel like you are looking into another world.
2. Then have students consider what their work is for each of these reading experiences: looking into a mirror, making sense of what they see in a funhouse mirror (a phrase I heard from Donna Santman [2007]), or turning a window into a sliding glass door.

   Mirror: What does your shared experience tell you about how the character is feeling, how they are acting, or what they are struggling with? What do you think they will do next?

   Funhouse Mirror: Name the differences in your experience and the character's. You may find these questions from Donna Santman's work on empathy to be helpful: "What do these differences tell you about the character's experience? How do these differences help explain or expose questions about how the character is reacting?" (Santman 2007)

   Window: What precise feelings and issues is this character experiencing? Has there ever been a moment where you felt that precise emotion—even if not as intensely or for as long or for the same reasons at all? What do the character's feelings or actions show you about the character? What does this reveal about who they are or how they are reacting?

   Sliding Glass Door: How does this text ask you to think or live differently because of what you have learned about this character's experience?

3. Model your thinking for whichever you think will be toughest for your students to practice independently. If you want students to engage in empathic reading practices, you will want to spend a couple of days with this work, and so you should have enough time to model at least two of these ways of reading.
4. Send students off to practice this work. Ask the class to find three scenes in the text they are reading that capture what the character is going through, or that they find hard to empathize with, and to practice the work set up above.

5. Have students discuss what they discovered in groups or partnerships. Then ask the groups to reflect on what they may have learned about empathy—why it is important and how to develop it. Have the class share out observations that you chart.

What Might This Look Like?

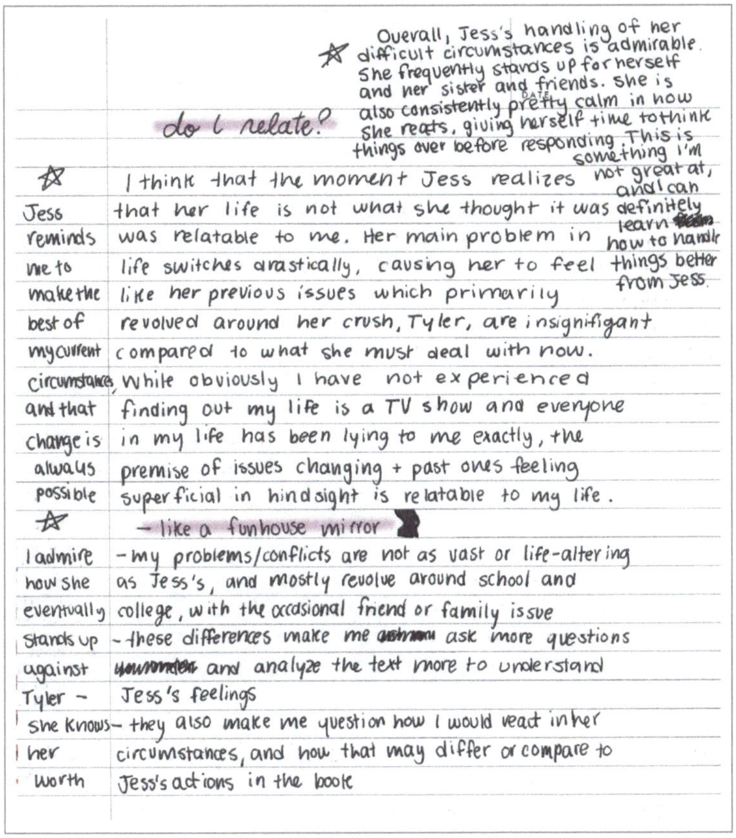

do I relate?

Overall, Jess's handling of her difficult circumstances is admirable. She frequently stands up for herself and her sister and friends. She is also consistently pretty calm in how she reacts, giving herself time to think things over before responding. This is something I'm not great at, and I can definitely learn how to handle things better from Jess.

I think that the moment Jess realizes that her life is not what she thought it was was relatable to me. Her main problem in life switches drastically, causing her to feel like her previous issues which primarily revolved around her crush, Tyler, are insignifigant compared to what she must deal with now. While obviously I have not experienced finding out my life is a TV show and everyone in my life has been lying to me exactly, the premise of issues changing + past ones feeling superficial in hindsight is relatable to my life.

— like a funhouse mirror

- my problems/conflicts are not as vast or life-altering as Jess's, and mostly revolve around school and college, with the occasional friend or family issue
- these differences make me ask more questions and analyze the text more to understand Jess's feelings
- they also make me question how I would react in her circumstances, and how that may differ or compare to Jess's actions in the book

Jess reminds me to make the best of my current circumstances, and that change is always possible

I admire how she eventually stands up against Tyler — she knows her worth

Annika weighs how much she relates to a character.

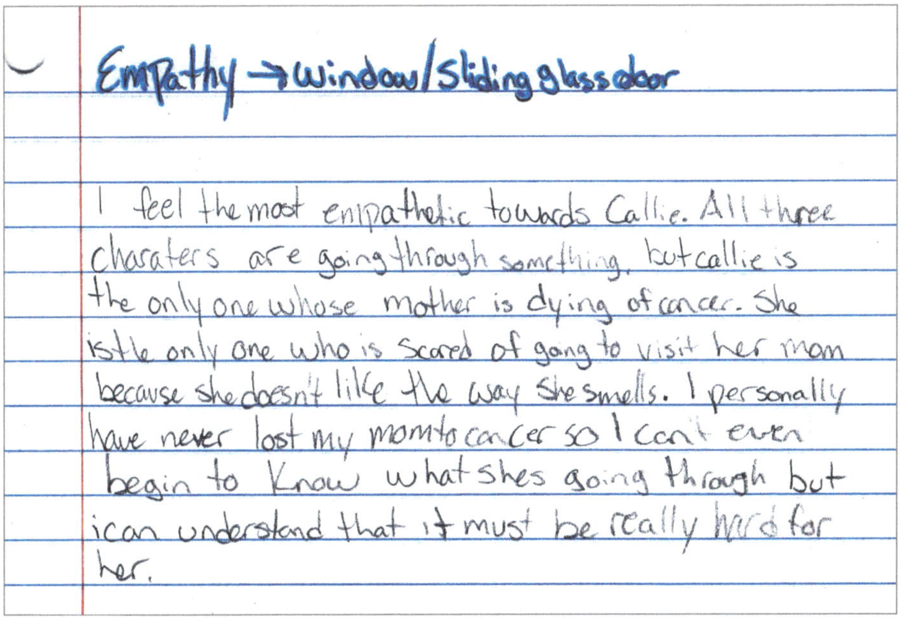

Empathy → window/Sliding glass door

I feel the most empathetic towards Callie. All three charaters are going through something, but callie is the only one whose mother is dying of cancer. She is the only one who is scared of going to visit her mom because she doesn't like the way she smells. I personally have never lost my mom to cancer so I can't even begin to know what shes going through but i can understand that it must be really hard for her.

Shay takes a moment to compare their experience to the character's.

Providing Feedback

If your students say or demonstrate . . .	Coach them on . . .
I can make connections between my experience and the character's and point to places where our experiences are very different. I can name what is similar and what is different between us.	Thinking about what is the same and different about their emotions and the character's and the way they see things Considering the ways that bias, oppression, and privilege may affect our understanding of someone's experience
I notice a change in the character's traits and emotions.	Noticing when the character sees something differently, when their opinion or worldview shifts, or when they think in a different way
I can use what is similar or different to think about what the character must be feeling and thinking, and I can be precise with my language when discussing emotions and thoughts.	Uncovering what is the same and different between their and the character's motivations and choices and beliefs Considering the ways that bias and privilege may affect our understanding of someone's experience
I can use what is similar and different to think about the character's motivations, choices, beliefs, and lessons. I can anticipate the way the character might change by the end of the text.	Doing this work in smaller or less obvious parts of the text Considering the ways that bias and privilege may affect our understanding of someone's experience

Optional Tool

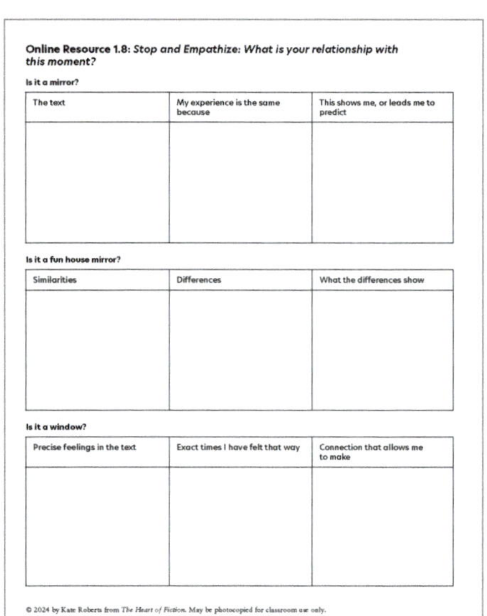

Online Resource 1.8: ***Stop and Empathize: What is your relationship with this moment?***

Is it a mirror?

The text	My experience is the same because	This shows me, or leads me to predict

Is it a fun house mirror?

Similarities	Differences	What the differences show

Is it a window?

Precise feelings in the text	Exact times I have felt that way	Connection that allows me to make

Stop and Empathize: What Is Your Relationship with This Moment? (OR 1.8)

AT THE END OF THE BOOK

In this section, we'll discuss the following strategies:

9. List the Lessons Learned

Practicing looking for layers of lessons in a text helps keep us from boiling down the novel into the one big thing we learned, or the moral of the story. This is also a good lesson when you are teaching theme, to make sure readers have thought deeply about where the character is before they consider the author's lessons for us.

10. Connect the Dots

It's important to lift our head up from character work and see what else is around from time to time. Here, we ask students to think about what other story elements are significant and how they connect to the characters.

11. React to and Critique the Text

Students are natural critics, and yet sometimes they do not feel like they can bring those superpowers to the novels we read in class. In this lesson, you encourage students to reflect on how well these texts resonate for them and to look for problematic representations in the text.

If you are like me, by the time you get to the end of the book you are so wrapped up in finding out what is going to happen that it can be tough to step back and do the kind of analysis you need to do in order to think big about the characters you have been following. By this point in our reading, we are lost in our books and just want to wash onto the beach of the ending (or off the cliff, depending on what we are reading).

So here is a reminder for us and our kids: what matters most is that we do the thinking we need to do, not when we do that thinking. For some kids it will make sense to stop when the thought occurs and make sure they trap it in writing. But others may want to wait until the end of things—the end of a chapter, even the end of the book itself. The work will be the same; the only shift is in whether the thinking happens in the moment or whether the reader doubles back to pick up thoughts dropped along the way.

9. LIST THE LESSONS LEARNED

THINKING ABOUT THE STRATEGY

The most obvious work we do at the end of the book when it comes to character is to take stock of what all this conflict and change has wrought on these poor souls. We now know what has happened. No more surprises, no more plot. So, what does this character take away from it all? What have they learned about life? About the problems they faced? About humanity, the people around them, themselves?

Often when we do work around the lessons a character has learned, we try to boil it down to the One Big Lesson. The moral of the story, if you will. Often we are so hungry to get kids to think about the theme of the text that we forget to linger in the many, many lessons they have learned along the way. After all, while the author may have had one big thing they wanted you to get from this book (though this is arguable), the fact is that it is also the little ideas along the way that most delight writers and readers alike. That one scene that came back briefly at the end. The loose thread that kept you guessing. The minor character and all that relationship offered.

About nine years ago I became a parent for the first time. You could say I suppose that there is one main lesson I have learned about parenting. If I had to put it into words, I would say the big lesson is that love will lead the way. Love those kids as much as you can and the rest will sort itself out. But if someone boiled down my entire experience of being a mom into that one line, I'd be, well, unimpressed. I've learned so much (mostly from making mistakes). Here's a partial list of the things I have learned so far from being a parent:

1. I set the tone.
2. Everything is temporary.
3. No one knows what they are doing.
4. Except that one mom in the music class, holy shit, she is amazing.
5. Everyone has different advice, so choose what seems right for you and your kid.
6. It's not the one moment of failure that messes them up; it's a pattern of dysfunction across the years. Be easy on yourself in the moment and then work on it.
7. Apologize when you mess up.
8. When everything is going out of control, play that song about butts.

You see where I am going with this? I could keep adding to this list; it could fill pages. And the same is true for the characters we get to know. To drill down their experience into one big lesson feels disrespectful. I may choose one to explore later, in writing or conversation. I may zero in on one that speaks to me most deeply, that changes my own perspective in life, but that doesn't mean I shouldn't pay tribute to all that has been learned before I do.

Finishing both *The Namesake* and *Aristotle and Dante*, I did some of this work. I listed out what I felt the main characters learned. And then I went through the list, ranking the lessons in order of importance, both in the book and in my heart. (See Figures 1.15 and 1.16.)

Finishing a book in this way helps me get my arms around the whole text. To survey the land of words I have just crossed, harvesting the bounty.

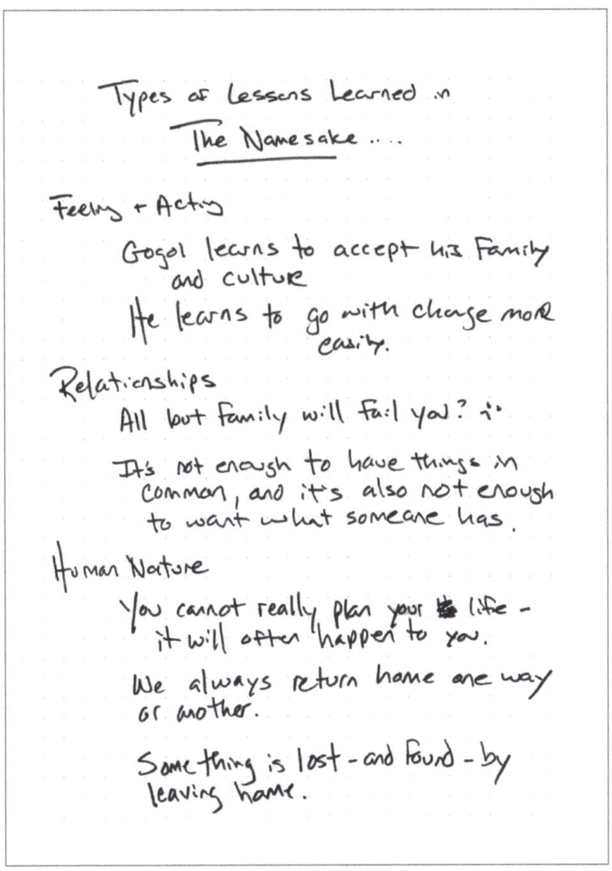
Types of Lessons Learned in
The Namesake . . .

Feeling + Acting

Gogol learns to accept his Family and culture

He learns to go with change more easily.

Relationships

All but family will fail you? :·

It's not enough to have things in common, and it's also not enough to want what someone has.

Human Nature

You cannot really plan your life - it will often happen to you.

We always return home one way or another.

Something is lost - and found - by leaving home.

FIGURE 1.15: *Model of a lessons learned notebook page*

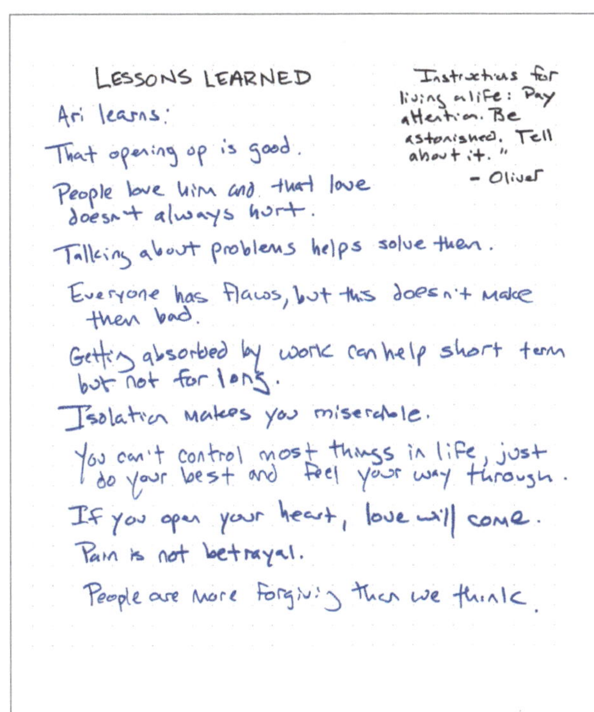
LESSONS LEARNED

"Instructions for living a life: Pay attention. Be astonished. Tell about it." - Oliver

Ari learns:

That opening up is good.

People love him and that love doesn't always hurt.

Talking about problems helps solve them.

Everyone has flaws, but this doesn't make them bad.

Getting absorbed by work can help short term but not for long.

Isolation makes you miserable.

You can't control most things in life, just do your best and feel your way through.

If you open your heart, love will come.

Pain is not betrayal.

People are more forgiving than we think.

FIGURE 1.16: *Model of a lessons learned notebook page*

9. LIST THE LESSONS LEARNED

TEACHING THE STRATEGY

Lesson Flow

Practicing looking for layers of lessons in a text helps keep us from boiling down the novel into the one big thing we learned, or the moral of the story. This is also a good lesson when you are teaching theme, to make sure readers have thought deeply about where the character is before they consider the author's lessons for us.

One way to teach this lesson:

1. Tell a story about an experience you had where you learned a lot. List out all of the things you learned. Explain that when we read a book, we need to collect all of the things a character has learned, not just the one big lesson.
2. Show students (on a chart or slide or with a document camera) a few categories of lessons that might be learned in a text (lessons about the characters' relationships with others, themselves, issues, society, human beings, topics).
3. Refer to a common text (like a prior novel or read-aloud or a movie or show you know everyone has seen). Model using the categories for lessons to come up with a few lessons the character in that text learned (model on some of the harder categories, like society or themselves).
4. Have students discuss with a partner a few other lessons the character learned in that text and have them share out as you list the lessons.
5. Send the class to work on the novel they are reading, beginning a list of lessons learned that they will add to as they finish the book.

What Might This Look Like?

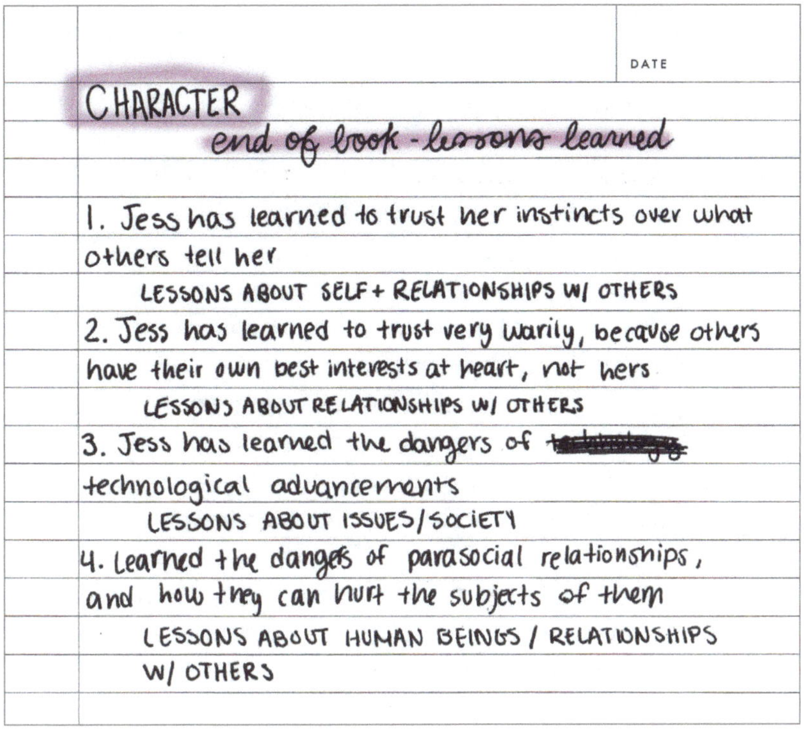
DATE

CHARACTER

end of book - lessons learned

1. Jess has learned to trust her instincts over what others tell her
   LESSONS ABOUT SELF + RELATIONSHIPS W/ OTHERS
2. Jess has learned to trust very warily, because others have their own best interests at heart, not hers
   LESSONS ABOUT RELATIONSHIPS W/ OTHERS
3. Jess has learned the dangers of technological advancements
   LESSONS ABOUT ISSUES/SOCIETY
4. Learned the dangers of parasocial relationships, and how they can hurt the subjects of them
   LESSONS ABOUT HUMAN BEINGS / RELATIONSHIPS W/ OTHERS

Annika lists out a variety of lessons the character has learned in the text using a menu of types of lessons characters tend to learn in texts.

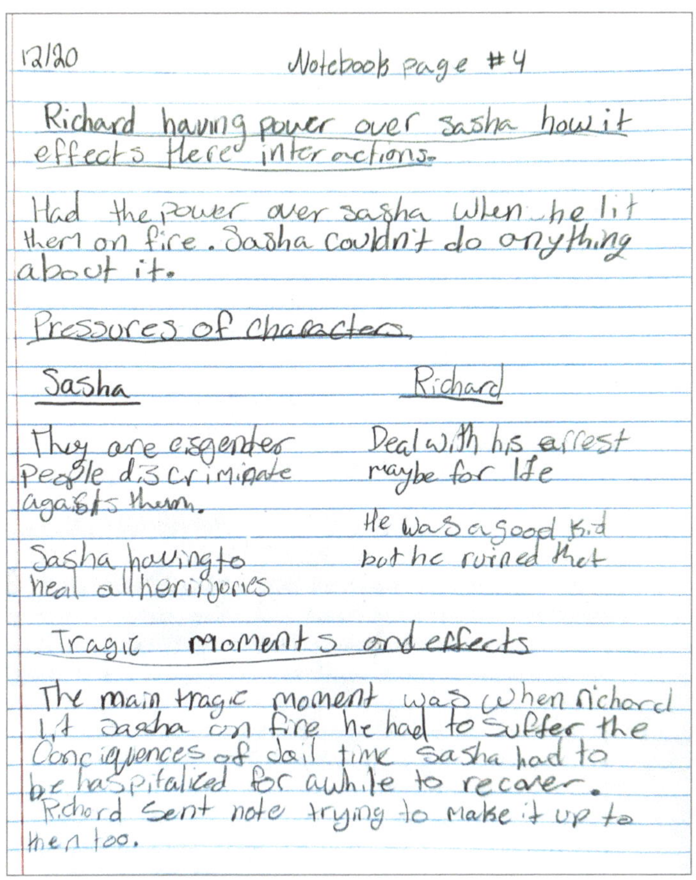
12/20 Notebook page #4

Richard having power over sasha how it effects there interactions.

Had the power over sasha when he lit them on fire. Sasha couldn't do anything about it.

Pressures of characters

Sasha	Richard
They are egenter People discriminate agaists them.	Deal with his arrest maybe for life
Sasha having to heal all her injories	He was a good kid but he ruined that

Tragic moments and effects

The main tragic moment was when richard lit sasha on fire he had to suffer the conciquences of jail time sasha had to be haspitalized for awhile to recover. Richard sent note trying to make it up to them too.

This student looks at an issue in the text between characters from multiple angles.

Providing Feedback

If your students say or demonstrate . . .	Coach them on . . .
I can name a clear, simple lesson the character learned. The lesson might be about how difficult something is or even a well-known phrase like don't judge a book from its cover.	Thinking about the precise language that could capture the lessons they see Adding on some more thinking by asking why, for whom, when, or how that lesson is true
I can name lessons the character learned by being precise with my language and adding qualifiers like why, when, who, and how to my ideas.	Connecting the lessons that characters are learning, looking for the ways they are linked
I can link lessons together and am able to see how the lessons characters learned are connected or contradictory.	Connecting to the lessons learned by examining which ones resonate for them in their lives and which do not

Optional Tools

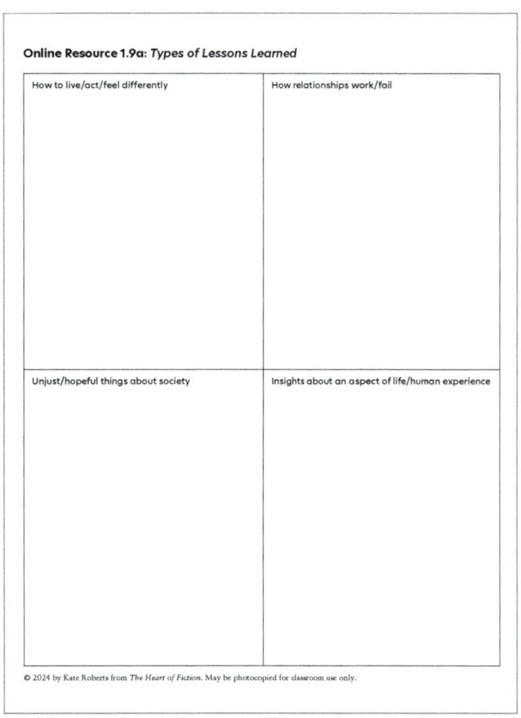

Online Resource 1.9a: *Types of Lessons Learned*

How to live/act/feel differently	How relationships work/fail
Unjust/hopeful things about society	Insights about an aspect of life/human experience

© 2024 by Kate Roberts from *The Heart of Fiction*. May be photocopied for classroom use only.

Types of Lessons Learned (OR 1.9a)

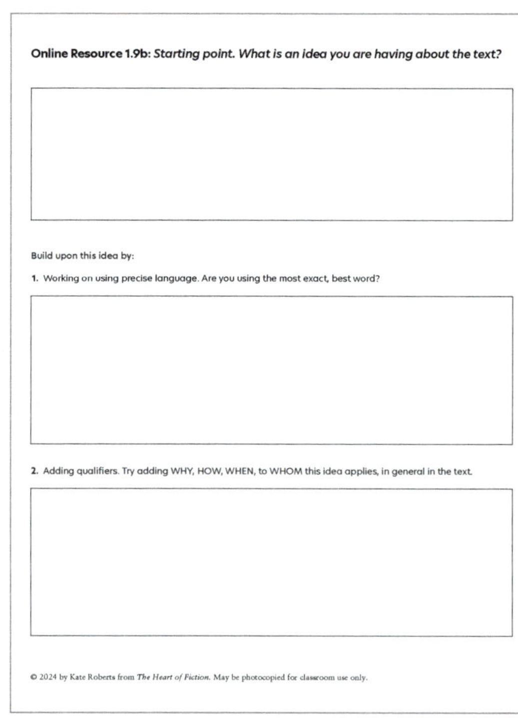

Online Resource 1.9b: *Starting point. What is an idea you are having about the text?*

Build upon this idea by:

1. Working on using precise language. Are you using the most exact, best word?

2. Adding qualifiers. Try adding WHY, HOW, WHEN, to WHOM this idea applies, in general in the text.

© 2024 by Kate Roberts from *The Heart of Fiction*. May be photocopied for classroom use only.

Starting Point (OR 1.9b)

10. CONNECT THE DOTS

THINKING ABOUT THE STRATEGY

This chapter is focused on teaching students to become more powerful readers of characters in the books they read. But it is rarely true that a reader thinks only about characters and nothing else. Each step of the way, I want students to touch base with the other elements of the text that matter most—to them, to me, to the state test even. However I frame this synthesis work, I want to be sure to explicitly teach kids to connect the characters in the text to something else.

Perhaps they will connect the characters to the theme. Here they will choose which lesson they feel the author most intended to teach their readers and then consider how the character's journey helped to develop that idea. Which moments in the text show the lesson fully formed, sure, but which lessons show the opposite of the lesson and its effects? Which show the slow march toward understanding? Which scenes offer the ways in which other people help or hurt the character on the road to this realization? If we are synthesizing character and theme, we need to consider the argument or logic of the lesson's journey across the text and discuss how the character acted as almost a puppet for that thinking.

It could be that students connect character to craft or literary technique. Here, it works in reverse to theme: it is the craft that is in service of the character. Looking across the traits and relationships and changes that matter most for this character, we can look back at the text and consider which techniques the author used to highlight, develop, or deepen our sense of them.

For *Aristotle and Dante*, I looked at theme, connecting the character's journey to what I think could be seen as a main theme of the text (see Figure 1.17). For *The Namesake*, I tackled craft (see Figure 1.18). Both experiences felt fun and difficult: like the thousand-piece puzzle I worked on last summer, I had to keep looking back at the text, then at what I was writing, then back at the text. But at the end, a pretty cool image began to appear from the pieces.

Asking students to synthesize across reading skills makes sure that we don't ignore the other important stuff as we read and also allows us to touch base with what our students remember (or need support remembering) about what they've learned in the past.

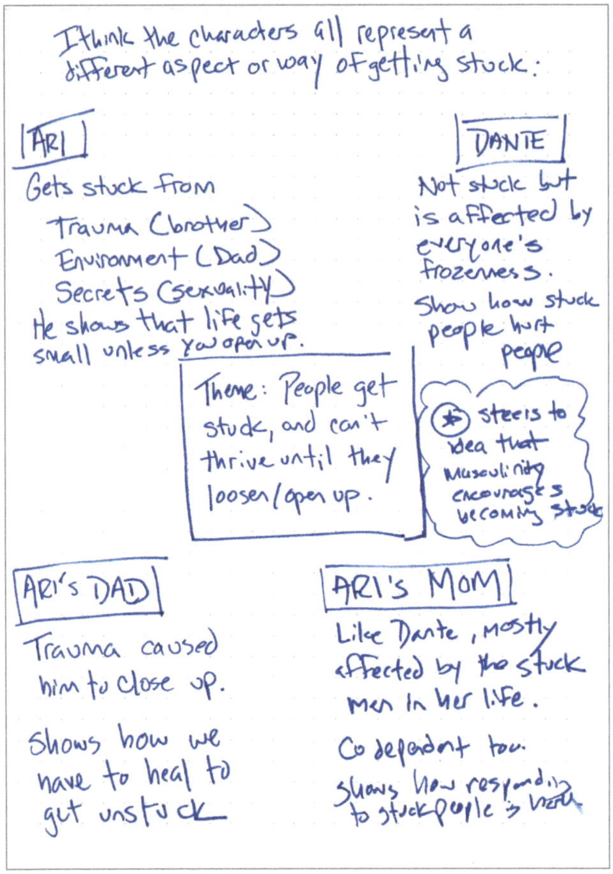

FIGURE 1.17: *Model of synthesis page*

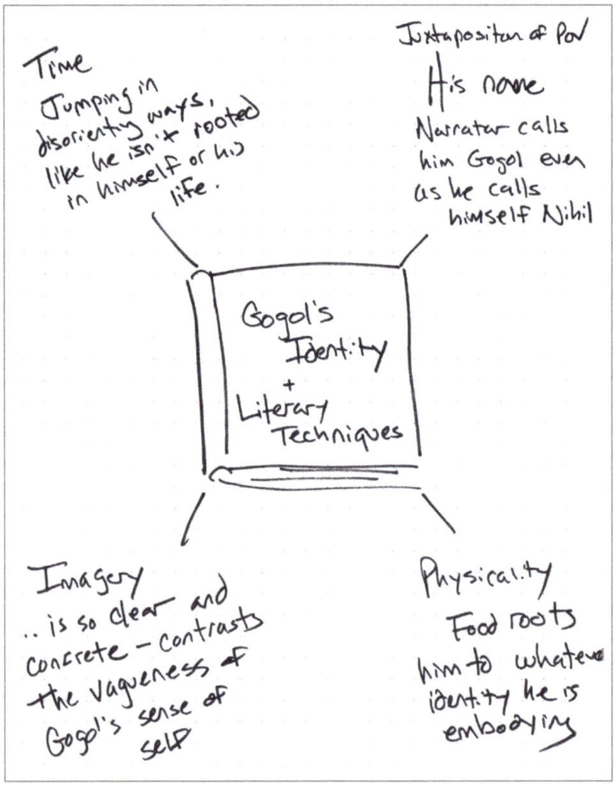

FIGURE 1.18: *Model of synthesis page*

10. CONNECT THE DOTS

TEACHING THE STRATEGY

Lesson Flow

It's important to lift our head up from character work and see what else is around from time to time. Here, we ask students to think about what other story elements are significant and how they connect to the characters.

One way to teach this lesson:

1. Ask students what they think would be more interesting in their books to think about: craft and literary techniques or themes. Set them up into groups accordingly.
2. Have the students do some individual writing about what they know about their topic (craft or theme). Then have students get into groups and, using their notes, remind each other of what they have learned in the past.
3. Give students the character questions that fit their topic (see list that follows) and have them get started working either on their own or with a partner if they are reading the same text.

   Character and Theme

   - Does the character change in the same way the theme develops?
   - Is the lesson the character learns also the theme?
   - Is the character's story a cautionary tale?

   Character and Craft

   - Does the technique reveal an aspect of their personality?
   - Is it a symbol for the character in certain ways?
   - Does it help us connect or relate to the character?
4. Go to each group at the beginning and model some of your thinking about the guide to get them started.
5. As a class, discuss what the groups found. If working on a whole-class novel, facilitate a whole-class discussion. If working on book clubs or independent reading, students can offer their thinking while the rest of the class looks for connection.

What Might This Look Like?

DATE

how characterization connects to theme

Jess develops confidence in herself as the book progresses. At the start of the book before the plot changes, she was filled with doubt – often feeling different and misunderstood by her peers. Others brush off her concerns about strange things she is noticing, and she does not have the confidence to push back against them yet. She is also unsure about what direction she wants her life to go in. Once Jess discovers what everyone has been hiding from her, she finds it easier to believe in herself and make her wants and needs from others known. However, she still struggles with doubt and guilt surrounding her escape from her town, and what happened to Kipps during it. Jess has always been a naturally selfless person, but learns the importance of determination to put one's self first in certain circumstances. Jess's story conveys the importance of resillience by showing her getting back on her feet and learning to depend on herself and speak up for what she wants.

Annika looks for connections between the characterization in the text and the themes it might develop.

Charater (Callie) → Theme

I believe the theme of this book is that Letting go is okay. In my opinion, Callie is the one who relates to this the most. She was refusing to let go and accept that her mother was dying, and in doing so she stopped eating. She damaged her body. But when she lets go and accepted that her mom wasn't going to be there for much longer She went to go visit her and she starts to slowly let People in.

Shay connects their thinking about character to a theme in the book.

Providing Feedback

If your students say or demonstrate . . .	Coach them on . . .
I can synthesize character with another element by unpacking how the element and the character are connected: *The theme is the lesson.* *The craft shows the character's trait.*	Considering how one element (like character) helps develop another (like theme)
I can synthesize character with another element by unpacking how the element and the character are connected: *The character's change is the way the theme is developed.* *The symbol reflects the character because _____.*	Thinking about why the author may have written this text this way—what they are trying to show their readers
I can synthesize character and another element by considering the author's purpose and by tracking how the author fulfilled that purpose using the character and the element: *The author wanted to teach us _____, so they had the character _____.* *The author wanted to show _____ about the character, so they used these techniques: _____.*	Looking for patterns and exceptions in the ways or reasons why the author writes

Optional Tools

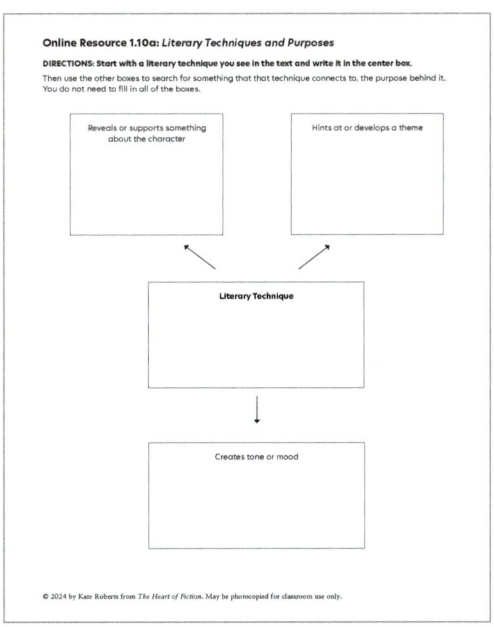
Online Resource 1.10a: *Literary Techniques and Purposes*

DIRECTIONS: Start with a literary technique you see in the text and write it in the center box.
Then use the other boxes to search for something that that technique connects to, the purpose behind it. You do not need to fill in all of the boxes.

Reveals or supports something about the character

Hints at or develops a theme

Literary Technique

Creates tone or mood

Literary Techniques and Purposes (OR 1.10a)

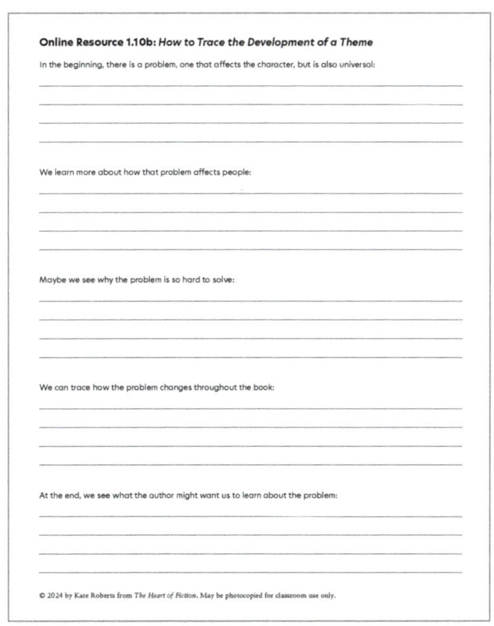
Online Resource 1.10b: *How to Trace the Development of a Theme*

In the beginning, there is a problem, one that affects the character, but is also universal:

We learn more about how that problem affects people:

Maybe we see why the problem is so hard to solve:

We can trace how the problem changes throughout the book:

At the end, we see what the author might want us to learn about the problem:

How to Trace the Development of a Theme (OR 1.10b)

11. REACT TO AND CRITIQUE THE TEXT

THINKING ABOUT THE STRATEGY

Some of the best school experiences I had growing up were when a classmate vehemently disagreed with the teacher's opinion of the book we were reading. Often I agreed with the teacher myself, but there was such a charge when Tom raised his hand and we knew he was going to launch an argument against the theme of the book we had read. It felt so rebellious, revolutionary even.

It shouldn't have felt this way. It shouldn't be that the books we give kids become idolized to the point that one understanding of them becomes enshrined in amber. Books are written by people. In a specific time and place, with a point of view on the world that is in every case so human. This means that in the exact same moment that there is truth in these books, there are also falsehoods, ideas that don't work anymore, incomplete perspectives.

I remember my Oxford tutor telling me, for example, that I could not hand in my paper of a feminist read on Henry James' *Turn of the Screw* because my interpretation did not exist in the text. I have heard teachers reject students' critiques of *To Kill a Mockingbird* as a seminal book on race because they hold the book in such high regard that any pushback on Atticus feels blasphemous.

But books aren't bibles. Instead of fearing these critiques, we should be inviting students to make them. As they end the book, what does not feel right? Which characters don't ring true? Which parts of the ending feel too easy? Whose perspective is not heard? What's another way of reading this book? What would be another way of writing this book? The wise educators at #DisruptTexts (Tricia Ebarvia, Lorena Germán, Kim Parker, and Julia Torres) teach us that we must "challenge the traditional canon in order to create a more inclusive, representative, and equitable language arts curriculum that our students deserve" (n.d.).

By allowing and teaching students to form their own opinions of the people and ideas presented in a novel, we allow them the dignity and truth of their own perspectives and lived experiences.

For example, in *Aristotle and Dante*, the thing that never rang true was the fact that Ari stayed so kind to Dante throughout, never thought about gay stuff, and then all of a sudden kissed him. There is something about Ari's journey that feels too sudden. I get being unaware of feeling attraction to the same sex. And I get awakening to that attraction. But there is something missing in the middle there—a process of feeling things and rejecting them that most queer people go through that doesn't appear in this story.

That doesn't mean it's a bad book. It doesn't even mean I'm right. But it's important to name the stuff that doesn't work for us in books if we really want to be engaged readers. A teacher who felt forced to teach *Huckleberry Finn* in his district worked to make sure that kids critiqued the text throughout; in fact, we joked that his whole unit could have been named "Should you hate Huck Finn?" You may agree or disagree with this take, but let me tell you—those kids were engaged.

Empower kids to notice the stuff that feels dumb. Unjust. Biased. Counter to the way they have experienced that thing. The easy endings and unrealistic changes and unlikely friendships. Teach them to become more critical readers of every text they take in.

11. REACT TO AND CRITIQUE THE TEXT

TEACHING THE STRATEGY

Lesson Flow

Students are natural critics, and yet sometimes they do not feel like they can bring those superpowers to the novels we read in class. In this lesson, you encourage students to reflect on how well these texts resonate for them and to look for problematic representations in the text.

One way to teach this lesson:

1. Show a video clip of teenagers from a TV show. Ask students if this clip captures exactly what it is like to be them. When they say no (as they surely will), ask them why—what does the clip get wrong? List the things the creators of that show are not getting right about your students' experience.
2. Tell students that even though the books they are reading are not all about teenagers, they still have the power and ability and responsibility to critique the way the author is representing people, society, and life.
3. Show students a list of critical reading questions they can ask of their texts. (Is this how people act in my life? Does this book match how problems are resolved in my experience? What is missing from this book? Whose voice is not heard? What feels realistic or not?)
4. Have students work to answer some of these questions in groups or on their own, depending on whether they are reading the same book as others, and what you feel would be most productive.
5. Create a class graph where each student adds the name of the book they are reading and how much they think the book accurately captures reality, on a scale of 1 to 5.
6. Discuss as a class or in groups what authors do that make their books feel more or less realistic. What makes a book feel right or wrong?

What Might This Look Like?

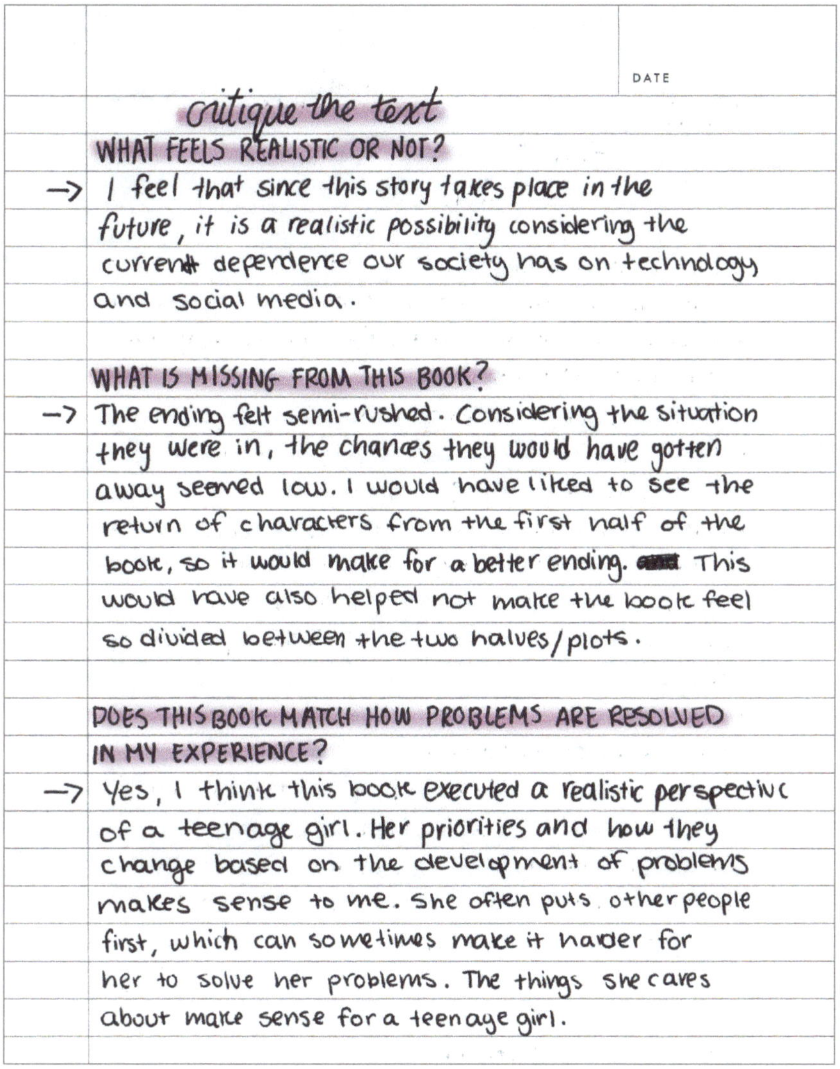

DATE

critique the text

WHAT FEELS REALISTIC OR NOT?

→ I feel that since this story takes place in the future, it is a realistic possibility considering the current dependence our society has on technology and social media.

WHAT IS MISSING FROM THIS BOOK?

→ The ending felt semi-rushed. Considering the situation they were in, the chances they would have gotten away seemed low. I would have liked to see the return of characters from the first half of the book, so it would make for a better ending. This would have also helped not make the book feel so divided between the two halves/plots.

DOES THIS BOOK MATCH HOW PROBLEMS ARE RESOLVED IN MY EXPERIENCE?

→ Yes, I think this book executed a realistic perspective of a teenage girl. Her priorities and how they change based on the development of problems makes sense to me. She often puts other people first, which can sometimes make it harder for her to solve her problems. The things she cares about make sense for a teenage girl.

Annika takes a moment to critique the text.

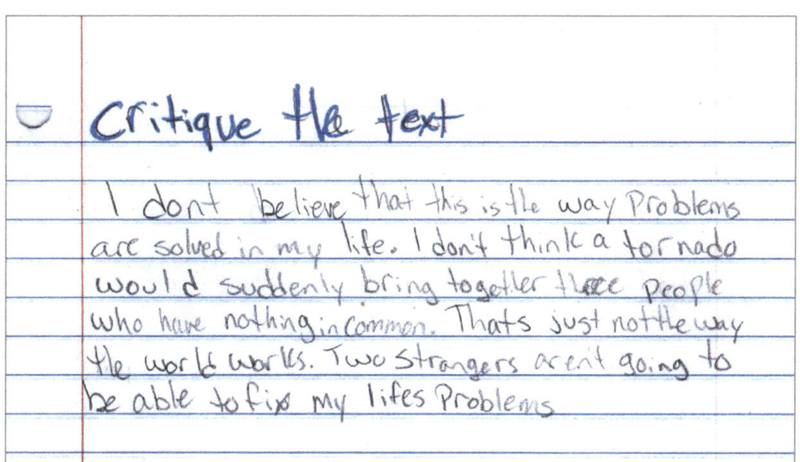

Critique the text

I dont believe that this is the way Problems are solved in my life. I don't think a tornado would suddenly bring together three people who have nothing in common. Thats just not the way the world works. Two strangers aren't going to be able to fix my lifes Problems

Shay evaluates whether the characterization in the text feels like a realistic depiction.

Providing Feedback

If your students say or demonstrate . . .	Coach them on . . .
I can name whether or not the book feels realistic based on my own experience.	Looking for exact parts of the book that they feel are or are not realistic Staying aware of the parts of the book outside of their own experience and realizing that they may have trouble critiquing what they do not understand
I can discuss what parts of the book feel realistic or not based on my experience and what I have learned about others from my reading, empathy, or research.	Looking for points of view that are missing in the text or that seem surface-level Staying aware of the parts of the book outside of their own experience and realizing that they may have trouble critiquing what they do not understand
I am able to weigh how realistic aspects of the book are as well as critique the points of view that are tokenized or missing in the text. I am aware of my limitations based on my experience and I research to find out what others think about the depictions in the book.	Looking for books that will help them understand more about a point of view or for books that capture a more realistic view of an issue or person Staying aware of the parts of the book outside of their own experience and realizing that they may have trouble critiquing what they do not understand

Optional Tools

Online Resource 1.11: ***Questions That Lead to Critique***

- Is this how people act in my life?
- Does the ending match how problems are resolved in my experience?
- Whose voice is heard most in this text?
- Whose voice is not heard very much in this text?
- What feels realistic in this book? Unrealistic?
- Are there any beliefs about right or wrong that you see in the story? Do you agree?
- What would you change about this book if you could?
- Does this book uphold or break down any stereotypes or biased views about the world?

Questions That Lead to Critique (OR 1.11)

What to Do When the Unit Is Done

So let's imagine that you have invited your students to engage with some of these lessons and supported them along the way. Hopefully, as suggested in the introduction, they have had repeated chances to try these strategies out. Hopefully, they have had a chance to try these strategies on more than one book. Hopefully, this work has been peppered with many opportunities for talk and writing and community building.

If this is all true, then at the end of the unit things can look quite . . . messy. Notebooks full of authentic and diverse notes, ideas looping back on one another, no structure or cohesion in sight.

It's at this point that I crave a little closure, a touch of order.

So what can we do to wrap things up in a way that feels fulfilling to our students and helps synthesize the work we have done? Here are a few ideas to end things after a deep meditation on the characters in a book.

Sigh. Sure, Write an Essay

Look, there is nothing particularly wrong with using essays as a way to punctuate our reading work. When done well, essays can be thoughtful pieces that tie together the threads of thinking woven across the weeks of the unit. The trouble is, we always do essays. And when we do, we often don't do them in ways that inspire students to write; we do them in ways that make writing seem laborious and too structured with no payoff. So, you can definitely end the unit with a character analysis essay and teach it in the ways you already have and, of course, it may be that your essay work feels vibrant, supportive, and joyful. But you also could take this opportunity to teach essay in creative, writerly ways. Katherine Bomer's book *The Journey Is Everything* (2016) and Allison Marcetti and Rebekah O'Dell's *Beyond Literary Analysis* (2018) both masterfully explore ways to help kids see essays as true explorations, as pieces of writing they can enjoy and be proud of. If we choose to ask students to write essays at the end of every reading experience, we will need to make that work the generative, creative expression of thought that it can be.

Synthesize the Notes

Another way to get at the good stuff of an essay without always confining it to five paragraphs of analysis is to show students how they might look through their notes and create a synthesized version of their thinking across the book. Students can categorize their thinking across their notebook and begin to look for common threads. Then, have them consider what kind of page might capture the essence of their thinking about the character. Do they have a strong theory? How could they express that visually? Finally, have students make a page or poster that both visually and with notations offers viewers a glimpse at their analysis of the character (see Figure 1.19 for an example). This work, developed by Maggie

FIGURE 1.19: *Synthesis page*

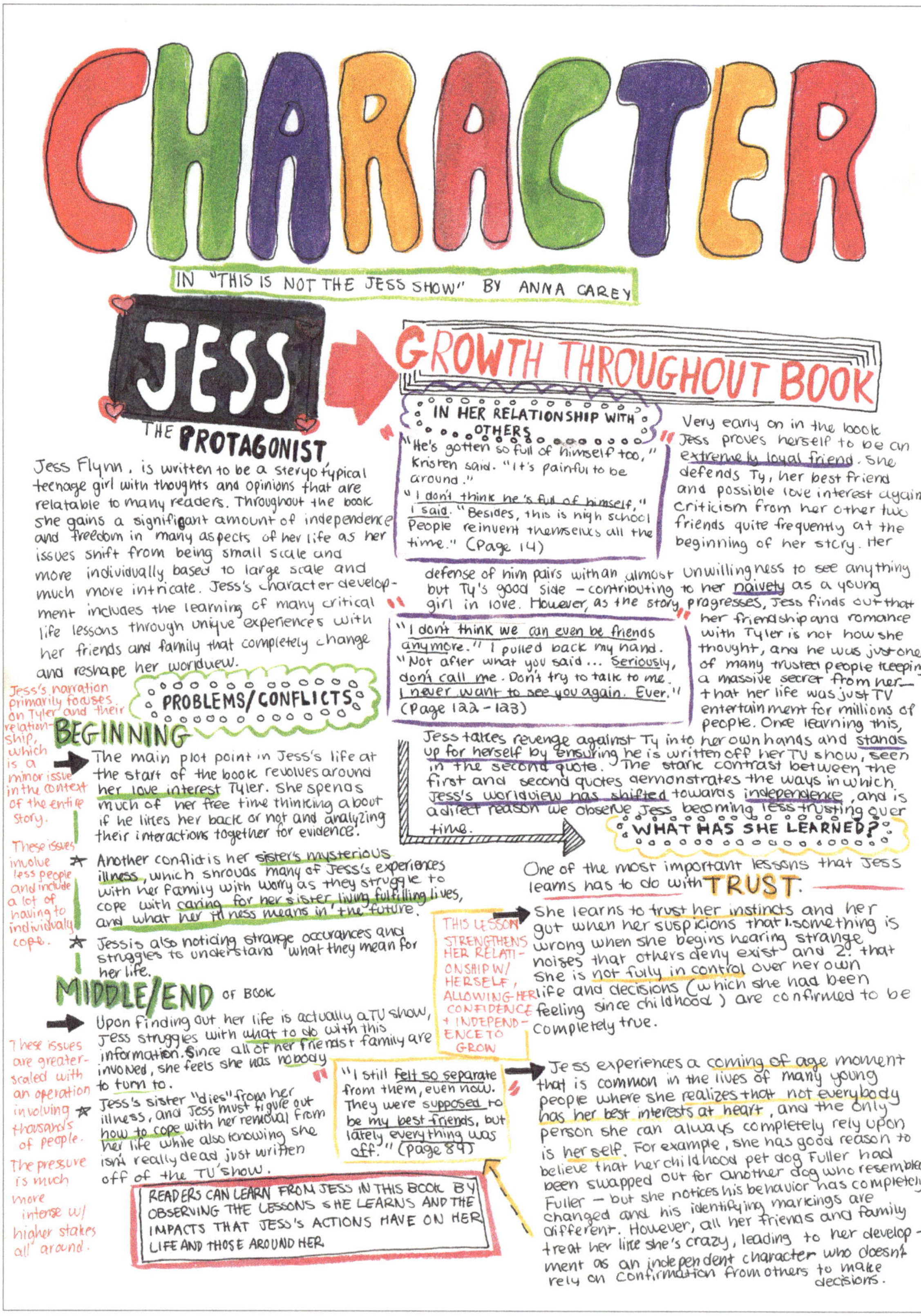

Here Annika synthesizes her thinking about character into a poster.

Beattie Roberts and Kristen Robbins Warren, can help students tie together their thoughts and offers a chance to bring much-needed creativity to analysis. (For more on synthesis pages, see "Thinking While Reading: The Beautiful Mess of Helping Adolescents Discover and Celebrate How Their Minds Work," by Maggie Beattie Roberts and Kristen Robbins Warren [2016].)

Make a Thing

Another option to close out the unit is to create a project. There are limitless possibilities here, as long as they come from collaboration between teacher and student and student and book. Perhaps students make posters that capture their thinking or a podcast recording the journey of their thinking. Maybe a recorded critique of the text or a series of TikTok videos from a character's point of view. Projects are usually highly engaging, creative ways for students to apply their understanding of the character to a different medium or platform. In other words, projects ask readers to use what they know about a character to live inside their skin a bit. To speak for them, expanding beyond the pages of the book. Often this works best when students have a choice of what kind of project feels the most interesting or useful. Offer a menu of options, give some examples, and leave some class time for students to do some of the work in class with you there to help guide them a bit. Then, celebrate and share projects together. For a more thoughtful discussion of projects, read Dan Feigelson's *Reading Projects Reimagined* (2014).

Whatever you do to end this time with students, strive to offer choice, creativity, and compassion. It is not necessary for students to leave with perfect analyses. It matters much more that students have an enriching experience that allows them to practice tying together their thoughts, theorizing and developing ideas, and expressing themselves in ways that feel gratifying.

At the End of the Day

Any educator with strong relationships with their students knows that what kids need most from us is to be seen and appreciated for the beautiful, flawed humans they are. Some of us know what this experience feels like well—we have had teachers every step of the way who saw us, appreciated us, celebrated what we brought to the table. Others of us had this experience occasionally. I fall into this category. Every once in a while, I had a teacher who changed my world with their ability to make me feel like what I had, what I was, mattered. Some of us have never had that experience, tragically. All too often, because of bias, white supremacy, and an educational system that often crushes teachers' spirits, Black, Brown, and Indigenous students, poor students, atypical students, students with disabilities, queer and trans students, and students who hold many of these identities at once go through their school career without teachers who convey, "I see you. I like you. You matter to me and to the world."

The thing is, forces like bias, white supremacy, and oppression cause us to stop paying attention to people as individuals. We clump people together without even noticing we are doing it. We calcify our thinking and act in reactive, unreflective ways.

But what we teach our students to do when analyzing characters in their books is an antidote to this kind of thinking. If we can look at our students and notice all of their traits, not just the one obvious one, if we can see their relationships and problems as a matrix that affects their behavior, if we can become attuned to little shifts, if we dig into what might cause them to be the way they are, we can build the relationships with our students that transform and motivate.

Of course, I want my students to use the strategies in this chapter in the books they read. And it is also true that I hope they will use them in their lives as well, as I did with my father the last time I saw him. When I live like this, striving to see people in their fullness and in their detail, I feel more connected, more present, and more alive. But I also want to live like this as an educator. I never want to forget that the students in the classrooms I serve are all individuals with universes of experience within them.

CHAPTER TWO

How to Teach Interpretation of Theme

What It Means to Interpret Themes

I cry during Superman movies. Every one. It's embarrassing, yet I've adopted it as a truth. When a new film comes out, I try to go to the theatre alone, when there aren't many people there, so that I can have my cry with the other people who go to see Superman alone. (It's a specific subgroup, to be sure.)

What is it about these movies, this story, that gets me? As a character, Superman is one of the cheesier of the bunch. The movies are often, well, not the best they could be. So how is it that from Christopher Reeve to Brandon Routh to Henry Cavil, I tear up?

In every iteration of his story, an idea runs through the flying red capes, bad disguises, and laser eyes: If you can, you must. Superman, Kal-El, Clark—he has these powers. He is able to do things that others cannot. And he is *good*; at his core, he is intact and good and strong. These are not things he earned; they have been given to him. And so he must—he *must* fight and he must protect and he must suffer and he must always rise above. He must always be Superman.

That is what gets me crying. I cry during Superman because of a theme: If you can, you must.

Theme, of course, is a well-worn path in the English classroom—that has taken a few turns. As a profession we have largely evolved from thinking that there are a few correct themes in books that readers must regurgitate. Almost all of the English teachers I know understand that theme is a wide highway—while there are certainly interpretations that are not supported by a book, there are many more that are, and most teachers hope to guide their students to discover the themes that speak to them. This is no small shift. For much of my schooling I was told what the themes were and asked to nod along.

Our students will often be happy to latch on to the themes we offer them. The work of uncovering, tracking, categorizing, and analyzing the ideas tucked within the events and figures of a book is difficult and many people won't jump at the chance to do it themselves. But if we hold back pre-fab interpretations, if we teach kids how to find the first inklings of what this story might be about, if we teach them how to analyze small bits of text in relation to those inklings, if we teach them how to then think across the full text to come to an overarching, relevant, and interesting interpretation, well then we'll have given them a skill set that could prove valuable for the rest of their lives.

After all, it is hard to find the time to reflect, isn't it? For me now, it is because there is such a crowded field—how do I fit in reflecting amid meals and work and homework and kid tantrums and wrestling matches? For our students, sometimes the packed nature of modern life makes it tough to find meaning, but it is also because they are at the beginning of it all. The themes of my life are so repetitive at this point that I would have to be obstinately avoiding them to not see the threads. Young people are just beginning to see issues repeat themselves with different proper nouns, but that doesn't mean they aren't there. If I think back to my adolescence, so many of the ideas that have run through my life began back then.

Yes, we should teach interpreting themes because it is a valued and rewarding thing to do with texts. But it is also the work that makes our lives more meaningful, less random, filled with purpose and insight. Socrates told us that "the unexamined life is not worth living," and while that may seem a bit extreme (especially as he said it very close to the time of the whole hemlock-imbibing thing), it is also certainly true. Or, maybe it's that the inverse is even more true—*the examined life is* so *worth living*. Give our students the tools to see the themes of their texts and their lives and let them loose. Let them have ideas and grow them and learn to complicate them and then strive to resolve contradictions. Like Nathan, who, as he was reading, began to make connections between different issues in the text he was reading. In Figure 2.1 he links issues of femininity to safety, while also finding issues that are definitely related, but less clearly, like fundamentalism and femininity.

What gets me about Superman is the theme that if you can, you must. Well, the same is true for our teaching. If we can teach students to develop their ability to take on and grapple with complex ideas in texts and life, then we must, right? Because what is life without meaning? Just a story? Full of sound and fury? Signifying nothing? I don't believe that, neither do you, and we can help our kids know that the power to see meaning is in their hands.

How Theme Works

As we begin to teach students to interpret themes on their own, we immediately see that they often need a lot of support. Sometimes the themes they find lean on clichés, sometimes the themes are crushingly simple, sometimes the themes are just off and are not supported by the text.

Let me be clear—this is not because kids aren't able to consider complex ideas, or because their thoughts are cliché, simple, or wrong. It is because they need us to teach them. As we begin, there are three things we should consider as we set our expectations for the unit:

1. This kind of interpretation is a very school-based thing. That's not bad; in fact, it can be great, but unlike the character work we did in the previous chapter, it is not something that people do naturally as they read. At least

not in the first read or not unless they are future English majors. My interpretation of Superman came from decades of being immersed and interested—both in the texts and in my reaction to them. I didn't watch one Superman movie and come out with my fully formed analysis of the text in relation to my childhood.

2. Most students will need to start rough and build toward complexity. Rare is the student who is able to raise their hand and answer the question "What is a theme in the text?" with an essay-ready thesis. Most kids will start with something like, "In *Macbeth*, guilt is bad." We should meet these rough-draft ideas with agreement and congratulation. Interpreting themes is abstract and unnatural work to do on a first read, so any step forward should be celebrated. Besides, a theme in *Macbeth is* that guilt is bad. So, yay!
3. Students will have to choose an idea to track in the book near the beginning if they have a chance of doing the work that needs to be done by the end. If we wait until the end of the book for students to think about the themes, then we are hoping or expecting them to reread vast swaths of the book to do the necessary work of close reading and tracking that one would need to do to be proficient at interpretation. This seems unrealistic, and so I begin having students look for themes from page 1 of the text, then choose a couple to track, and then decide later how they are connected or which one to base their interpretations around.

With these ideas in mind, let's get started. The effort to find themes begins before we crack the cover of our book, as we ready ourselves for what is to come.

BEFORE YOU START READING

In this section, we'll discuss the following skills:

1. **Center Your Own Experience**

   Offering students a chance to reflect on which universal issues are most important to them right now can help them find the themes they relate to most as they begin reading.

2. **Develop a Text Set**

   For most of the texts our students will read, there is a community of people who are already in deep discussion. Help them find support as they read.

You might choose to ignore this section. You might want students to dive into the text and get oriented to the characters and world of the story before asking them to prepare themselves thematically. But you also might want your students to have a heads-up before they jump. If you choose to use this section with your students, first know that any prep we do for themes in a book must be held with a very loose grip. It's meant to be a flirtatious glance at possible ideas, not a first date with a future thesis statement.

If you would like to give your students a running jump into the themes of the novel they are reading, try these lessons with them.

1. CENTER YOUR OWN EXPERIENCE

THINKING ABOUT THE STRATEGY

It might be self-centered of me, but I really started reading only when I could choose the books and courses I took. Once I got to college and could direct my own reading life, I read, ultimately becoming an English major. The obvious reason is because I had choice and could study what I was interested in. But it was also because more and more often, not only could I choose what I read but I could choose what I *thought about what I read*.

Although I had been taught in high school to never use *I* when writing papers, in college I found this not to be true—while some professors had an aversion to the actual pronoun, all hoped that I focused my analysis on ideas that took root in my own heart and mind. I wound up reading about characters' lives but writing about mine.

When students are about to read a novel in class—whether they chose it or were asked to read it—we can offer them an opportunity to begin by exploring what issues are the most important to them right now. Because while certainly it helps to build the schema for the setting of the text before reading, it is equally helpful to build a bit of the ideological scaffold for the book.

This is a lesson where that list of common themes in literature can come in handy. While usually these premade racks of words don't really help students click into the themes of the books they read, using them to see which issues resonate for us in our lives can help focus our attention. Have students reflect on a list of issues that they have seen in texts or that tend to be pretty common and pick out one or two that they feel they can connect to, that they struggle with, or that they are proud of how they handled. Students can also do a search for the common themes in the books they are about to read, and use that list if it feels more directly helpful.

Looking at the themes easily found for *The Namesake*, I chose to center my experience on stability and change (see Figure 2.1).

We can still engage in this *theme schema* work even if we haven't already looked up the common themes, however. It can help students to be attuned to themes in a book if they are aware of the themes in their lives. Without knowing what awaits, I can still list out a few of the issues that I am most concerned with, confused about, and engaged in; I can still freewrite about those issues; and I can still bring that foundational awareness into my reading. If this is the course you take, the trick is to try for the most universal language to capture the themes in your life, as the more universal your concerns are, the more likely those themes will emerge in a text.

For example, while it is more precise to say that parenting is a huge theme in my life, it would be more universal to say that I am interested in thinking about responsibility. Marriage? Precise. Communication? Universal. Help students find the truly universal themes in their lives to help them enter a text with themes they care about in mind.

In this way, my writing and thinking can set me up to see things in the text I may not have before. See my freewrite in Figure 2.2 for an example.

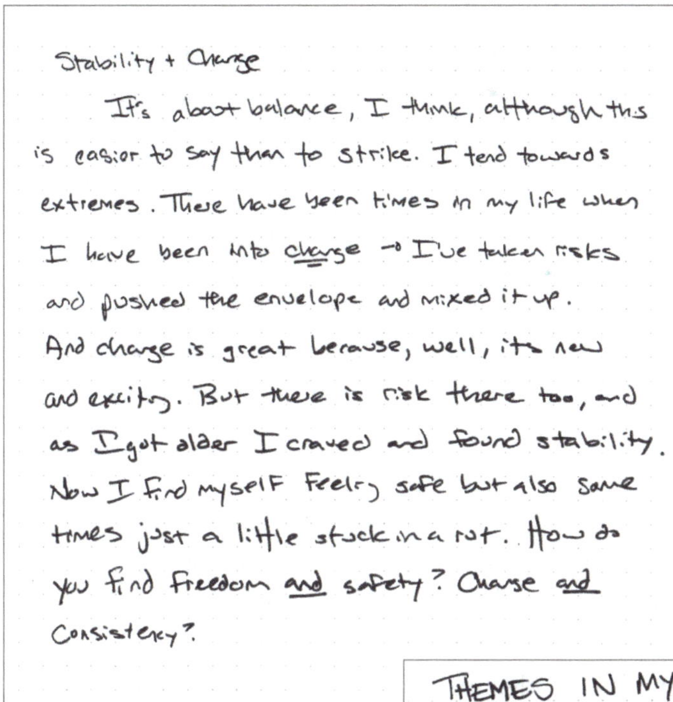

Stability + Change

It's about balance, I think, although this is easier to say than to strike. I tend towards extremes. There have been times in my life when I have been into change → I've taken risks and pushed the envelope and mixed it up. And change is great because, well, it's new and exciting. But there is risk there too, and as I got older I craved and found stability. Now I find myself feeling safe but also sometimes just a little stuck in a rut. How do you find freedom and safety? Change and Consistency?

FIGURE 2.1: *Freewrite on common themes in* The Namesake

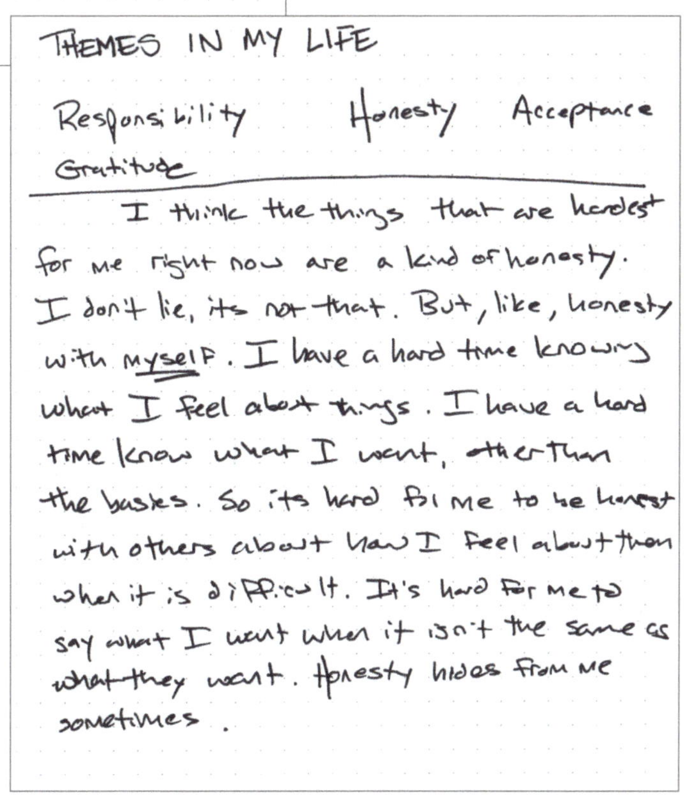

THEMES IN MY LIFE

Responsibility Honesty Acceptance Gratitude

I think the things that are hardest for me right now are a kind of honesty. I don't lie, it's not that. But, like, honesty with myself. I have a hard time knowing what I feel about things. I have a hard time know what I want, other than the basics. So its hard for me to be honest with others about how I feel about them when it is difficult. It's hard for me to say what I want when it isn't the same as what they want. Honesty hides from me sometimes.

FIGURE 2.2: *Freewrite about current issues that matter to me*

1. CENTER YOUR OWN EXPERIENCE

TEACHING THE STRATEGY

Lesson Flow

Offering students a chance to reflect on which universal issues are most important to them right now can help them find the themes they relate to most as they begin reading.

One way to teach this lesson:

1. Introduce the lesson by letting students know that for most people, loving a book and loving reading is about connecting to the story, characters, or themes. Give an example of a time when this was easy because the book was so similar to your life and a time when the connection was less direct.
2. Model taking a well-known issue from a well-known book and reflecting on what your experience has been with that issue, including any stories, beliefs, or conflicts as you do.
3. Ask students to practice this work with a partner. Each student will pick an issue from the book they are currently reading. Then they will talk with their partner about stories, beliefs, and conflicts they have. Each partner will have a chance to bring up an issue to discuss.
4. Give students time to write out a reflection on either an issue they discussed with a partner or a different issue that is in the book.

What Might This Look Like?

DATE

MY OWN EXPERIENCE

social commentary

• Through research, ~~this~~ I've seen that this book deals with the daily problems of a teenage girl (which I can obviously relate to, as a teen girl) as well as social commentary. On the internet in 2021, there is a lot of discourse and analysis of what is and what is not morally or politically correct. I have experience discussing such topics with my parents, friends, and peers/teachers in school. I would like to try to relate the commentary Jess experiences in the 90s to that going on today, analyzing how it has changed or stayed the same, or if any of the events in the book from the 90s have impacted social commentary today. Some topics I can personally/significantly relate to that could be mentioned in the book are sexism, celebrity culture, and privacy (especially in an online world.)

resources

- This is Not the Jess Show on Goodreads summary and reviews
- This is Not the Jess Show on Amazon reviews
- This is Not the Jess Show Review + Overview on Common Sense Media

Annika reflects on the issues that she might relate to in the text.

2

1. Center your experience: I think I can most connect to the theme of standing up for what's right. At school and at home, I try my best to make the right decisions and help people around me. I feel even if I make a bad choice I can somehow fix it. One time I had to be the one person to blow the whistle on someone who used an inappropriate name as there name of a game we were playing in a class, and while I was caused I little bit of trouble afterward I knew it was the right thing to do because it improved the community.
2. Develop a Text Set: There has been a play based on to kill a mockingbird, multiple movies, and there is a graphic novel interpretation.

Miles connects a memory from his life to some of the issues he expects to see in the text.

Providing Feedback

If your students say or demonstrate . . .	Coach them on . . .
I can give brief summaries of times when I faced this issue and one-word descriptions of how I feel about the issue.	Small-moment writing, where we pause for every frame of the story to add action, description, dialogue, or thinking Being precise with their language when describing emotions
I can make broad, general statements about how I feel and what I believe.	Using thought prompts to push their thinking: This is important because ______ . The reason for this is ______ . On the other hand ______ .
I can write entries that explore deeply what I believe and struggle with about an issue.	Trying to find connections between the issues that come up about this text: How do these issues intersect in their life?

Optional Tools

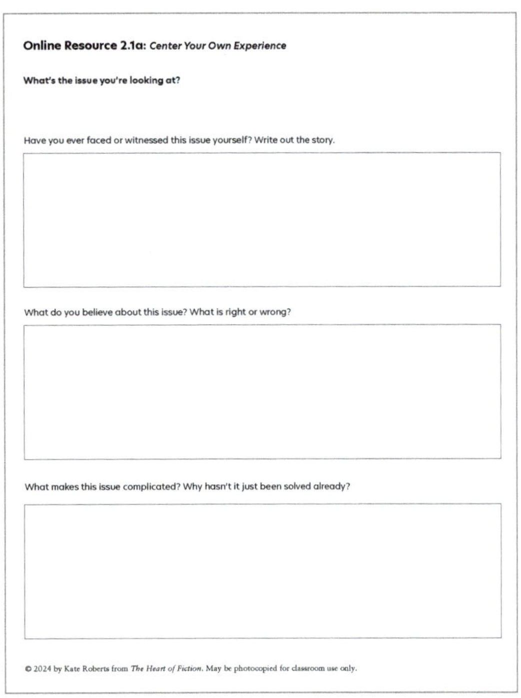

Online Resource 2.1a: *Center Your Own Experience*

What's the issue you're looking at?

Have you ever faced or witnessed this issue yourself? Write out the story.

What do you believe about this issue? What is right or wrong?

What makes this issue complicated? Why hasn't it just been solved already?

Center Your Experience (OR 2.1a)

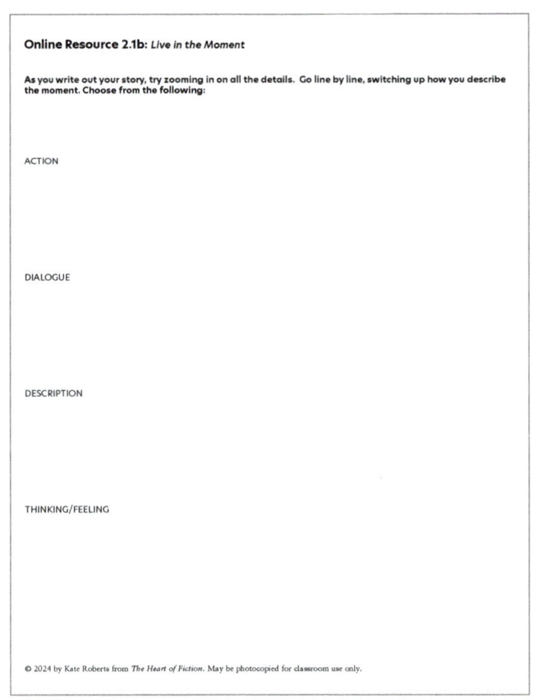

Online Resource 2.1b: *Live in the Moment*

As you write out your story, try zooming in on all the details. Go line by line, switching up how you describe the moment. Choose from the following:

ACTION

DIALOGUE

DESCRIPTION

THINKING/FEELING

Live in the Moment (OR 2.1b)

2. DEVELOP A TEXT SET

THINKING ABOUT THE STRATEGY

I am a sci-fi, fantasy, superhero consumer. Books, films, shows, video games— you name it, I am there. There is no greater intellectual joy for me than to be fully immersed in a world given to me by someone else, stopping to look up and listen to ideas that people are throwing out there for consideration.

An example: During the COVID-19 pandemic I decided to rewatch the Marvel movies (phases 1–3) in chronological order. If you don't know what that means, just know that it's a lot of films to watch. As I watched each piece, I have sources that I go to that help me think bigger about the text than I would on my own. There is a podcast I listened to that unpacks each film through the lens of one idea. There are websites and essays I consulted to read up on what others have picked out that I may have missed. These companion texts help me root my own interpretation and thinking, and they help me discover new ideas.

It is not that I get my ideas from these essayists. Certainly my thinking is shaped by the discussion, but more often I hear my own thoughts more clearly by having something for them to hit against, like some kind of thought sonar.

The books our students read are rarely obscure texts that no one has heard about. If they are whole-class novels, then chances are they are very well-known books that have a long tradition of thinking and criticism surrounding them. If the books are chosen by the students, then they are often popular books that also have lots written about them. There are often film adaptations of books, graphic novel versions, online playlists.

Helping students collect some text sets that they will want by their side as they begin a theme study of a novel does two things: it offers readers backup for both their reading and their thinking, and it offers new ways of looking at the text that can help inform their interpretation.

Have students do some research on people, publications, podcasts, movies, films, and social media platforms that have devoted time to the books they are about to read. Looking for texts for *Aristotle and Dante*, I found a few podcasts and videos quite quickly (see Figures 2.3 and 2.4).

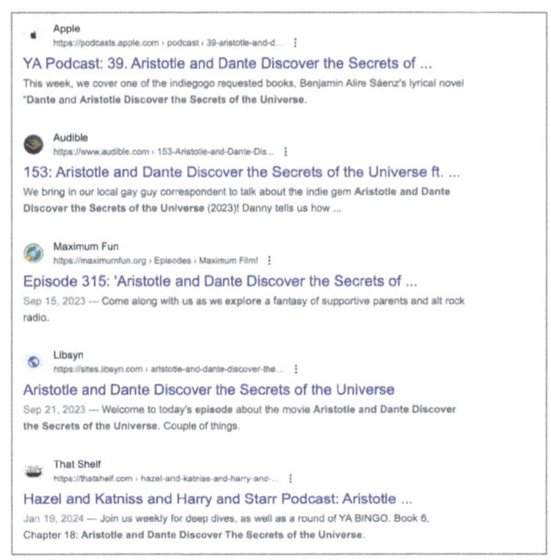

FIGURE 2.3: *List of podcasts from my quick online research*

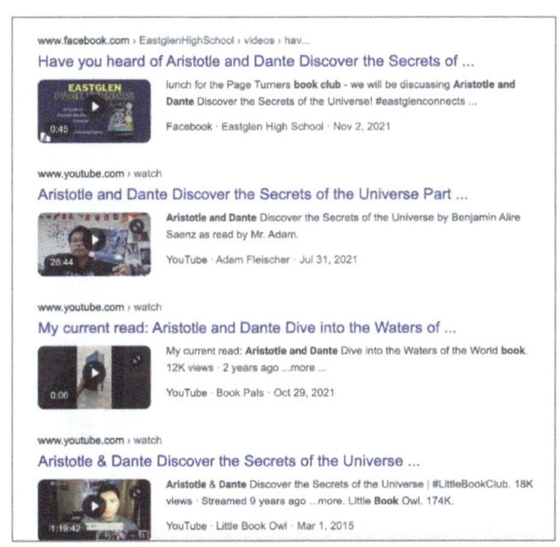

FIGURE 2.4: *List of YouTube videos from my quick online research*

2. DEVELOP A TEXT SET

TEACHING THE STRATEGY

Lesson Flow

For most of the texts our students will read, there is a community of people who are already in deep discussion. Help them find support as they read.

One way to teach this lesson:

1. Introduce the lesson by having students share out a time when they looked up more material around a text, person, or moment in pop culture (listening to a podcast about Marvel movies, watching TikToks about the latest YouTube star controversy).
2. Create a list together of the reasons why this was helpful. Point out that it isn't that these other sources tell you what to think, but that by listening to what other people think about something, you get to be in conversation, and this conversation helps you see what you think about the text.
3. Model how you find companion texts for a book you are reading. Highlight the types of materials you are looking for: essays, podcasts, YouTube essays, movie interpretations, graphic novels, and so on.
4. Give students time to look online for available materials that might help support their thinking and challenge their interpretations as they read.
5. Set up a structure for the rest of this unit where once a week, you encourage or assign students to use their companion texts to rethink the text or clarify their thinking. Ask students to write a quick response during this time where they name what the companion texts offered them.

Providing Feedback

If your students say or demonstrate . . .	Coach them on . . .
I am struggling to find any companion texts for my book.	Looking for a different kind of text: podcast, YouTube review, SparkNotes, adaptation, audiobook, etc.
I found one companion text and I think it will be fine.	Looking for a few different kinds of companion texts so that they can choose which one feels most interesting to use as they read
I found a bunch of companion texts.	Surveying the materials they have to see which ones might be the most helpful to them based on how in depth the materials go, what kind of support they need, or what is most interesting to them

Optional Tools

Online Resource 2.2: ***Develop a Text Set***

Check the following:

- ☐ Podcasts
- ☐ Video Essays/Reviews
- ☐ Adaptations: Movies, TV Shows
- ☐ Graphic Novels
- ☐ Summary sites

Rank order of interest:

1.

2.

3.

What help do I think I will need most from my companion texts?

Develop a Text Set (OR 2.2)

AS THE BOOK BEGINS

In this section, we'll discuss the following skills:

3. Consider Character and Conflict

While it may seem negative, most themes begin in the problems of the text. Here you can help students uncover the layers of conflicts that are arising from page 1.

4. Look for Universal Problems

Helping students move from the specifics of the text to the universal issues that will become themes can be tricky. This lesson offers a scaffold for students who are having trouble seeing the abstract in the particular.

5. Rank the Issues That Are Arising

At some point, we have to decide which issues feel the most urgent, interesting, or significant so that we can narrow the field of our interpretation. Here we help students rank the issues based on a set of criteria.

I have a friend who just started therapy. He had never been before, and it is rocking his world. The experience of looking at his entire life—all of his relationships and choices and reactions—through the lens of what he is learning there is incredibly painful. "It's like I have to relive my whole life," he said recently, burying his head in his hands.

Sometimes when we are teaching young people to interpret themes in their books, we accidentally force them into being like my friend who started therapy late. We wait until the end of the book to suddenly spring theme into the equation. They have focused on plot and character, and they have paid attention to a literary technique here and there, and then—bam—we hit them with "Now that you are almost finished, please go back and look at every important scene through the lens of a complex and significant issue in the book." It's too much.

Instead, we can teach students to have a theme mindset from the first page of the book. To be on the lookout for important issues from the start, to begin naming the ideas they will want to track throughout their reading.

3. CONSIDER CHARACTER AND CONFLICT

THINKING ABOUT THE STRATEGY

Themes live in the problems we face, how we face them, and the consequences of those choices. Our problems begin at the beginning—of our lives and the texts we read. While the proper nouns change, many of the problems I face today are similar to the ones I encountered when I was a kid. Here is a template of one problem that has followed me since time immemorial:

> I am overwhelmed by ______. I don't know how to handle ______, so instead I withdraw, get grumpy and sarcastic.

This in and of itself is not a theme, but it is a repeating problem that I can see began at, well, the beginning.

In the texts we read, it is the same. Rarely do authors spend time developing problems in Chapter 1 that they do not revisit across the text. This means that we can teach students to begin noticing the problems a character faces from the start.

This may inspire you to lean on some old favorites when it comes to teaching conflict. And certainly, teaching students that many people use terms like *individual* versus ______ to describe the kinds of conflict in a text might be helpful. But I find that sometimes we need a little bit more coaching than this to make the kinds of problems we are trying to find shine a little brighter.

Teach students that as they begin a book, they can write down a list of the problems they notice right away. If they struggle to name a problem, guide them toward moments where the character's life seems difficult, or they are feeling a negative emotion, or it seems like this place is messed up in some way. Then see if they can locate the source of that difficulty, that feeling, that messed-upness. Don't worry right now about vocabulary or whether they capture things perfectly. We have a long way to go and this is just the beginning. If need be, you can offer students some categories of problems that people face, like family, fitting in, money, inequality, power, and relationships, and see if they can find some less obvious problems.

In *Aristotle and Dante*, for example, on page 1 I could see Ari struggling with not liking the world, feeling alone, being irritated by everything, and not feeling like he has really lived. That's one page, and, as I read the book, I saw that these problems helped construct the themes of the book.

In *The Namesake*, similarly, the problems that are introduced on page 1 form the foundation for the themes in the text. By page 1 Ashima is homesick and trying to recapture the past but feeling what is missing. As we read the novel, we move through iterations of these same issues (and others, of course) with Ashima, Ashoke, and Gogol.

The seeds of theme are often sowed in the first lines of the novel. Teach students to find them and get ahead of the game.

3. CONSIDER CHARACTER AND CONFLICT

TEACHING *THE STRATEGY*

Lesson Flow

While it may seem negative, most themes begin in the problems of the text. Here you can help students uncover the layers of conflicts that are arising from page 1.

One way to teach this lesson:

1. Show students a first scene from a movie (say, the first scene in *Black Panther*).
2. Guide students in a discussion naming the issues that come up in that first scene (obeying convention versus doing what you think is right; family betrayal; helping community in the best ways).
3. Point out that those issues are important in the text as a whole.
4. Have students practice reading the first scenes or chapter of their book and do the same thing—list the problems they see the character facing. Chances are these will be significant issues in the text.
5. Encourage or assign students to stop after each beginning chapter and list out the conflicts and problems and issues they see. Ask them to notice which problems are being repeated.
6. Give students time to read, talk, or write about the book they are reading while you confer or pull small groups.

What Might This Look Like?

DATE

CHARACTER

chapter one

- the first problem/conflict she (the main character, Jess) introduces to us is that she's fallen in love with her best friend
  - → she contrasts this against other major world issues/events that are less important to her
  - → very typical teen girl so far
- Jess is very observant
  - → noticing strange noises
- no strong feelings towards her ill sister, Sara
  - → she describes her medical setup + Sara's caretaker, Lydia to the reader, but there isn't any hint of worry surrounding this topic yet
- Jess cares the most about her own issues
  - → she's not exactly self-absorbed, but she seems to be surrounded by world/family issues that are much bigger than her love life that she spends less time discussing
  - → foreshadowing that her perspective on conflicts may shift throughout the book? Since it seems to be so exaggerated on a small, more personal scale now

Connecting the issues in the text to the character's experience helps enrich our understanding of the themes that are emerging in the text.

As the book begins:

1. Consider character and conflict: Chapter one: Jem Finch: loss Jean Finch: too early to tell Atticus Finch: to early to tell Dill: Family most issues are not put in this chapter
   Chapter two: Jean Finch: has a really bad school teacher School Jem Finch: Not important in this chapter Walter Cunnigham: Has to deal with his poor family and
   Chapter Three: Jean Finch: her family is being a little annoying and she still doesn't like school Jem finch: His annoying sister
   Chapter 5: Jean is dealing with here friends leaving her behind, Jem is dealing with issues with his father, and dill has nothing wrong
   Chapter 6: Jem is dealing with adolescent problems and dill is leaving, I would also like to point out how time is moving very quickly in this book
   Chapter 7: The infamous duo are dealing with school and figuring out who is giving them gifts
   Chapter 8: The duo are dealing with there secrets their first snow, and a fire at a friends house
   Chapter 9: Atticus is dealing with his family and a new court trail while Jean is dealing with school issues and an annoying cousin
   Chapter ten: We learn about Atticus's secret past and we see a dog die

Miles lists out the conflicts at the start of the book.

Providing Feedback

If your students say or demonstrate . . .	Coach them on . . .
I see one concrete problem the character is facing.	The different kinds of problems characters can face: external, internal, problems with others, ways they wish the world were different, etc.
I can name an internal and external conflict.	Reading a bit more closely—going line by line and looking for issues that the character is having Using precise language when describing problems
I have a list of problems the character is facing.	Looking for connections between the problems—which might affect each other? Making some predictions based on how stories tend to go: What do they think the character will learn? (This is their forecasted theme.)

Optional Tools

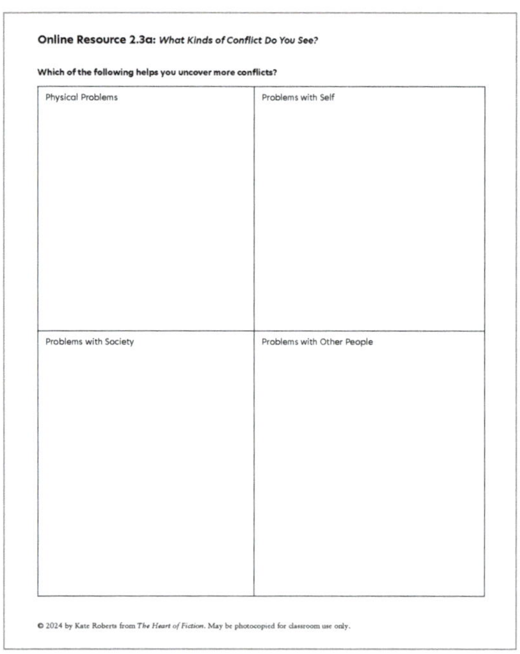

Online Resource 2.3a: *What Kinds of Conflict Do You See?*

Which of the following helps you uncover more conflicts?

Physical Problems	Problems with Self
Problems with Society	Problems with Other People

© 2024 by Kate Roberts from *The Heart of Fiction*. May be photocopied for classroom use only.

What Kinds of Conflict Do You See? (OR 2.3a)

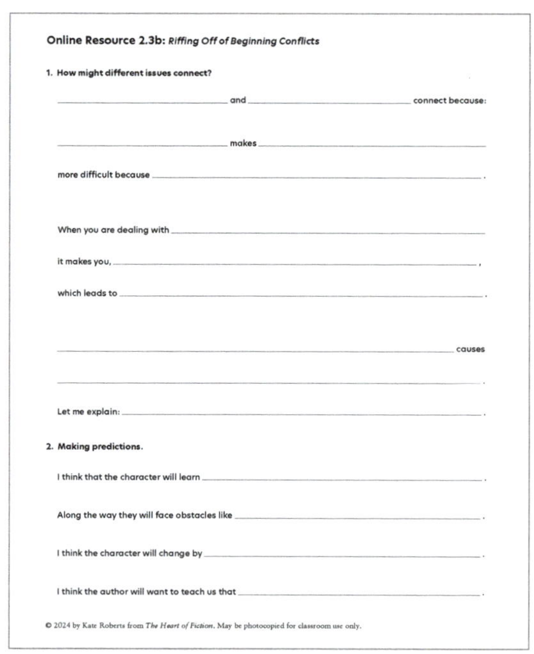

Online Resource 2.3b: *Riffing Off of Beginning Conflicts*

1. How might different issues connect?

_______ and _______ connect because:

_______ makes _______

more difficult because _______.

When you are dealing with _______

it makes you, _______,

which leads to _______.

_______ causes

_______.

Let me explain: _______.

2. Making predictions.

I think that the character will learn _______.

Along the way they will face obstacles like _______.

I think the character will change by _______.

I think the author will want to teach us that _______.

© 2024 by Kate Roberts from *The Heart of Fiction*. May be photocopied for classroom use only.

Riffing on Beginning Conflicts (OR 2.3b)

4. LOOK FOR UNIVERSAL PROBLEMS

THINKING ABOUT THE STRATEGY

Chances are you lived through the COVID-19 pandemic and you struggled. Everyone in the world was struggling—to some degree—with the same thing. Sort of. But also, not at all, right? Because we also had very different experiences. Some lost loved ones and jobs and were alone. Others had jobs but juggled working full time and homeschooling children. We each had our particular mental health struggles. In a way, our experiences were very different, and yet there is something that held us together in this time, something universal, though lived through the prism of very different circumstances and marked as always by privilege and oppression.

While our stories were specific, there were themes that felt universal. I personally struggled with some issues that were particular to me. But everyone struggled with loss. It might even be fair to say that we all experienced the idea that loss can change you for better or worse, depending on privilege, personality, and chance.

These universal themes in our lives live in our novels as well. When we read novels, we encounter characters facing problems that we relate to or that are unfamiliar to us. But even if the plot veers into uncharted territory, we often can relate to the bigger issues in the text. It's these issues that we encourage students to name at the beginning of the book. Certainly they will not be able to say, "This book is about how loss can change you for better or worse, depending on privilege, personality, and chance," after reading the first chapter, but chances are they will be able to see "loss," "how loss affects people," "choices people make in the face of loss," and so on. It's this handle on the universal that we can teach students to look for at the start of the book, and having a strong grip on these ideas will serve us well as we dive into the narrative.

In *Aristotle and Dante*, for example, right away, I can see universal issues of identity, insecurity, openness and honesty, vulnerability, family, and fitting in. I don't need to know these characters completely to pick up on these themes if I know what I am looking for, if I have already used the previous strategy and identified problems coming up in the text.

We can teach students a relatively simple trick that proves rewarding, although it might take a little practice. Have them take a problem they noticed in the book, like "Ari doesn't feel like he has really lived." Then have them try to break that problem down into as many universal words and phrases that they can. Reading Ari's thoughts on the limits of his life, I write down, "dissatisfaction, grumpiness, yearning for something, insecurity, self-esteem." Now for sure I don't know which of these ideas are going to be central to the text yet, but I am almost certain that all of them will be resolved in some way by the end, with some kind of message attached. They are all the beginnings of theme.

In *The Namesake*, then, I can take one of the problems that arises early on, like "Ashima is trying to find her way in a strange country with a husband she does not know well yet," and break it down into a few universal issues—assimilation, nonconformity, identity, loneliness, pride, racism. When students do this work on all of the interesting or major problems they see emerging in the text, they will have both a nice long list to consider as the issues they want to track as well as a good sense of the issues that will keep coming up.

Around May in 2020, my eldest son began feeling the wear of the changes in his life. At bedtime he complained, "I just want the virus to be over."

I comforted him as best I could, but the thing that helped most was when I said, "You know, buddy, every kid in the world is dealing with this right now."

"In the whole world?" he asked. And while certainly every child's story was different, I could confidently tell him that there was something universal going on, that he was not alone.

4. LOOK FOR UNIVERSAL PROBLEMS

TEACHING THE STRATEGY

Lesson Flow

Helping students move from the specifics of the text to the universal issues that will become themes can be tricky. This lesson offers a scaffold for students who are having trouble seeing the abstract in the particular.

One way to teach this lesson:

1. Introduce the lesson by asking students to list some problems they have faced in their lives. Have a T-chart up that you can write on, with one side labeled "My Problem" and the other, "Universal Problem."
2. Sort students' responses and guide the class in a discussion of the difference between a problem that affects them personally and a problem that is universal. Show how we can move in both directions when discussing problems, for example, how my personal problem "can't get a full night of sleep" can be translated to the universal issue "staying healthy."
3. Ask students to pair up and create this same T-chart for the book they are reading. Have them list out the problems the characters are facing and then translate those specific problems into the universal.
4. Discuss with the class the universal issues they came up with for their books, and invite students to add other issues they may have missed to their chart if they fit the book as well.
5. Give students time to read, talk, or write about the book they are reading while you confer or pull small groups.

What Might This Look Like?

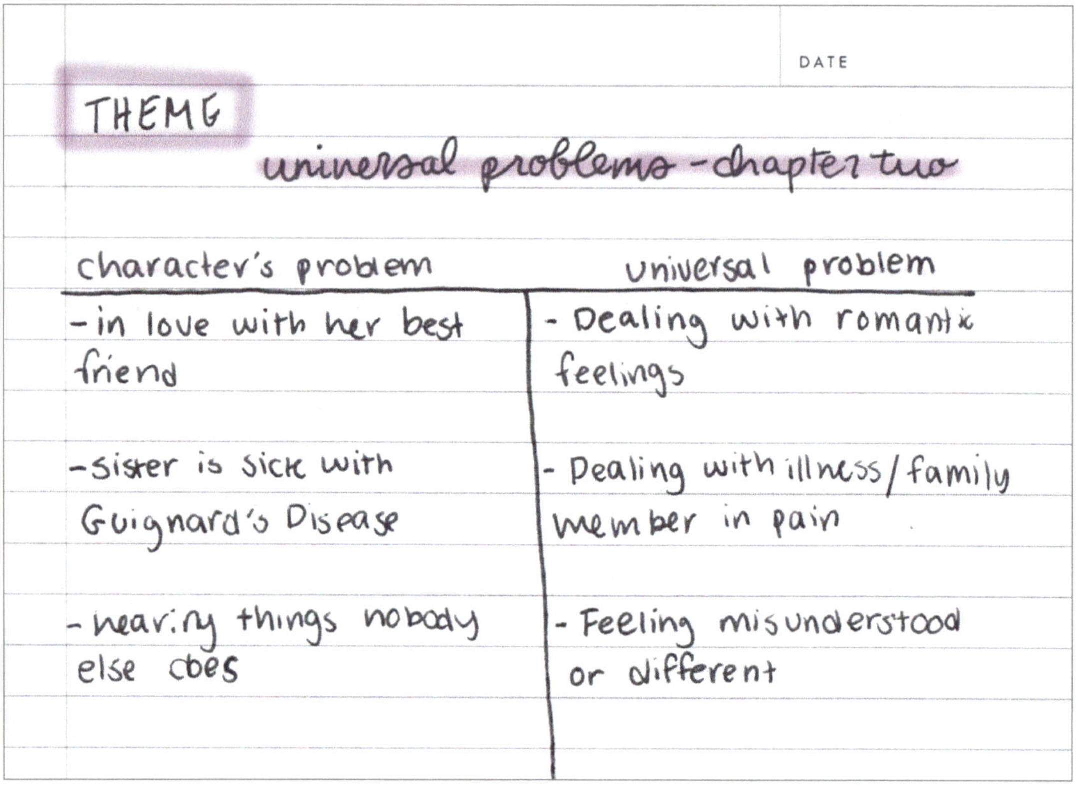

DATE

THEME

universal problems - chapter two

character's problem	universal problem
- in love with her best friend	- Dealing with romantic feelings
- sister is sick with Guignard's Disease	- Dealing with illness/family member in pain
- hearing things nobody else does	- Feeling misunderstood or different

Annika steps back to name some of the universal problems in a text.

Looking at universal problems

Universal problems	Jean	Jem	Atticus
Jean: New school years Jem: Puberty	The starting of school	Growing up	
Jean/Jem: Who is this guy		This is shared between Jean and Jem: Figuring out who is giving them presents	
Jean: New teacher Jean/Jem: Secrets	The school she is currently going to isn't teaching her well	This is shared between the two: They are dealing with trying to keep things a secret	
Atticus: Trying to win the trail and trying to protect his family			A new trail relating to an African American man

Miles begins to work on tracking the universal problems in **To Kill a Mockingbird.**

Providing Feedback

If your students say or demonstrate . . .	Coach them on . . .
I can name the problems in the text, but I'm not quite sure how to make them universal.	Thinking about the topic of the problem the character is facing (If they are fighting with their mom, for example, the topic is family.) Using a short list of universal issues to help jog their thinking (No more than three or four—love, loss, money, injustice—should do the trick.)
I can name a universal problem in the text.	Reading just one paragraph of a text and pulling out a universal issue represented there Finding a target number of problems, like three to four, within a short time frame, such as five minutes
I can find layers of universal problems in the scenes of a text.	Considering which problems feel most important to the text and relevant to them Considering what the text is starting to say about these problems

Optional Tools

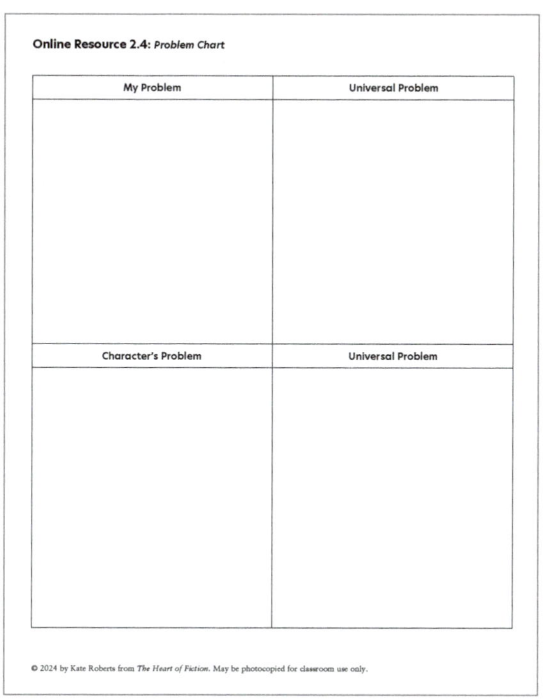
Online Resource 2.4: *Problem Chart*

My Problem	Universal Problem

Character's Problem	Universal Problem

Problem Chart (OR 2.4)

5. RANK THE ISSUES THAT ARE ARISING

THINKING ABOUT THE STRATEGY

Embarrassingly, many of the issues that plague me today existed in my life from the very beginning. It's a little exhausting. How many times can I feel as though I don't quite fit in? Doesn't one just get over their self-reliance once it is no longer needed? Why haven't I learned to just ask for what I need?

It appears as though the issues we encounter when we are young, the ones that stick to our particular personality and experiences and brain chemistry, don't just fade away. They stay like the muscle memory of riding a bike or an unpleasant odor for which you can't find the source.

However, for most of us, their importance changes over time. When I was younger, fitting in felt like the most important problem man has ever faced, whereas now I am struggling much more with other things. The fitting-in thing is still there (just find me at any education conference and we can discuss), but it feels less urgent, less interesting even, at this point in my life.

We can have the same attitude about the issues that arise in a text. At a certain point (near the end of the beginning, usually) we know what the issues are in this story. We also know that we will not be able to track and discuss all of them unless, like me, you find yourself studying *Jane Eyre* four different times across the course of your college career. But we will want to begin tracking at least one issue, perhaps a few, and so we will want to make some decisions.

We can teach students that once they have a nice list of issues that feel both very much in the text and universal, we can begin to rank them in order of importance.

Of course, this begs the question, of importance to whom? The simple answer is to have students rank the issues in the book in order of importance to the character or author. Like, which problems feel like a really big deal in this text? If I did this work in *Aristotle and Dante*, I'd probably rank the problems Ari is facing in this order: (1) opening up, (2) connecting to his family, and (3) having a negative outlook. Depending on how active I am able to be and interested in being in this book, I could decide to focus on one or two of these as I continue in the book.

But that is not the only metric of importance that matters to a reader. Often the major themes of the book are not the ones that interest me. We can also offer students a chance to track the ideas that have the most relevance or interest for them right now. If I take *The Namesake* on this journey, I am going to prioritize differently than if I were focusing on Ashima's and Gogol's biggest issues. I might focus on this list: (1) the American dream/mirage, (2) accepting ourselves, and (3) being homesick for a home that doesn't exist. It's the list of issues that most emotionally resonate for me—the ones I am the most interested in.

For this is certainly, ultimately, what we hope students will get out of a unit that helps them interpret themes—not just the ability to begrudgingly tell us what Shakespeare has to say about jealousy but the experience of encountering a text that is dealing with the same stuff they are interested in right at this moment. The joy and pain of seeing their own heart living another life. The wisdom gained by seeing in words the thing that they could not express but feel.

We can offer the opportunity for this experience to students, along with the assistance in uncovering the author's purpose, whatever that is, as if anyone could possibly know.

5. RANK THE ISSUES THAT ARE ARISING

TEACHING THE STRATEGY

Lesson Flow

At some point, we have to decide which issues feel the most urgent, interesting, or significant so that we can narrow the field of our interpretation. Here we help students rank the issues based on a set of criteria.

One way to teach this lesson:

1. Introduce the lesson by discussing how different problems are more or less important at different stages of our lives. Demonstrate on your own life, explaining how the problems that mattered most to you when you were younger are less important now and vice versa.
2. Refer to the list of universal problems from the previous lesson, and ask students to put them in order of importance.
3. Offer students guidance as to what makes an issue more or less important: it seems to be affecting a lot of the story, it matters most to the character, the author seems to care a lot about it because they repeat it a bunch, or it matters the most to the reader.
4. If reading a whole-class text, discuss. If reading choice books, have students go right to reading, looking for these ranked problems as they do.
5. Give students time to read, talk, or write about the book they are reading while you confer or pull small groups.
6. Close out class by asking students to jot down the issue they think is most important as well as three scenes so far that seem to highlight that issue.

What Might This Look Like?

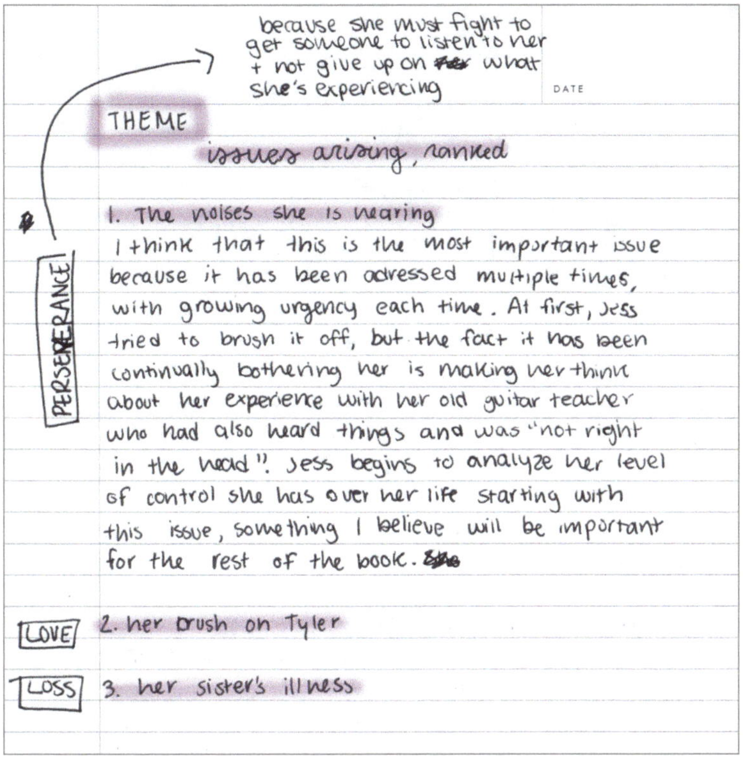
because she must fight to get someone to listen to her + not give up on what she's experiencing

DATE

THEME

issues arising, ranked

PERSEVERANCE 1. The noises she is hearing

I think that this is the most important issue because it has been adressed multiple times, with growing urgency each time. At first, Jess tried to brush it off, but the fact it has been continually bothering her is making her think about her experience with her old guitar teacher who had also heard things and was "not right in the head". Jess begins to analyze her level of control she has over her life starting with this issue, something I believe will be important for the rest of the book.

LOVE 2. her crush on Tyler

LOSS 3. her sister's illness

Annika ranks the issues in her text to determine which she will track closely.

Rank the issues arising

1. Protection. Trying to win the trial and trying to protect his family: "Jack, and I hope and pray I can get Jem and Scout through it without the bitterness, and most of all, without catching Maycombs's usual disease" (Pg 117 Lee) "The jury couldn't possibly take Tom Robinson's word against the Ewells'" (Pg 117 Lee
2. Who is this guy: This is most important because it is really important for us to understand for later in the story
3. Secrets
4. New teacher
5. Puberty
6. New school years

Miles ranks the issues in his text to determine which he will track closely.

Providing Feedback

If your students say or demonstrate . . .	Coach them on . . .
I can put issues in an order, but I'm not quite sure why.	Using the menu of ranking criteria (see "Optional Tools") to help name a reason Focusing on the issue that seems to be coming up the most—chances are if it keeps coming up, it's important
I can put the issues in an order that makes sense to me, and I know which one I want to track.	Talking a little about how their ranking fits the criteria Looking for a few scenes where they see that issue in the text
I can put the issues in an order that makes sense, and I am thinking about tracking more than one.	Strategizing what kind of tracking system they will use for multiple issues—different-colored sticky notes, a chart in their notebook, etc. (The system will need to mark scenes for each issue and allow for some writing about each scene.)

Optional Tools

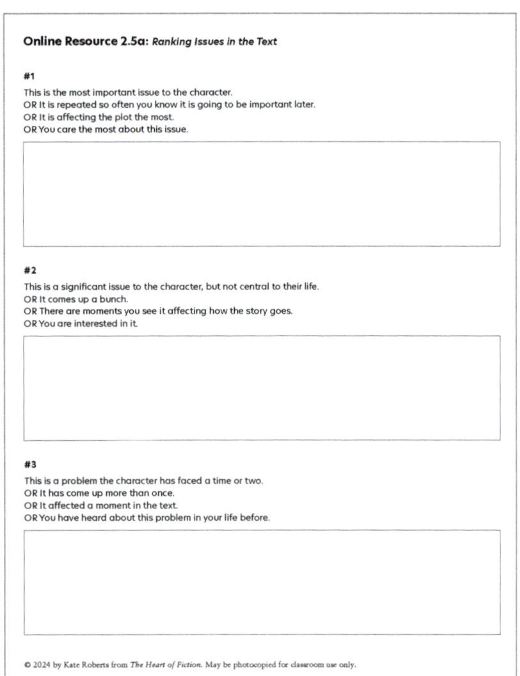
Online Resource 2.5a: *Ranking Issues in the Text*

#1
This is the most important issue to the character.
OR It is repeated so often you know it is going to be important later.
OR It is affecting the plot the most.
OR You care the most about this issue.

#2
This is a significant issue to the character, but not central to their life.
OR It comes up a bunch.
OR There are moments you see it affecting how the story goes.
OR You are interested in it.

#3
This is a problem the character has faced a time or two.
OR It has come up more than once.
OR It affected a moment in the text.
OR You have heard about this problem in your life before.

© 2024 by Kate Roberts from *The Heart of Fiction*. May be photocopied for classroom use only.

Ranking Issues in the Text (OR 2.5a)

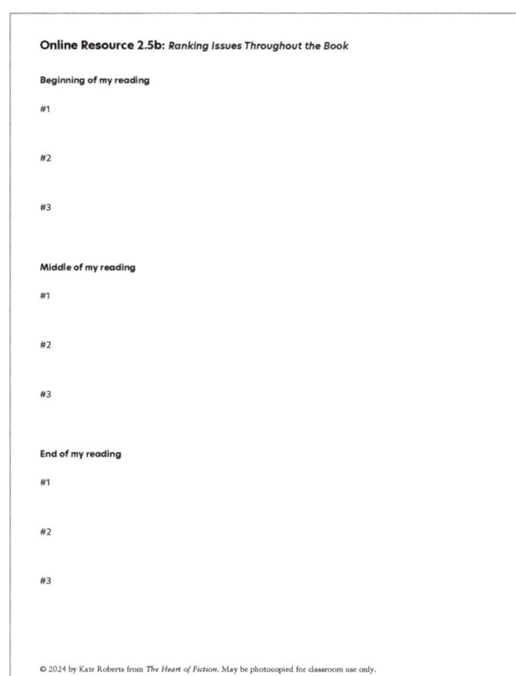
Online Resource 2.5b: *Ranking Issues Throughout the Book*

Beginning of my reading
#1
#2
#3

Middle of my reading
#1
#2
#3

End of my reading
#1
#2
#3

© 2024 by Kate Roberts from *The Heart of Fiction*. May be photocopied for classroom use only.

Ranking Issues Throughout the Book (OR 2.5b)

IN THE MIDDLE OF THE BOOK

In this section, we'll discuss the following skills:

6. Track and Analyze Critical Scenes

It is important that students analyze the scenes that express key issues as they read. Here, we offer students a breakdown of how to do this analysis work.

7. Examine the Intersections

Issues and themes don't live in isolation. Teach students to search for the ways that the issues influence each other to help them come away with more complex thinking.

8. Dive into Complexity

When we offer a concrete, practical way to scaffold sophisticated analysis, students are able to give complexity a go.

When thinking about theme, readers often think of the middle of the book as Jan Brady. The middle child. Left alone, ignored. The end of the book is where all the action is. That's when, supposedly, we find out what the theme is. It's Marcia. So popular. And the beginning is the adorable baby sister whom you can't help but pay attention to. Oh, sweet little Cindy.

The middle of the text, however, when thinking about theme, is where all of the good stuff lives. This is where the ideas get developed, complicated. It is where the seeds of our actual interpretation will be sown, and it is where we first will see the sprouts of our analysis. It is, then, where we should do the most work as readers and interpreters of theme.

We usually don't, though. And then at the end we are a little bit overwhelmed at the thought of thinking through hundreds of pages to come up with what the author is really trying to say. Let this section, then, be an invitation to you and your students to roll up your sleeves and dig into the beautiful mess of the middle.

6. TRACK AND ANALYZE CRITICAL SCENES

THINKING ABOUT THE STRATEGY

It's tough to interpret the lessons we learn just from the end of things, isn't it? Let's take a relationship ending. I have a friend who got divorced. When it first happened, they said mean things about their ex, they were full of hurt, like most of us are at the end of things that we wanted to last. But months later, so much had changed. They were compassionate and understanding and had a big picture of the whole relationship, not just the messy end.

What had changed? Time and reflection. My friend was no longer just looking at the issue of marriage through the last moments. They were examining the whole story—the various scenes of their life together. Each scene had a different message—how they met, how they made the decision to marry, the birth of their children. And each scene added layers of meaning to the big issue of marriage. It is complicated. The ending just wraps up the journey; it does not define it.

When we are reading a novel, there is a temptation to wait until the ending to figure out what it is about. We hope that by getting to know the characters and following the plot, we will inherently understand the *story*—the threads of meaning that make great books more than just a series of events. But often by the end of the book, we are like my friend—in our emotions, in the moment. A character dies and we mourn. A parent is forgiven, and we feel tightness in our chests with a mix of relief and resentment. Or we did not connect that much to the text at all, and so as it concludes we shrug and move on with our day.

And yet we can read—and live—in a way that collects meaning as we go. We can develop our awareness that life—and books—have threads of meaning that may not make sense yet but will eventually if we pause and reflect as things happen to us, to the characters we read, to others.

Once students have a sense of the issues that are important for them to track in the text, teach them to stop when they see scenes where that issue seems to live, and teach them to slow down and consider what these particular scenes have to say about it all.

The first part is easy enough. Students can pause after each chapter or so and look back, thinking, *Was the issue I am tracking relevant in any of these scenes?* If the answer is *no* after a couple of chapters, have them reflect on the issue to see if they maybe want to choose a more prevalent issue, or ask them to look again.

The second part of this lesson is much trickier and is a central muscle we want to develop in students' thinking when they are interpreting themes. Let's say I know that in *Aristotle and Dante* I want to track the issue of pushing people away. When I find a critical scene—a moment when my issue is essential—it may not be so clear what the scene is really saying about that issue. Most people need explicit strategies for unlocking the messages a scene has around an issue. They may need, for example, to be taught some kinds of ideas that tend to live in scenes. Often a scene has a reason or cause for the issue. Or sometimes it shows an effect. Other times it offers a solution. If I know these kinds or brands of connections that I can make from a scene to an issue, I can begin to think things through. (See Figure 2.5.)

This lesson should be repeated throughout the book. It can be a standing assignment: after every chapter, we pause, look for the issue we're tracking, and analyze the critical scenes. We will return to these analyses as we near the end, but more than anything else in this chapter, this lesson will bear the fruits of interpretation, allowing us to pluck the theme from its branches.

Pushing People Away

This scene unpacks WHY we push people away. We push them away because it doesn't feel good when we are close. There is criticism, judgment, expectation. All of a sudden we feel and see what we are supposed to be and it is painful that we are not that. All of a sudden who we are is not enough. When it feels like this to be close, of course we push people away.

FIGURE 2.5: *My entry analyzing a critical scene*

6. TRACK AND ANALYZE CRITICAL SCENES

TEACHING THE STRATEGY

Lesson Flow

It is important that students analyze the scenes that express important issues as they read. Here, we offer students a breakdown of how to do this analysis work.

One way to teach this lesson:

1. Introduce the lesson by telling the stories of two moments when you struggled with the same issue. Highlight how our issues may stay consistent, but what we learn and the ideas we have about them change, and the same is true in books.
2. Model taking an issue, finding a scene that embodies that issue, and exploring what the scene is teaching you about that issue. Consider these questions:

    - Is there a reason this issue is difficult in this scene?
    - Is there a cause of the issue in this scene?
    - Is there an effect of the issue in this scene?
    - Is there a solution offered in this scene?

3. Ask students to find a critical scene for an issue they are tracking. They may work with a partner or independently.
4. Give students time to try this strategy on their scene.
5. Share with the class a few of the ideas that students have.
6. Ask students to keep reading and repeating this work, at least once per chapter, for the rest of the day and for the rest of the book.

What Might This Look Like?

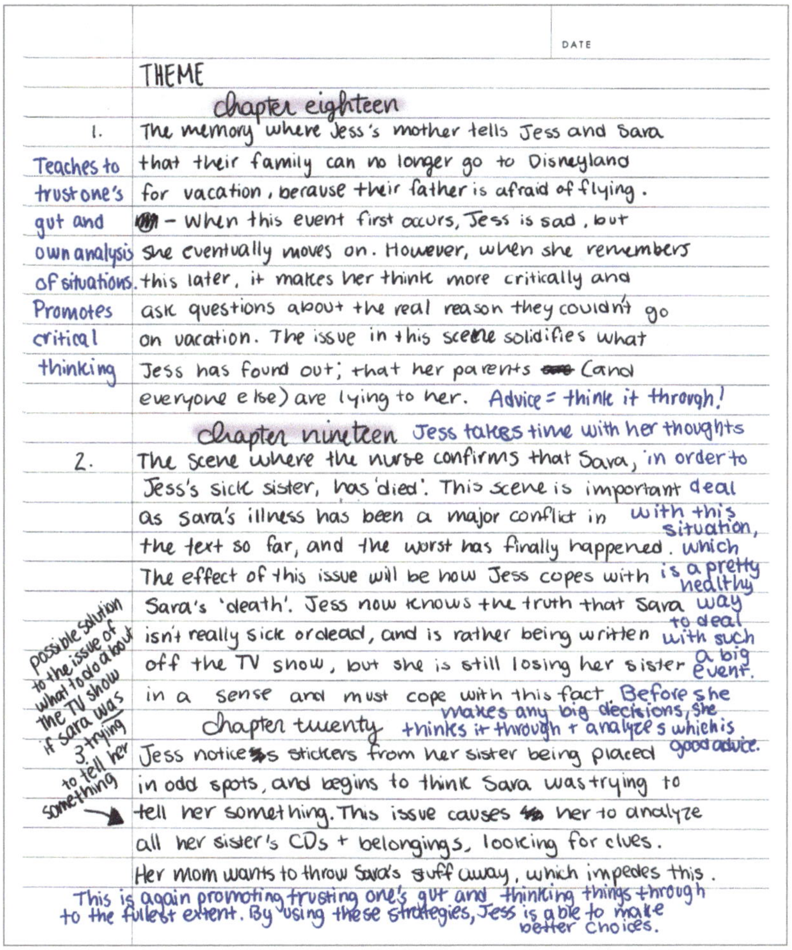
DATE

THEME

chapter eighteen

1\. The memory where Jess's mother tells Jess and Sara that their family can no longer go to Disneyland for vacation, because their father is afraid of flying. – When this event first occurs, Jess is sad, but she eventually moves on. However, when she remembers this later, it makes her think more critically and ask questions about the real reason they couldn't go on vacation. The issue in this scene solidifies what Jess has found out; that her parents (and everyone else) are lying to her. Advice = think it through!

Teaches to trust one's gut and own analysis of situations. Promotes critical thinking

chapter nineteen Jess takes time with her thoughts

2\. The scene where the nurse confirms that Sara, Jess's sick sister, has 'died'. This scene is important as Sara's illness has been a major conflict in the text so far, and the worst has finally happened. The effect of this issue will be how Jess copes with Sara's 'death'. Jess now knows the truth that Sara isn't really sick or dead, and is rather being written off the TV show, but she is still losing her sister in a sense and must cope with this fact.

in order to deal with this situation, which is a pretty healthy way to deal with such a big event. Before she makes any big decisions, she thinks it through + analyzes which is good advice.

chapter twenty

3\. Jess notices stickers from her sister being placed in odd spots, and begins to think Sara was trying to tell her something. This issue causes her to analyze all her sister's CDs + belongings, looking for clues. Her mom wants to throw Sara's stuff away, which impedes this.

possible solution to the issue of what to do about the TV show if Sara was trying to tell her something

This is again promoting trusting one's gut and thinking things through to the fullest extent. By using these strategies, Jess is able to make better choices.

Annika analyzes scenes that fit with her working theme.

1. Track and analyze critical scenes:

Chapter 12: The issue of this chapter is ignorance. The cause of this "Issue" is when Cal, their African American maid takes them to an African American church. Another cause of the children not knowing much about African American culture is the fact that the two communities, the black and the whites, are separated. So a cause is segregation causes ignorance. The effect this causes is that the white community and the black community become a little bit closer because of these little kids. So an effect of ignorance is that you leave it to the kids to figure things out. So in this scene we learn that sometimes not knowing all the history of an issue can help you get over it. And also that being ignorant can make you more or less racist, bc the kids ignorance makes them more innocent and less racist. The ignorance protects them from the rqcism in a way

Chapter 13: The issue in this chapter is being judged. The cause of this issue is that aunt Alexandra thinks that the kids are not being raised right. So maybe family can judge you more than other people sometimes. Another cause is that racism makes people even more judgemental. The effect of this is their life is changed and aunt Alexandra has a big role in the family. Another effect this might have is on the grandmother herself but we don't know at this moment.

***Miles analyzes scenes in* To Kill a Mockingbird.**

Providing Feedback

If your students say or demonstrate . . .	Coach them on . . .
I am having trouble finding a scene with my issue in it.	Reflecting on their issue and looking to see if another one is more present in the text Chunking the text they've read so far into beginning, middle, and end; naming what happened in each chunk; and reflecting on whether the issue lives in any of those parts
I can find a scene, but it's hard to know what it is telling me about the issue.	Working with some sentence frames: The reason ______ is difficult in this scene is because ______ . ______ is caused by ______ in this scene. In this scene, ______ happens because of ______ . If you are facing ______ , you should ______ , according to this scene.
I can think about the issue in the scene, but I tend to use one strategy each time (reasons the issue is difficult, for example).	Trying on different ways of analyzing a scene by using the above sentence frames Freewriting or talking a bit to get some other thoughts going

Optional Tools

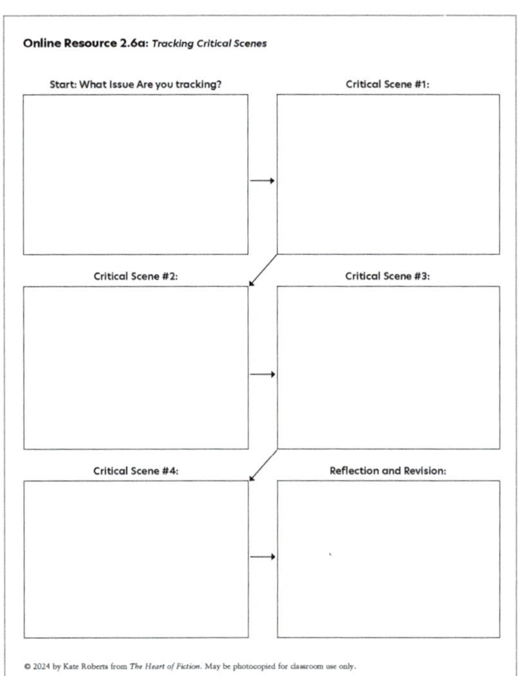

Online Resource 2.6a: *Tracking Critical Scenes*

Start: What Issue Are you tracking?

Critical Scene #1:

Critical Scene #2:

Critical Scene #3:

Critical Scene #4:

Reflection and Revision:

Tracking Critical Scenes (OR 2.6a)

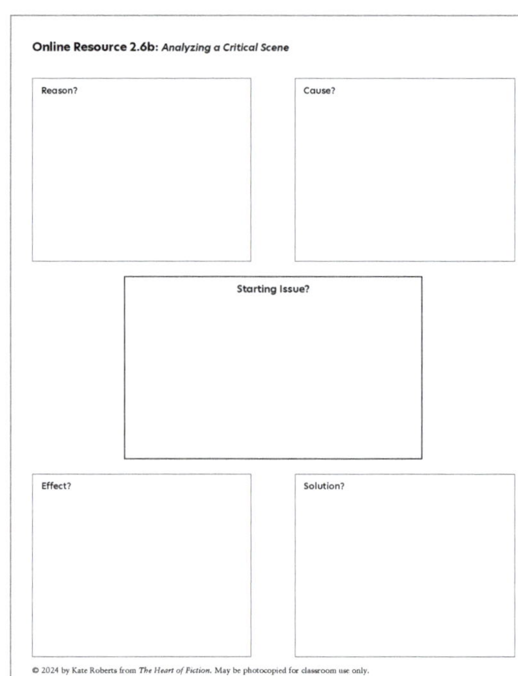

Online Resource 2.6b: *Analyzing a Critical Scene*

Reason?

Cause?

Starting Issue?

Effect?

Solution?

Analyzing a Critical Scene (OR 2.6b)

7. EXAMINE THE INTERSECTIONS

THINKING ABOUT THE STRATEGY

These last few years I have faced some minor health issues. There have been discomforts and a few breakdowns of systems that used to work just fine in the ol' bod. As I explore how to feel better in this next chapter that people keep calling middle age (rude), it turns out that there is not just one thing that needs fixing, one disorder or disease or bad habit that needs a tweak before healing. Instead, there is a delightful matrix of issues that interact with and affect each other. Diet and exercise and stress and genetics all work together to make up "how I feel." There is an intersection of causes and issues that creates a complicated ecosystem affecting my health.

It's never just one thing. The same is true in books. Sometimes when we think about theme, we can focus on one issue at a time. "This book is about loss." When we do this, our thinking can stay a little simple, one directional. As teachers we hunger for that elusive qualifier *insight* in our thinking; we crave themes that demonstrate our students have dived into issues and tried to capture nuance, and instead we get "Don't judge a book by its cover."

At this point in the series of lessons I've laid out, students have picked an issue or two to track, and they are practicing finding critical scenes for that issue and unpacking the ideas that live between the lines. Once students have a handle on that work, we can add a layer—we can teach students that themes intersect with each other in a text and that as we read we can look for issues that connect in scenes and begin to build a more layered approach to our interpretation.

For instance, in *The Namesake* I am tracking the idea of the American dream/mirage. I have been collecting ideas around this issue in the critical scenes I've found. Figure 2.6 contains an example of a scene I analyzed using the work from the previous session.

> Gogol does not date anyone in high school. He suffers quiet crushes, which he admits to no one, on this girl or that girl with whom he is already friends. He does not attend dances or parties. He and his group of friends, Colin and Jason and Marc, prefer to listen to records together, to Dylan and Clapton and The Who, and read Nietzsche in their spare time. His parents do not find it strange that their son doesn't date, does not rent a tuxedo for his junior prom. They have never been on a date in their lives and therefore they see no reason to encourage Gogol, certainly not at his age. Instead they urge him to join the math team and maintain his A average. His father presses him to pursue engineering, perhaps at MIT. Assured by his grades and his apparent indifference to girls, his parents don't suspect Gogol of being, in his own fumbling way, an American teenager.

The disconnect b/t parents' dream + kids / Dreams are often secret / The real American Dream is being cool not getting ahead? / Multiple American dreams?

FIGURE 2.6: *Scene from* The Namesake

If I go back and look for intersections with other ideas, however, I can see that along with the issue of the American dream/ mirage there is also clearly the issue of family and obligation here. We can teach students first to take this layering approach to critical scenes: what other issues live here? Have them annotate about a few more issues—or even one more issue—that they see coming up alongside the main issue they are tracking.

Then, we can begin to explore the connections between these issues. How do they fit together here? Is there a way that one enhances the other, makes it more intense? *Is* there a causal relationship between them? An effect one has on the other?

As I think through the scene from *The Namesake*, I start to explore the intersection of family and the American dream. My synthesis doesn't have to be perfect; I don't have to figure it all out. This lesson is helping young people craft more complex ideas, ideas with some parts to them, contradictions, some nuance. By definition as we practice this, we might get off track. It is the practice that makes the work better. Figure 2.7 shows the rough-draft thinking I did for the scene from *The Namesake*. Notice how I am striving to find the intersections between the issues, taking risks and seeing what happens.

Wanting students to be insightful about literature and not giving them time to approximate that level of analysis is contradictory. Students need lots of time and practice to develop the ability to see connections between ideas, practice we can give them especially in the middle of the books they read.

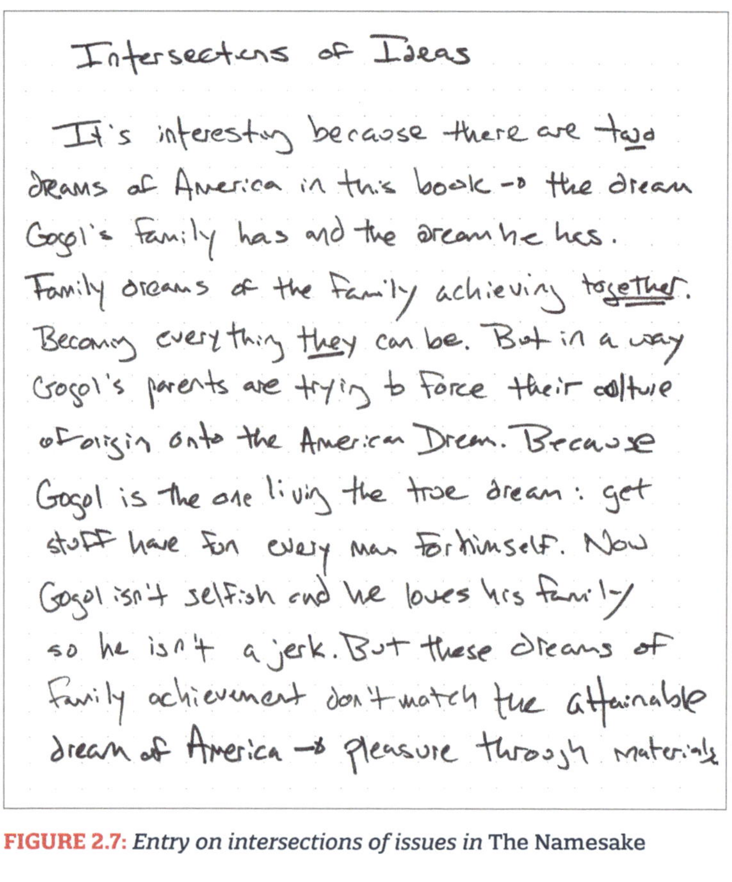
Intersections of Ideas

It's interesting because there are two dreams of America in this book → the dream Gogol's family has and the dream he has. Family dreams of the family achieving together. Becoming everything they can be. But in a way Gogol's parents are trying to force their culture of origin onto the American Dream. Because Gogol is the one living the true dream: get stuff have fun every man for himself. Now Gogol isn't selfish and he loves his family so he isn't a jerk. But these dreams of family achievement don't match the attainable dream of America → pleasure through materials

FIGURE 2.7: *Entry on intersections of issues in* The Namesake

7. EXAMINE THE INTERSECTIONS

TEACHING THE STRATEGY

Lesson Flow

Issues and themes don't live in isolation. Teach students to search for the ways that the issues influence each other to help them come away with more complex thinking.

One way to teach this lesson:

1. Introduce the lesson by telling a story of a time when your problems fed off each other. For example, you might talk about a time when not having enough money made it harder for you to go see family when they needed you. In this case, the issues of family and money intersected with each other.
2. Model looking at a scene you have recently analyzed for one issue. Reread the scene with your students, showing them how you look for complementary issues in the scene that intersect with the one you are tracking.
3. Ask students to practice this work on a scene they have analyzed (either with you as a class or on their own). They can work in pairs or independently.
4. Fold this work into their existing job of analyzing critical scenes as they read. Again, about once per chapter, they can find a scene and analyze it through the lens of the issue they're tracking, now also looking for intersecting issues as well.
5. Give students time to read, talk, or write about the book they are reading while you confer or pull small groups.
6. At the end of class, show students a few examples of long writes that strive to capture the analysis of both the tracked issue as well as the intersecting issues. Ask them to begin a long write now, to be finished either at home or the next day.

What Might This Look Like?

complimentary issues

REALITY IS SUBJECTIVE

In recent chapters, the issue of Sara's sickness and ultimate death have been intersecting with the reality that Jess's life is not technically real, and is actually a TV show. Even though everyone in Jess's life are actors, Jess still feels that her and her sister truly loved each other. She is noticing ~~[struck out]~~ suspicious things about Sara's behavior, and possible clues she left behind that may relate to the TV show.

Jess's TV show orchestrated Sara's death for plot and character development and to make Jess more interesting to the viewers of the show. Jess knows this now, which will influence her choices and descisons that will in turn influence how the show turns out.

Margin notes: commentary on how everyone's reality is different and can be subjective. Thus, the text is saying we should be aware and sensitive to other points of view. / POWER & CONTROL / Makes the reader analyze the amount of control they have over their own life and the factors that may be influencing them. / promotes self-reflection / Makes me think if I am the most powerful person over my own life or someone else?

counterpoint to the issue

Jess must counter her grief for her sister she must pretend is dead, with coping with the fact she loved her sister deeply but was lied to by her every single day of her life. These are extremely complicated feelings for Jess to have to deal with at such a young age, and they will affect how she proceeds through her life.

Annika tries to explain how different issues in her book intersect with each other.

2. Examine the Intersections

Chapter 12's "issue" is extremely related to the problem of trying to win the trial for Tom Robinson. The reason why this is so is because Tom Robinson is an African American who attends the church in chapter 12 often and has a wife struggling which is why during communion they force everyone to give them more money for the wife. Racisim and Law is something that intersects closely to one another, especially during this time period. Most people on the jury of a trial were probably racist during this time, so most aferican aericans who were tried for a crime were arrested or put to the chair . This is so unfair and maybe that is how these two issues intersect. Racisim makes the law not fair.

Chapter 14's issue is related to dills family problems I mentioned that was earlier in the book. The reason why these things are connected is because dill feels like he is not loved by his family and so he runs away which is sort of illustrated in the early chapters of the book. It was also made oblivious that he likes the finch household way better than his own because that's where he ran away to and that's where his friends are.

Miles tries to explain how different issues in his book intersect with each other.

Providing Feedback

If your students say or demonstrate . . .	Coach them on . . .
I'm doing OK with my tracked issue, but I am having trouble finding another issue in the same scene.	Listing all of the topics brought up by this scene and then asking which of these topics are causing problems or bad feelings
I can find another issue that intersects, but I am having trouble saying much about it.	Using a sentence frame to see if it helps: In this scene, the issue of ______ is made even harder because of ______ . ______ affects by ______ . In this scene, the solution to ______ is ______ .
I can name the way that two issues intersect in a scene.	Writing or talking out the details and angles: the way these issues cause each other, how they make the other more difficult or easy to deal with, the effects they have on each other, etc.

Optional Tools

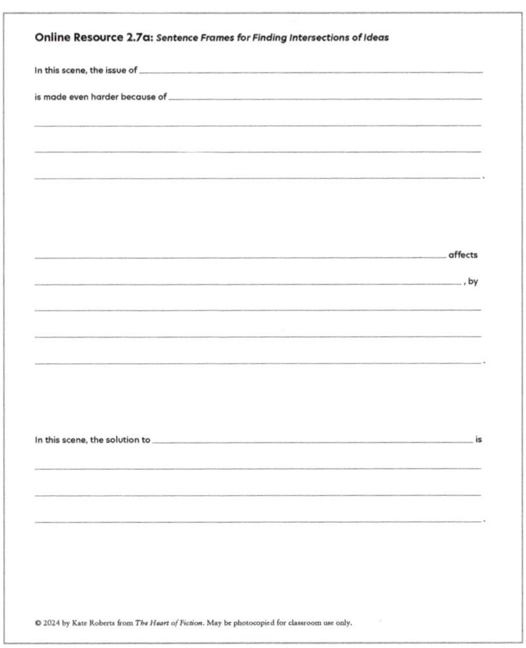

Online Resource 2.7a: *Sentence Frames for Finding Intersections of Ideas*

In this scene, the issue of ______

is made even harder because of ______

______ affects

______ , by

In this scene, the solution to ______ is

© 2024 by Kate Roberts from *The Heart of Fiction*. May be photocopied for classroom use only.

Sentence Frames for Finding Intersections of Ideas (OR 2.7a)

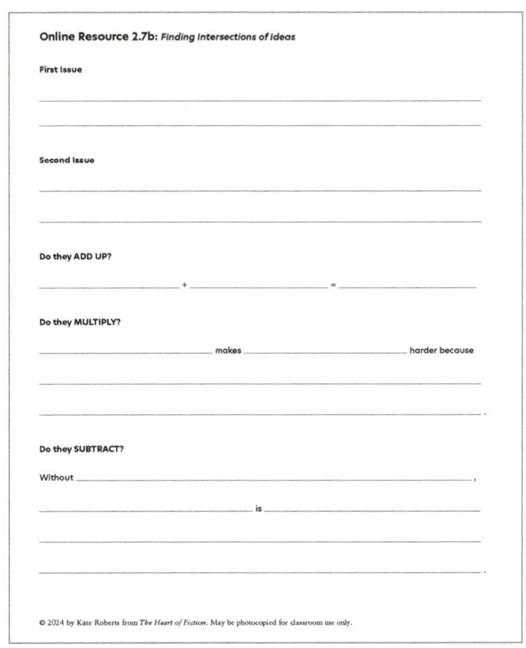

Online Resource 2.7b: *Finding Intersections of Ideas*

First Issue

Second Issue

Do they ADD UP?

______ + ______ = ______

Do they MULTIPLY?

______ makes ______ harder because

Do they SUBTRACT?

Without ______ ,

______ is ______

© 2024 by Kate Roberts from *The Heart of Fiction*. May be photocopied for classroom use only.

Finding Intersections of Ideas (OR 2.7b)

8. DIVE INTO COMPLEXITY

THINKING ABOUT THE STRATEGY

My eldest son once told me that he saw someone steal gloves from the left-behind pile and he didn't know what to do about it. I asked him what he thought his choices were, and he listed them: tell the teacher, ignore it, or talk to the kid. He said, "I don't know what the right thing is to do." We worked together to unpack it, because it wasn't clear what the right thing was. On the one hand, telling the teacher felt right because maybe she should know, but then this kid was a friend, and maybe he needed them. Should he be punished? Would there be a better way to handle it? "It's complicated," my six-year-old said.

It is complicated. And my six-year-old knows it. All kids do. They know early on that big issues are not easy to solve, that it is hard to figure out relationships with other people, and how to belong and be yourself, and how to do what's right while taking care of yourself.

I say this because sometimes, when we are teaching students how to analyze an issue (in texts, the world, our lives), they don't always show us how deeply they understand the complexities of life. Sometimes they *say* things like, "Friendship is important," or "Prejudice is bad," and it feels as though maybe they believe that the message is that simple, when we know there are layers and contradictions and complexities that feel out of reach.

We have to start with the idea that our kids do in fact often intuit how layered these issues are. They know that friendships are important but also really difficult. They know that sometimes you watch your friend do things you know are bad for them, but they won't stop and you don't know what to do. They know that sometimes friends turn on you, and your world is toppled. They know that friendship sometimes feels like a gift and other times a pain and that any human relationship has good parts and bad. And they know that not all friendships are the same.

What they don't know is how to put all of that into words that reflect the exact complicated ideas that seem to be developing in the book they are reading.

We can help them practice by exploring what makes a theme complex in the first place. A simple theme takes on a through line, like loss, and reflects back the main, universal thing that the text seems to repeat in different scenes. *Loss affects us in many ways.* A complex theme takes that through line and explores what the text might be saying about something that doesn't feel so easily answered, something not so obvious. Two ways to teach into this idea of complexity come to mind. One is to take our issue and look to see if there is a counterpoint developed in the text. In other words, if loss is our main issue, is there anything in this text about loss versus holding on?

Versus is the key here. Is there a *versus* to the issue we are tracking in the text? When I think about *Aristotle and Dante*, by the middle of the book I can absolutely see that Dante is the *versus* to Ari's pushing away. All of a sudden, the book is not just about how pushing people away makes you lonely; it's about finding the balance between pushing people away and *needing to be close*. I can start to explore which scenes strike which balance between these two counterpoints as I read.

Another way to think of theme complexity is to pause in the middle of the book and ask ourselves what questions this book is trying to answer about the issue we are tracking. In *The Namesake*, I am tracking the American dream/mirage. But what is this text asking about this issue? Perhaps it is how much of the American dream is a mirage? In what ways does the American dream affect what we accept as happiness? Or who gets the dream and who gets the mirage? I can now think about how the critical scenes answer these larger questions, collecting ideas as I go.

Regardless of how we teach students to think about complexity, intersections, and critical scenes, students are going to need to have a system for tracking their thinking from the middle to the end of the book. Have them figure out whether they will trap their analysis in a notebook, on a chart, or on sticky notes. This is the hard-work part of the unit, the place where we roll up our sleeves and start to get messy. Knowing how to contain the mess will help when we are ready to clean things up into a cohesive interpretation.

8. DIVE INTO COMPLEXITY

TEACHING THE STRATEGY

Lesson Flow

When we offer a concrete, practical way to scaffold sophisticated analysis, students are able to give complexity a go.

One way to teach this lesson:

1. Introduce the concept of complex ideas by telling a story about a time when you thought something was simple but then realized it was way more complicated than you thought.
2. Model a starting point: an idea you have about a text that is good but maybe doesn't capture the complexity of the text.
3. Tell students that there are two ways to make our ideas more complicated: by finding the counterpoint and by looking for questions the book is asking about the issue.
4. Demonstrate finding a counterpoint for the issue you began with. This means asking, "Is there a *versus* here?" Brainstorm some together as a class.
5. Demonstrate finding questions the text asks about the issues. Brainstorm some together as a class.
6. Ask students to take some of their thinking and to try both of these strategies to see what comes up. Have them freewrite thoughts from these beginning complex ideas.
7. Share a class list of beginning points for complexity.

What Might This Look Like?

DATE

themes in the book

Throughout the book, Jess must unravel and grapple with many events alone when she discovers she can't trust the majority of her friends and family as they have been lying to her her whole life. This speaks to themes of the resillience and strength of Jess as she is determined to make it out of her town no matter what. Jess learns to depend on herself and trust her gut. In the second half of the book, a new theme starts to develop - a commentary on technological advancements and parasocial relationships in society. A big reveal/plot twist is that the book is actually set in 2037 instead of the 90s, and America is Jess's TV audience who is invested in her life and know everything about her through their screens. We see how this discovery mentally affects Jess, sending her close to the edge of spiraling as she grapples with being famous against her consent. We see how her fans act, and can draw the conclusion that their obsession with a TV show star who was being manipulated is unhealthy, and that parasocial relationships are damaging for everyone involved. These relationships are fostered by the heavy advancements in technology in 2037, therefore implying that society must be careful in our dependence on technology going forwards.

Annika makes her theme thinking more complex by using the structure of the novel to build her ideas.

Dive into Complexity

The idea/issue I am going to use to make it more complex is Growing Up and Scout's new school teacher, as well as a new year of school entirely. Scout feels that the teacher is mean and is also not teaching the students well which I agree with. So there is growing up vs. being a kid. But in a way it is better to be a kid because growing up just means accepting bad teaching and racism. So maybe the book is saying that you should stay a kid and innocent for longer because growing up means accepting bad stuff. A counterpoint one could make is that the teacher has been taught and went to college for teaching. Some questions asked are What does it mean to grow up, and how is being innocent protecting you from life? It seems like the book is saying that growing up means accepting unfairness and racism and agreeing with the adults around you which I don't agree with.

The idea/issue I would like to make more complex is Aunt Alexandra's Underlying racism. It is made obvious throughout the story that Aunt Alexandra is racist, as many of the people in the town. One could argue that it is a product of the time and that she is still a good person. Some questions the text asks are is Aunt Alexandra a nice person, and how did she become this way. I think the reason she became racist is because of years and years of being convinced that African Americans were less than her. Systemic racism and white washing of history is probably what caused her to be extremely racist. I think that latter on in the book her view is changed as she becomes a better person by being surrounded by the family.

Miles finds ways to make his thinking about an issue more complex.

Providing Feedback

If your students say or demonstrate . . .	Coach them on . . .
I am having trouble coming up with something more complicated than the idea I started with.	Listing all of the topics brought up by this scene and then asking which of these topics are causing problems or bad feelings
I came up with something, but now I'm done.	Looking for the other side; for example, if their idea is negative, have them look for a positive counterpoint Using question stems like these: How should we deal with ________? Why do people ________? Is ________ worth the ________?
I have a bunch of ideas and questions, but I'm not sure what to do with them now.	Freewriting to see which ideas hold water Choosing which revised ideas to track from now to the end of the book

Optional Tools

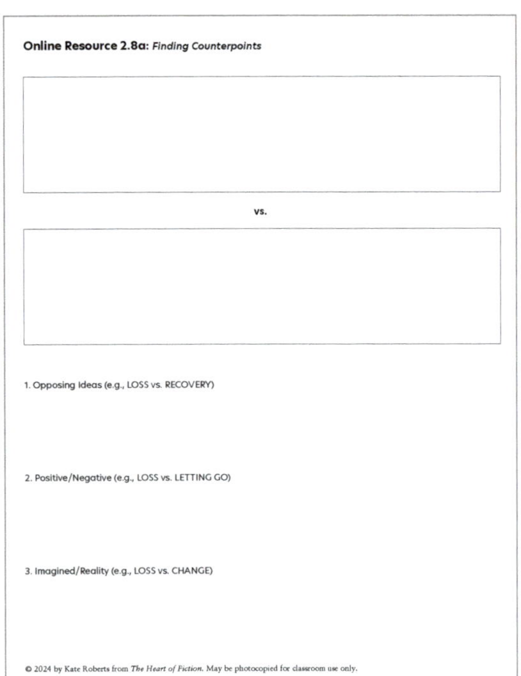

Online Resource 2.8a: *Finding Counterpoints*

vs.

1. Opposing Ideas (e.g., LOSS vs. RECOVERY)

2. Positive/Negative (e.g., LOSS vs. LETTING GO)

3. Imagined/Reality (e.g., LOSS vs. CHANGE)

Finding Counterpoints (OR 2.8a)

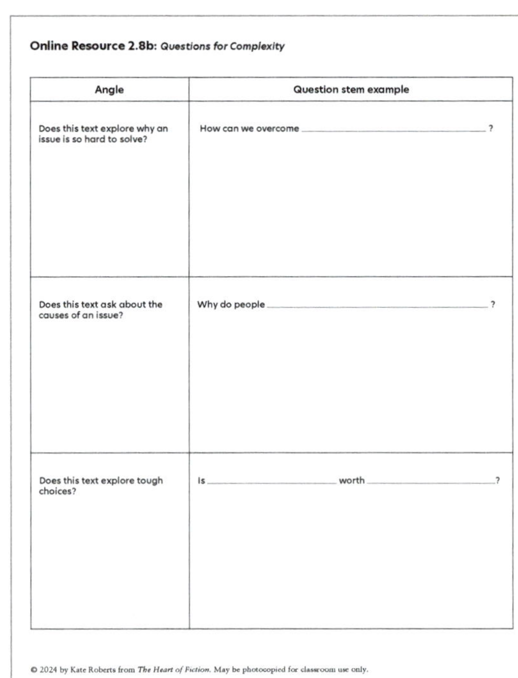

Online Resource 2.8b: *Questions for Complexity*

Angle	Question stem example
Does this text explore why an issue is so hard to solve?	How can we overcome ________?
Does this text ask about the causes of an issue?	Why do people ________?
Does this text explore tough choices?	Is ________ worth ________?

Questions for Complexity (OR 2.8b)

AT THE END OF THE BOOK

In this section, we'll discuss the following skills:

9. Organize Your Thoughts

Here we offer students a chance to look over their thinking across a book and start to notice patterns and categories of analysis.

10. Consider the Outcomes

Interpretation of a theme involves both outlining the path of an idea across a book and forming a reflection based on the ending. This lesson helps students use the results of a story line to see their analysis in a new light.

11. Rank, Rephrase, and Realize

Naming what the theme of a text is can be intimidating. Offer students a process to help them craft, problematize, and revise their thinking into something grand.

A few years ago my wife and I picked up the book *Red*, by Michael Hall (2015), to read to our boys. It's the story of a crayon that is blue but has a red wrapper. Finally another crayon sees who he really is and asks him to draw a blue ocean. Red finds his truth and it is a happy ending.

We loved it. It was so clearly an allegory about growing up LGBTQIA+. We had great discussions with our boys and found lots of text details to support our interpretation.

Except that we were "wrong." Hall (2015) writes on his website that this story captures how it felt to be a kid with dyslexia trying to fit in in a world that expected him to do things he could not. We aren't the only ones who have "misinterpreted" the text. One district at least has even gotten homophobic complaints from parents after a kindergarten teacher read the book aloud.

Of course, I put *wrong* and *misinterpreted* in quotes because neither is true. Interpretation is a strange thing once the book has ended and we are reflecting on the whole book. On the one hand, we want to make sure our thinking is grounded in the text, is comprehensive, and feels close to the author's intentions based on what we see between the covers. On the other hand, we want our interpretations to feel authentic and unique and ours—we want the freedom to relate to the text and to find relevant ideas in the novel even if it was written centuries ago.

This is a delicate balance and will take some work. The strategies that follow might help.

9. ORGANIZE YOUR THOUGHTS

THINKING ABOUT THE STRATEGY

Hopefully by the end of the book our students have a mess on their hands. Perhaps the mess is a book stuffed with sticky notes or a notebook with byzantine charts. The end of a novel should find us awash in ideas.

I hope for this chaos because we are finished. There will be no more scenes, no more information. We've got the goods, and now we are going to begin to make some conclusions about what this book is about. We are about to make some judgment calls—about what matters most, what the author intended, what themes are most worth reflecting on.

We do this in our lives too, if we are lucky, at the end. We age, we look across the years, and we find patterns. We try to make sense of it all. We look for meaning that can give us peace, and if we don't find it, we name the tragedies. We name it all so that we can say, before we go, "I was here, and this is what it meant."

The last time I visited my father before he died, we watched a movie in his one-bedroom apartment in Albuquerque. It was a good movie, right up my dad's alley. When it was done, he needed a cigarette, and we walked out to his patio. It offered a small peek of the immense desert sky. My dad dragged his tar-stained oxygen tank with him as he lit up his millionth cigarette.

He said he loved the movie, then his face contorted in grief. He looked at the sky, then at me. "I never thought I would go with such a whimper," he said.

But you know what? He should have. He should have known. Because the pattern of his life since he was thirty-five was leading to this moment. I knew it. But my father, my beloved father, was looking only at the beginning of his life for clues to meaning. When he was young, adventurous, rebellious, full of promise. In his interpretation of his life, he ignored the last thirty years. The ones where he sat alone, drinking and smoking the days away, resentful that the world wasn't offering him more.

In that moment on his patio, I was frustrated. I wanted to yell at him: "But it was all leading here. Why haven't you been paying attention?" I wanted him to have insight that could help me move on from the grief that was waiting for me, instead of this willfully narrow take on his life.

I know that's a lot for a lesson on organizing your notes. But when we are at the end—of our books, our relationships, our lives—we should look at the whole, if we want to be wise. We should look back. In the case of our reading work, we can teach students to make piles or color-code annotations that go together and then name why they go together. (See my examples in Figures 2.8–2.10.) Students will need time to make these categories. They can work in groups, and they should be sure to also look for the exceptions, the parts that don't fit into one category or another. This work is essential for students to get a bird's-eye view of the span of their thinking around the themes in a text. If we want interpretations that feel like they hug the entirety of the novel, that are unique, that hold complexity, then we have to offer students practice in being able to find the patterns of thought that are there.

And while I don't have illusions that this work will necessarily transfer to our ability to do the same with our lives, it can't hurt. Just knowing that I can look for the categories and patterns in my life helps me see the direction I'm going in. It's mostly good, thankfully. But I see the trouble too. I see the places that hold seeds for regret. There are patterns. I don't want to get stuck at the end feeling surprised when the signs were there all along.

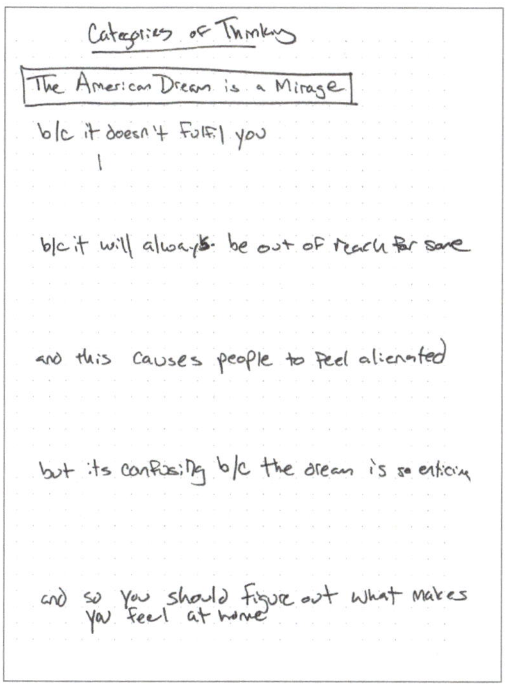

FIGURE 2.8: *Example of organizing notes in a notebook*

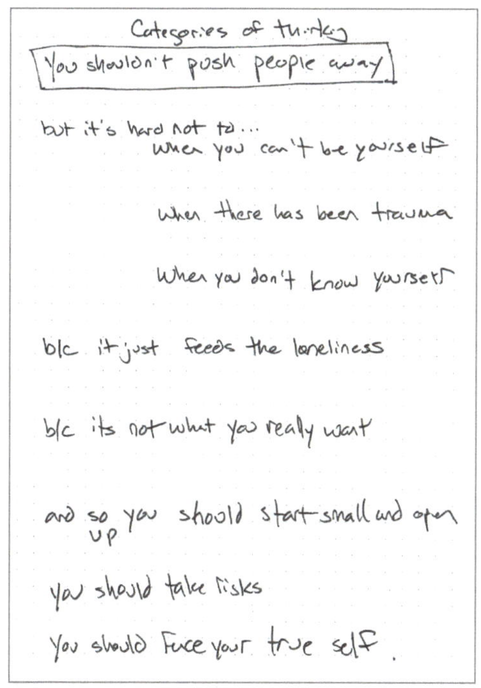

FIGURE 2.9: *Another example of organizing notes in a notebook*

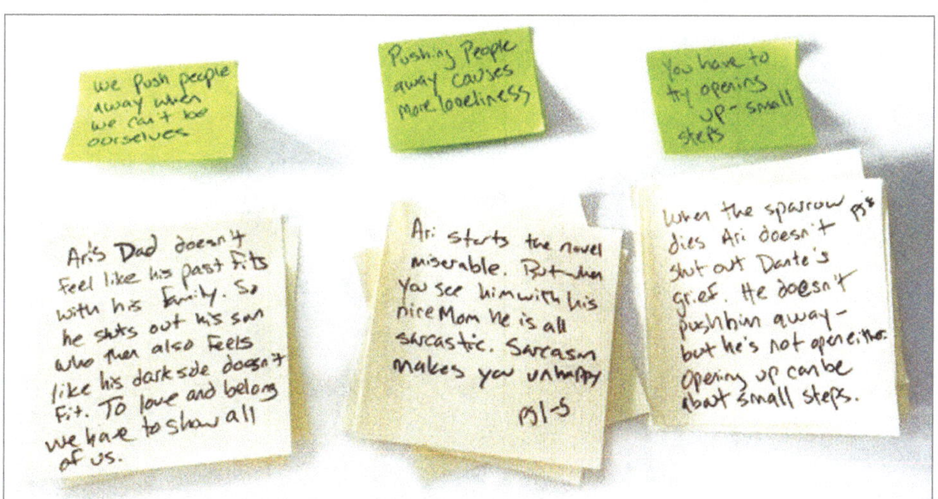

FIGURE 2.10: *Example of organizing notes by grouping sticky notes*

9. ORGANIZE YOUR THOUGHTS

TEACHING THE STRATEGY

Lesson Flow

Here we offer students a chance to look over their thinking across a book and start to notice patterns and categories of analysis.

One way to teach this lesson:

1. Introduce the lesson with a story that needed to be seen from the end to be understood. Point out that when we interpret something, we try to find an idea that captures the whole story, or as much of the story as we can.
2. Tell students that they will be looking over their notes to find categories and patterns. The goal is to have at least three big ideas by the end of class.
3. Demonstrate one way of organizing their notes. Some options include
    - Color-coding notes by category or idea
    - Grouping notes together in stacks
    - Creating a chart that collects ideas, scenes, and subordinate ideas
4. Give students time to work. Students should spend some time working independently, but they can work together if they are reading the same book.
5. Work with students in groups to repeatedly model ways to group notes.
6. Celebrate students' ongoing progress with a museum display: students leave their work on their desks and walk around the room to check out each other's work.
7. Offer enough class time for them to continue this work until they are done.

What Might This Look Like?

DATE

THEME

possible themes for... (what does she learn?) (IDEAS)

herself

- determination consistent throughout the book
- Confidence in herself/what she wants grows start → end
- develops her moral compass for what is right and wrong throughout the book
- ~~[illegible]~~ resilience to get through life
- what is her free will & what choices have been made for her?

relationships with others

- learns to be careful who she trusts, as many will take advantage b/c they want what's best for themselves
- the secret she discovers about the people around her makes her grow up + change her proirities quickly

society

- technological advancement can be detrimental if taken too far and left uncontrolled
  - can be used to hurt people in a way that normal people will be complicit in and even egg on
- para social relationships are unhealthy for everyone involved, and they can be a dangerous result of technological advancement

3 themes:

- courage and perseverance
- coming of age
- technology can be used for evil

Annika pulls ideas from her notes and groups them under categories of issues that run through the text.

As the book begins:

1. Consider character and conflict: Chapter one: Jem Finch: loss Jean Finch: too early to tell Atticus Finch: to early to tell Dill: Family most issues are not put in this chapter
   Chapter two: Jean Finch: has a really bad school teacher School Jem Finch: Not important in this chapter Walter Cunnigham: Has to deal with his poor family and
   Chapter Three: Jean Finch: her family is being a little annoying and she still doesn't like school Jem finch: His annoying sister
   Chapter 5: Jean is dealing with here friends leaving her behind, Jem is dealing with issues with his father, and dill has nothing wrong
   Chapter 6: Jem is dealing with adolescent problems and dill is leaving, I would also like to point out how time is moving very quickly in this book
   Chapter 7: The infamous duo are dealing with school and figuring out who is giving them gifts
   Chapter 8: The duo are dealing with there secrets their first snow, and a fire at a friends house
   Chapter 9: Atticus is dealing with his family and a new court trail while Jean is dealing with school issues and an annoying cousin
   Chapter ten: We learn about Atticus's secret past and we see a dog die

Miles color-codes his notes.

Providing Feedback

If your students say or demonstrate . . .	Coach them on . . .
I can pick out notes that feel important, but I am not sure how they connect together.	Looking for one-word categories—for instance, if the big issue I am tracking is "American dream," then maybe a bunch of my notes have to do with "dreams" while another set has to do with "unsatisfying"
I can connect notes into one-word categories, but my groups feel too simple or general.	Being precise with their word choice—for example, if their original category is "difficult," help them work to describe what kind of difficulty their notes capture, like "how hard it is to fit into someone else's dream"
I can find interesting patterns of ideas, but they feel repetitive.	Looking at notes from different angles, like causes of the issue, effects, solutions, and lessons

Optional Tools

Online Resource 2.9: *Organizing My Notes*

Issue/Idea	Scene	Scene	Scene

Organizing My Notes (OR 2.9)

10. CONSIDER THE OUTCOMES

THINKING ABOUT THE STRATEGY

While it is true that we can make meaning as we read, and as we live, it is also true that the ending of things defines the final meaning we make. Our eldest son was in kindergarten when the pandemic hit. He spent half of his first real year of school learning remotely. We made lots of meaning along the way, to be sure. There were moments of triumph and gratitude and perseverance. There were moments of frustration, boredom, even despair. But we weren't really sure what the year meant until it was done. There was an online celebration. His wonderful teacher made a video montage of photos from across the year. All the kids showed up. My son brought his fox stuffy, as usual. As the video played, the kids in the photos were together, doing inquiry, playing, sitting on the rug, and then . . . all of the photos were of computer screens. And yet still so much learning, laughter, fortitude. So much community. All the grown-ups were in tears. All of the kids looked proud (or more interested in dancing to the music).

If you had asked me at any given day what the meaning of that year was going to be, I would probably have focused on how that week was going. Or I would have admitted that I just didn't know. But the ending showed me, at least a little: it was a year of us doing our absolute best. And that was enough. It was also not enough. It was beautiful. It was sad. When we are interpreting the themes in a book, the ending will have a lot to tell us. In particular, the outcomes will. What happens to the characters? What happens to the characters the author loves? What about the ones they hate? How does the story resolve? What's the tone at the end? Does the author seem to like this ending or think it's sad?

Once we have answered these questions, we can bring that to our thinking about the issues in the text. For example, as I consider *Aristotle and Dante*, it strikes me that Ari has opened up, including around his feelings for Dante, and Dante has gotten, essentially, what he wanted: closeness. So, Ari changed and Dante stayed the same, and it is definitely seen as a good thing in the book—the tone is sweet and romantic. As I consider the issues of pushing people away, as I begin to really consider what this novel has to teach me, I feel certain that at its root Sáenz wants us to heal enough to let others in.

In *The Namesake*, it's trickier. There is a feeling of dissatisfaction at the end of the novel that surprised me. (Spoilers ahead) Gogol, who wanted to find the American dream, is divorced and grieving his father and closer to his family than ever, but he's kind of adrift. Ashima is going back to Calcutta. The novel kind of peters out. It's like the dream just wilts.

Ah. See that? I have been tracking the ideas that underpin the issue of the American dream for the novel. I have lots of ideas. But now at the end I can see how they fit together a bit more clearly. The dream wilts at the end. All of that effort, the striving by all of the characters, and for what? For something, to be sure, and there is more work to do, but I am onto something now. By using the outcome of the novel to view my thinking about the text with a final lens, I can start the work of creating a cohesive idea about a theme of the text.

We can teach our students to unpack the ending of the novel in some predictable ways and then use that analysis to help them reflect on their thinking across the book.

10. CONSIDER THE OUTCOMES

TEACHING THE STRATEGY

Lesson Flow

Interpretation of a theme involves both outlining the path of an idea across a book and forming a reflection based on the ending. This lesson helps students use the results of a story line to see their analysis in a new light.

One way to teach this lesson:

1. Introduce the lesson by telling a story where things turned out alright and then telling the same story with a different ending where things turned out badly. Point out how the outcome changes the message of the story. In texts, how things end often gives us a glimpse into what the author wants us to see.
2. Model thinking through the ending of a text the class knows. Explore what this ending might be saying about the author's point of view on the issues of the text.
3. Highlight that the author's opinion about what happens also matters. The author might reveal their point of view by presenting some things as tragic or dark and others as victories.
4. Give students time to do this same work on their text. Have them list out what happens and then write or talk about what this might reveal about the author's point of view while you confer or pull small groups.
5. Gather as a class and consider how the author's point of view might shift how we see the development of the theme. (See "Optional Tools" for specific development frames.)

What Might This Look Like?

DATE

outcomes of the story

the problems ⟶ what happened? [+ author's POV]

1. Jess is hearing things other people aren't ⟶ Jess was correct, and people have been lying to her. The author is communicating the importance of trusting your gut.
2. Sara is sick and dies ⟶ She doesn't really die, and was just getting written off the TV show. By including this, the author shows the readers how cruel the people running the show are to make Jess think her sister died.
3. Nobody is allowing Jess to leave the town/TV set ⟶ she becomes determined to escape (and does so). This reveals the main plot point of the book, and begins to introduce some of the more complex themes of the book.
4. Kipps gets shot in the shoulder ⟶ Jess comes up with a plan to save him, and even thinks about sacrificing herself. The author wants readers to see that Jess's situation is not all bad – she found someone she really cares about who is on her side. This scene shows how selfless Jess is as well. The author wants to give Jess a happy ending with Kipps.

Annika maps out the outcomes for various characters.

At the end of the book:

1. Organize your notes: This section just color codes areas that relate to one another in the theme so the final product will have the organized note. Just to tell you Blue means it's related to racism, Red means it's related to family, and Green means growing up.

2. Consider the outcomes: The book *To Kill a Mockingbird* ends very abruptly. Mr. Ewell is "Murdered", Tom Robinson is killed and we get to see Boo Radley one time. While Abrupt I feel the ending makes a lot of sense, the story really was about how Jem Finch broke his wrist, in some roundabout way. I think it's interesting how the author does this using one relatively small thing, to teach us about racism and what's right. Another reason I love this conclusion is because of Boo Radley. I knew that Boo had to show up once in the book and I was proven correct. I think it was handled perfectly with him being the one to help Jem at the end of the book. I barely mention Scout but she did some cool stuff too and was the one to tell everyone what happened. She also got to talk to Boo in the end. The problems that were presented earlier in the book are also resolved fine too, if not a little sad with some of them. In the end, I feel like Aunt Alexandrea became a lot less racist at the end of the story which also connects to the theme of taking baby steps to get to the solution. The Resolution to the trail was extremely sad and what happened to Tom was also extremely sad. I think what these outcomes tell me about the author's view on things is that people, even if they start out bad, can change, and that while a random act of kindness can help people, they still might end up hurt in the end. The problems, even though I didn't like the way they all were resolved, still were finished well and well. I think I really like to kill a mockingbird and I hope to read it again.

Miles works to find the connections between what happens at the end of the book and the themes the author might be hoping to develop.

Providing Feedback

If your students say or demonstrate . . .	Coach them on . . .
I can name what happens at the end of the book, but I am having trouble seeing how that shows the author's point of view	Asking whether the author is happy or sad about the outcomes for the main character and if the author seems to like the main character or not
I have a sense of what the author feels about the ending of the book, but I'm not sure what this means about their point of view on the issue I am tracking.	Considering what the author thinks should happen around the issue they are tracking—for example, they can ask, "What does the author wish were true about the world?"
I have a sense of the author's point of view, but it feels simple or too general to be useful.	Making ideas more complex or nuanced by playing with word choice and being precise with every word Adding on thinking by adding qualifiers to their thinking, like why, when, for whom, and how

Optional Tools

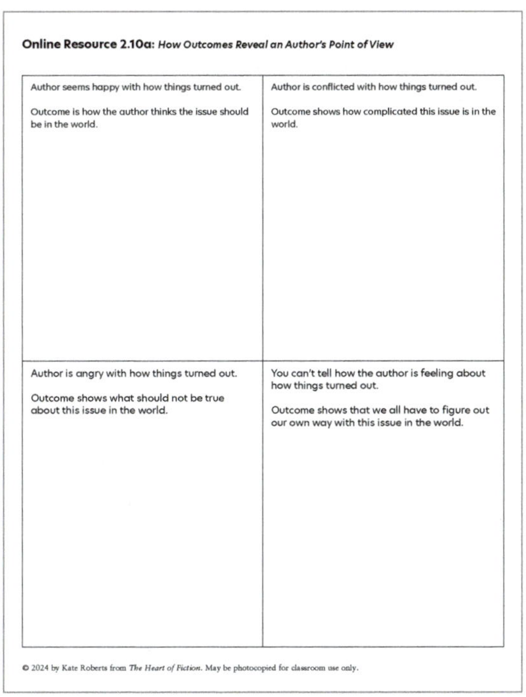

Online Resource 2.10a: *How Outcomes Reveal an Author's Point of View*

Author seems happy with how things turned out. Outcome is how the author thinks the issue should be in the world.	Author is conflicted with how things turned out. Outcome shows how complicated this issue is in the world.
Author is angry with how things turned out. Outcome shows what should not be true about this issue in the world.	You can't tell how the author is feeling about how things turned out. Outcome shows that we all have to figure out our own way with this issue in the world.

How Outcomes Reveal an Author's Point of View (OR 2.10a)

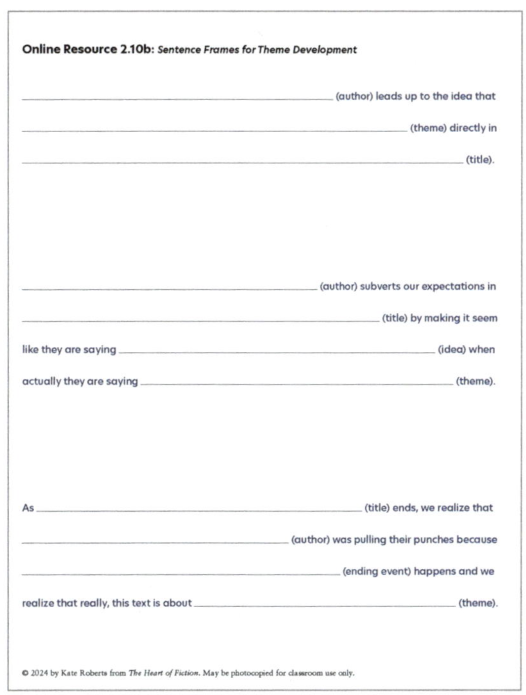

Online Resource 2.10b: *Sentence Frames for Theme Development*

__________ (author) leads up to the idea that __________ (theme) directly in __________ (title).

__________ (author) subverts our expectations in __________ (title) by making it seem like they are saying __________ (idea) when actually they are saying __________ (theme).

As __________ (title) ends, we realize that __________ (author) was pulling their punches because __________ (ending event) happens and we realize that really, this text is about __________ (theme).

Sentence Frames for Theme Development (OR 2.10b)

11. RANK, REPHRASE, AND REALIZE

THINKING ABOUT THE STRATEGY

When I turned forty-four, I had a really good year. For maybe the first time in my life, I faced no real problems. Irritations, sure. The grind of life, yes. But nothing was really wrong. On my birthday, as I reflected at the end of the year, a host of thoughts came up. *It's going to change. Enjoy it. It's going to get taken away. You need to keep giving back. You took advantage of what you had* . . . among others.

That night, I tried to put these thoughts together into some kind of theme for the year, what I thought it all meant. Some of these ideas rose to the top. They felt more important. For example, I felt a kind of pride in the hard work, healing, and openness of my journey, but I felt equally humbled by the luck, love, and privilege that eased the way and opened doors. Meanwhile the fear that everything would be taken away was there, like neurotic background noise. Underneath it all, *Enjoy it; it will change* beat like a drum.

The next day these thoughts kept tumbling around and I started to try to put it all into words as I bought groceries and did my day. To do this, I had to allow myself to have rough-draft ideas, and then I had to work to critique them. I began with *Sometimes things are good. They will change someday, so I should enjoy it while it lasts and give back.*

But this felt clunky and didn't capture the gratitude and responsibility I felt to my communities. So I reworked it all in my head a bit. *If you experience truly good times, enjoy it while it lasts, because nothing does forever. You need to always know your responsibility to the world.*

Better. But could I fit them together, into a synthesized theme for that point of my life? *One way to enjoy life when it is good is to be sure to remember your responsibilities to others and the world.*

But did I agree with this? Rereading it, it feels so . . . punishing. Like, the only way to enjoy life is to be hard on yourself? That's not what I really believed.

And so there was this realization: *Enjoyment maybe isn't the goal. Or maybe it's about enjoying all of it—the tough stuff, the responsibilities, the easy times.*

If there was a theme for my birthday when I was forty-four, it would be this maybe: *Enjoyment isn't about ease; it's about connection and presence, although ease is really nice too sometimes.*

I do the same kind of work when I try to synthesize my thoughts about an issue in a book into a theme. First, I rank my ideas—which seems most important? Then, I begin to craft and revise a synthesis of these ideas into a working theme. Through it all, I am looking for realizations—sparks that help me see how it all fits together.

Figures 2.11 and 2.12 are my examples of this work from *Aristotle and Dante* and *The Namesake*. As we help students do this work, we should remember that this kind of analysis, critique, and synthesis is quite difficult, and that approximations should be celebrated. It is not about, at this point, whether or not students craft perfectly stated themes, but that they have a chance to practice the reworking and rewording that comes with writing anything well.

I can't teach students to have a realization; that is not something you can force. But often, in my experiences, fostering the conditions we have so far in this chapter allows for spontaneous epiphanies from us more often.

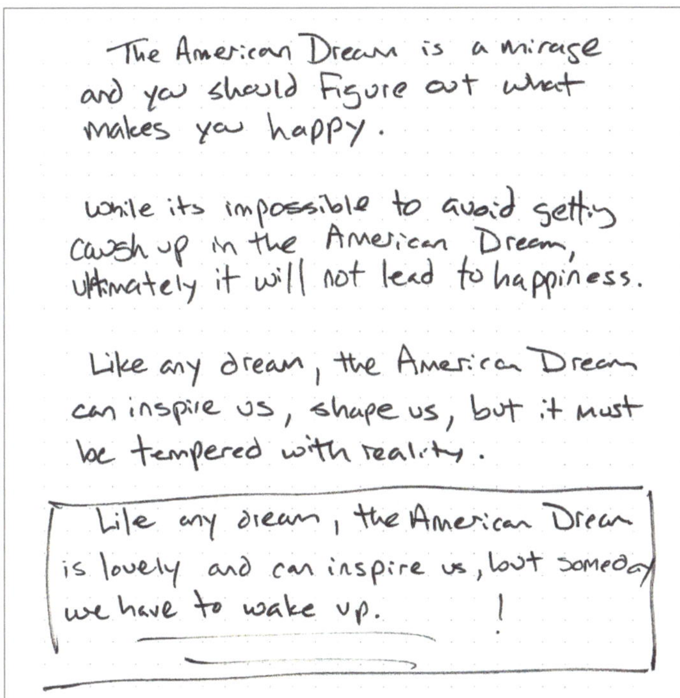

FIGURE 2.11: *Revising the final theme for* The Namesake

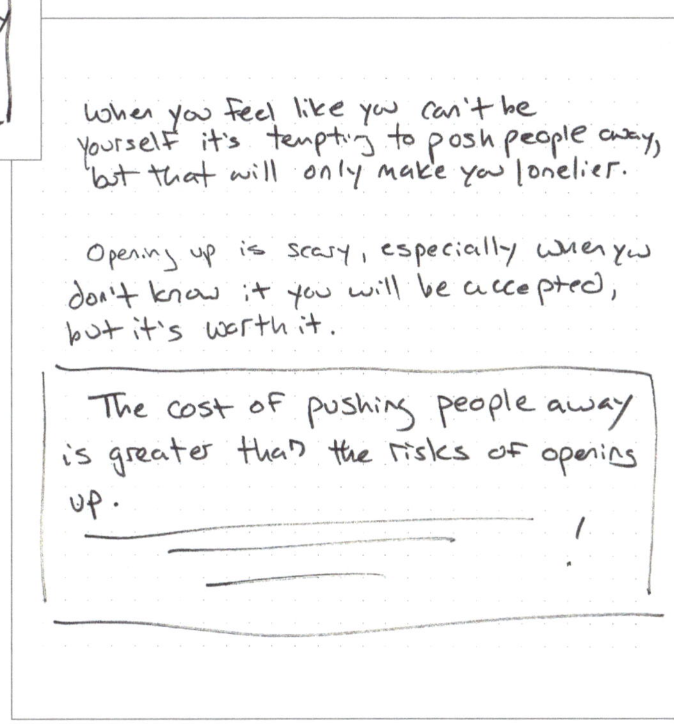

FIGURE 2.12: *Revising the final theme for* Aristotle and Dante

11. RANK, REPHRASE, AND REALIZE

TEACHING THE STRATEGY

Lesson Flow

Naming what the theme of a text is can be intimidating. Offer students a process to help them craft, problematize, and revise their thinking into something grand.

One way to teach this lesson:

1. Congratulate students on how much thinking they now have about theme. Explain that now we have to make sense of all this thinking.
2. Model how you take the categories and groups of thinking from the previous lesson and rank them in order of importance.
3. Give students time to do the same for their thinking across the text.
4. Model how you start to join these ideas together for a rough draft of a clunky theme. Be sure not to model too good of an idea at first. Give kids time to try this.
5. Model how you make your clunky rough-draft idea better by making sure it highlights what is highly ranked. Then show them how you keep revising your idea until it is comprehensive, true, and well put.
6. Ask students to try this work, first independently.
7. Have partners work together to revise their themes, asking each other: "Does this capture the most important ideas? Does this feel true to you? Is this the best way to phrase your thinking?"
8. Collect final themes as a class, display them, and celebrate.

What Might This Look Like?

DATE

ranking theme categories

1. coming of age - switch in priorities / scale of issues throughout the book
2. perseverance and resilience – the reason she was able to make it out of the set/her town
3. self confidence / trusting one's gut
4. technology can be bad if taken too far (parasocial relationships)
5. free will vs choices made for you
6. morality
7. being careful who you trust

theme rough draft

The theme of the book centers on coming of age due to a shocking/hard to grapple with event, and persevering through it to become a better + happier person. The event and status of the main character's life was caused by an advancement in technology leading to something morally wrong becoming approved of by society.

final theme

The theme of *This is Not The Jess Show* is perseverance, shown through a Coming-of-Age story where the main character struggles against a restrictive, technology based society that wants to hurt her.

Annika prioritizes, synthesizes, and revises her theme work.

Rank, Revise, Realize:
Themes ranked:

1. Racism
2. Family
3. Growing up
4. Protection

In this book an idea I think the book is teaching us is the idea of growing as a person and growing as a family, with protection connecting to all of it. When I first read this story I did not think it would be as heartfelt and thoughtful as it was. I also didn't know how all the themes in this book connected but I think I have a grasp on that know. To Kill A Mocking Bird is telling you the tale of what it is like to grow as a person as well as a family, with protection tying it all together. One might say, Miles, but how can you say such a thing, that doesn't make any sense. But I'll tell you my boy/girl, It is quite possible. To grow as a person, one might need protection from a bad element of life, such as shielding your children from racisim. Another way one might grow as a person is exposure to a different life style. A good example of this is Aunt Alexandrea, who while at the start of the book seemed like an old mean lady, by the end of the book, because of exposure to the Finches, she became a less mean old lady. Okay Miles you convinced me thar protection is important to growing as a person, but what about growing as a family, that has to be impossible. Wrong again, I would say. Protection is extremely important for a familys growth. Without the shielding the father/mother figure provides there would be pandemonium. Of course thats in the real life, what about in the book. Well, in the book without Atticus's attempt to do away with racsim in his familys life, he was able to grow to very nice and impressionable kids. So thats how the theme of protection relates to growing as a person and growing as a family.

Miles' first attempt at putting together his ideas about the text's theme.

Providing Feedback

If your students say or demonstrate . . .	Coach them on . . .
I can rank my ideas, but I am having trouble synthesizing them.	Looking for relationships between the ideas they have ranked: Does one cause the other? Does one idea make the other one more or less intense? Is one idea a solution or consequence of the other?
I can synthesize my ideas into a rough draft, but it feels like a list of ideas instead of a synthesized theme.	Trying some sentence frames to practice the syntax of synthesis: When ________ [is true], ________ [is also true], because ________ . (Example: When the American dream causes people to feel alienated, it does not fulfill you, because it is the connections to others that really help us live fully.) If ________ , then ________ . ________ makes [harder, easier, etc.]. (Example: If the American Dream doesn't work for everyone, then people feel alienated, and makes the dream a tool of inequality.)
I can synthesize my ideas, but my theme sounds clunky.	Revising down the page: taking a fresh page and putting the theme up top, rephrasing it a bunch of different ways all down the page, then circling the one that sounds the best and truest and most comprehensive

Optional Tools

Online Resource 2.11a: *Syntax of Synthesis*

When ________
________ ,
________ because
____
________ .

If ________
________ ,
then ________
________ .

________ makes
________ (hardier/easier).

Syntax of Synthesis (OR 2.11a)

Online Resource 2.11b: *Ranking and Revising Our Themes*

Order of Importance:
1.
2.
3.
4.
5.

Revising Themes

First try

Second try

Third try

Fourth try

Fifth try

Ranking and Revising Our Themes (OR 2.11b)

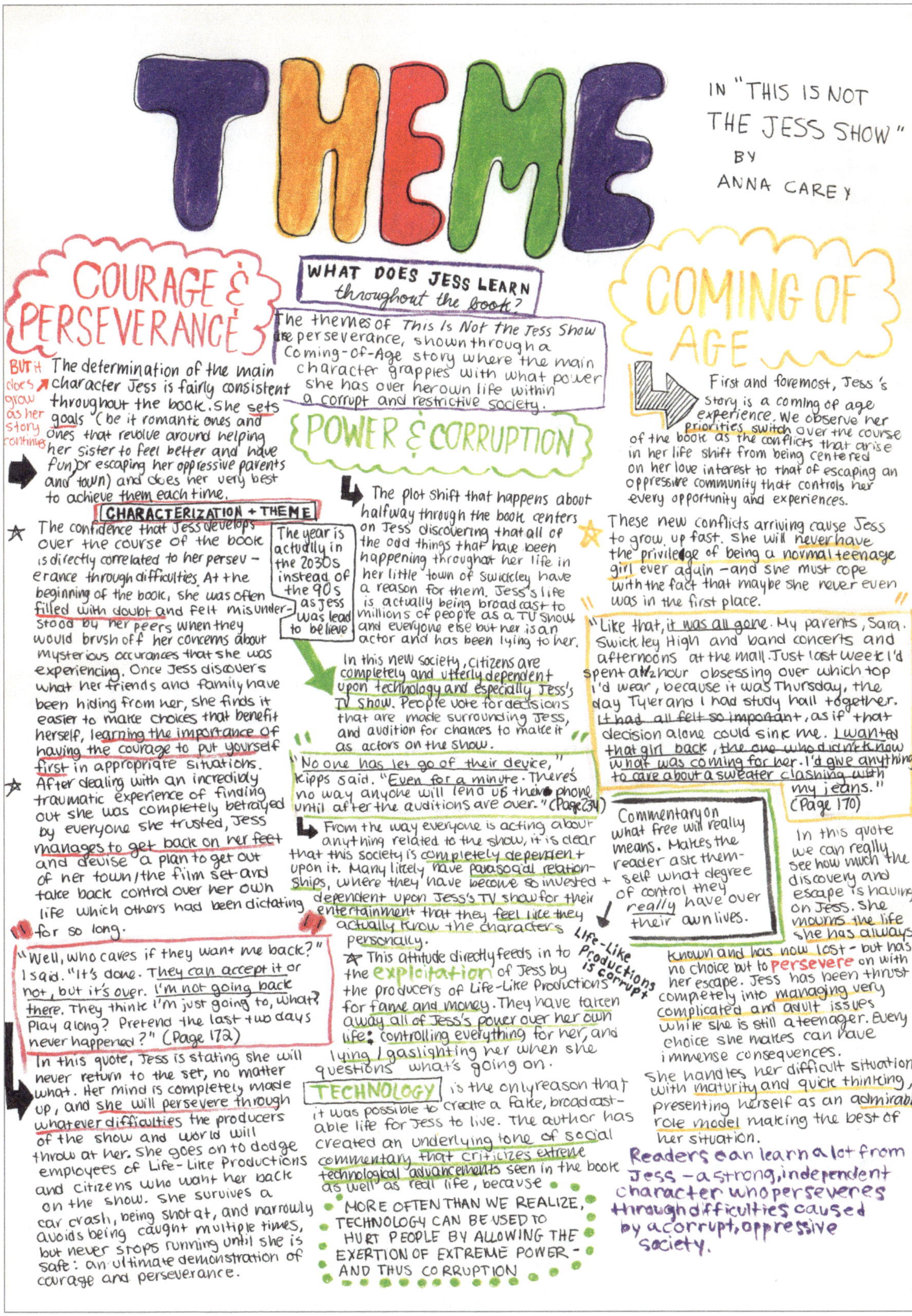

FIGURE 2.13: *Annika works to capture her thinking about the theme in the book she read.*

What to Do When the Unit Is Done

Let's consider where your students are at the end of this unit. As opposed to the character unit in the previous chapter, at the end of this sequence of lessons, your students should have something pretty cohesive. They should have a theme that has been reworked and revised. They also should have a few supporting ideas for that theme (the categories from Lesson 10, "Organize Your Thoughts"). They have marked critical scenes along the way that serve as evidence for these ideas as well. In short, the theme work here gets students prepared to discuss the themes in the book as well as that elusive skill that pops up in standards and assessments—the development of the theme in the text.

There is still some mess to clean up. Hopefully, as noted in the introduction, students have had repeated chances to try these strategies out. Hopefully, they have had a chance to try these strategies on more than one book. Hopefully, this work has been peppered with many opportunities for talk and writing and community building. Now we can consider what work might reflect all of the reading and thinking they have done.

Write an Essay—A Better One

To be honest, theme essays have been the bane of my teaching existence. I have struggled to teach students how to write about theme without their whole essay becoming a slightly angled retelling of the book. "A theme in the book is ____. For example, in the beginning you can see ____." Students vary in their syntax and vocabulary and their ability to stretch out an idea, but many times their essays feel like they do not reflect the thinking we have done together across the text.

Now, however, we have charted a different course. As students read, they stopped and analyzed scenes, and they collected subordinate and supporting ideas toward a greater theme in the text. Then, they organized them so they'd have a sense of which ideas supported the theme they have embraced. This means that kids can write essays that have more analysis than retelling, more substance than summary. They can consider a discussion of the development of the theme through a sequence of ideas (in the beginning, they look at the causes of the issue; in the middle, the effects; and at the end, they learn the lessons). Or they can look for a logical structure to their thinking in the book ("Because of [idea one], there is [idea two], which leads to [idea three]."). Either way, students have more to discuss and less to rehash.

Synthesize Your Notes

Perhaps, though, we don't want this to be the time of the year when students write an essay in response to their reading. At the same time, we don't want to lose all the good thinking we have done to the ether of time. Students could create a one-page synopsis of their thinking about the theme in the text, where they display the theme, the supportive thinking that props that interpretation up, and powerful quotes that exemplify this thinking (see Figure 2.13 on page 143). Advancing Literacy (formerly The Teachers College Reading and Writing Project), calls these visual essays, and they allow students to offer up all of the analysis that goes into an essay without needing to always write all of the connective tissue. It's a good way to move on without ignoring the great work kids did, and it's a great way to put a punctuation mark on the unit.

Make a Thing

As in the character work from the previous chapter, another option at the end of a book is to make something. What that might be is up to you, your students, and your collective imagination. Often people choose for this spot to be a place of creativity, multimodal expression, and choice. Some projects that suit theme work well include multigenre projects, podcasts, poetry, and short stories. (For more on ways to think creatively and progressively about ways students can write, check out M. Colleen Cruz's *Independent Writing* [2004] and Shawna Coppola's *Writing Redefined* [2019].) The defining characteristic of these projects is that they center around the theme and involve the other stuff—the supportive ideas and the critical scenes. Another defining characteristic? The attempt at some fun.

A note about projects: From the start you will want to consider how much teaching you want to put into the actual project itself. How much class time will be devoted to the projects? This is important because sometimes I get hung up on the quality of the genre or modality of the project but haven't taught enough of the conventions for the thing they are making to help kids make better stuff. If I don't teach deeply how to make a great podcast, I can't get upset about not having great podcasts. On the other hand, I could let go of the technical quality of the projects and instead lean into the choice, fun, and independence that are possible when we say, "Hey, here is a list of stuff you could make to show your thinking about the themes in a book. Choose one and try it out!"

Any of us who made a mixtape in middle school or a photo collage in high school or has gone to one of those painting parties knows the fun and learning that happen when you don't worry so much about how good you are but just jump in and try a thing. We can give that to our students and create a layer to our reading work that is full of joy.

At the End of the Day

My first year teaching, when my students would leave at the end of the day, I would slump to the floor against the lockers where no one could see me and cry. Almost every day I did this. There were two ideas that felt so true to me, crashing into each other on the seas of my heart.

> I love these kids.
> I don't know how to teach.

I have worked with thousands of teachers over the years, and I have realized that we all have a few of these controlling ideas in our first few years of teaching, don't we? They shape us. They shape what kind of teachers we will become, even though we enter the profession with our own personalities and traits and default settings. I am so grateful that these were the ideas that came to the surface during my first of year, because there were others that would have been more damaging to myself and students. I could have followed the lead of *These kids can't* ______ or *This doesn't work* . . . or even the seductive *When I was a student* . . . .

The ideas we pay attention to sculpt us into different versions of ourselves. They become the themes of our lives. If I am honest, after I teach now I still feel those two ideas beating within. *I love these kids. I don't know how to teach yet.* They keep me going.

Themes are not things that just arrive to us at the end of a book or our lives. They are things we develop and follow and choose to see. They are controlling beliefs that get contradicted. They are built of experience and faith and epiphanies and monotony. Themes—in books and in life—are the answers to the eternal question: What is the point? And they are available to us, all of us, if we take things one step at a time.

CHAPTER THREE

How to Teach Craft Analysis

What It Means to Analyze Craft

I'm not going to lie: a good percentage of my relationships are run over text message. While this might be an exaggeration, distance, the busy life we all lead, and my introverted nature make texting an easy way to stay in touch and get to some of the best parts of connecting with others. There are the text threads where we go over the problems we are facing. There are the planning texts. And there are the long, rambling, wonderful jokes. Thank goodness for the joke threads. Nothing makes me feel less alone than a well-chosen GIF or the perfect meme.

It's interesting, isn't it, that at this time in human history, so much of our interconnectedness is in written words? We communicate through typed sentences now, much more than in phone calls, and more than in person.

This means that *the way* we write is often just as important as what we write. Our craft communicates multitudes.

How many of us have received a "K" in response to a question and knew immediately that something was wrong? How many of us have laughed hysterically because of a well-worded phrase? How many of us have felt the gut punch of pain because of a simple sentence laid out plainly—"I don't know" or "We have to talk"?

It may seem corny to say craft is all around us, but, well, craft is all around us. Teaching students to be able to name it, feel its effects, and then try to name those too, only helps them enjoy their world more. *Craft*, *voice*, *literary technique*—all of these terms strive to capture the thing that makes a text more than simply a story told, ideas communicated. These terms try to capture the stuff in a text that makes us *feel*.

When we teach students to notice, appreciate, and consider the ways in which creators create, we teach them the secrets, inside jokes, winks and nods of artists. At the same time, a study of craft offers students an articulated glimpse into something much harder to define. Discussing physics, scientist Michio Kaku said, "The universe is a symphony of vibrating strings" (2011). As human beings, we get ever closer to understanding and quantifying that music. When we can quantify it, we will also, it stands to reason, be able to control it. Isn't it the same for writing, for any art? There is always something a bit out of reach in the works that speak to us. I can analyze the craft, but there is a "symphony of strings" that sings a particular human song.

Analyzing craft, we hope, can help us attune our ears to the songs of humanity in the writing we read. While we will get better and better at quantifying the techniques we see, the ultimate goal is not those things we can define; it is the sense of the song that is just out of reach.

How Craft Analysis Works

Craft is at once precise and elusive. Sure, we can name the techniques we see. We can point at a line and exclaim: "Imagery!" We can even pinpoint why the technique is there. We can say "The imagery in 'But there was no stopping water breaking from a breaking womb and there was no stopping now' (Morrison 2007, 61) juxtaposes the unstoppable transformation of birth and abuse from the point of view of the birthed and abused." We can notice and name the repetition of stopping, breaking, stopping, breaking. But we can't teach students to feel the heartbreak and tragedy that the line evokes when you come to it in *Beloved*.

We can't teach this because it's personal. More than anything else, I think, the ways in which readers respond emotionally to one book rather than another are based in the voice of the author. The craft, rhythm, voice, and technique. All the stuff that makes lines sing or be silent in my own very personal little heart.

It's like music, isn't it? For years I was obsessed with a single pause in Etta James' "At Last." Near the end of the song she pauses midline, and for whatever reason that pause felt to me like it held everything about being in love. I loved that pause. Yet I can tell you that the numerous people I have tried to convert to my weird religion of the pause in "At Last" did not hear it the way I did. They liked it maybe. Many placated me and said, "Oh, that's cool."* But they didn't hear it like I did.

Now what if I found myself teaching a music appreciation and analysis class to a hundred teenagers? Of course I'd be excited to teach Etta James' "At Last." It is a favorite song and it contains a lot that I think kids could learn from. Nothing wrong with that.

But let's say now that "At Last" was one of only a handful of songs I taught them. And because I decided that "At Last" was really important, especially that pause part, I spent a really long time on the song. We'd listen to a line a day and break it down. I'd point out every move she makes in that song and how the choices she makes in terms of technique reflect her bigger messages. I'd spend so long on this one song, making it more important than all the other songs, that by the time we got to *the pause*, the students might be sick of it. Most of them anyway. Maybe I'd have had a class that complied with a shrug and analyzed each line dutifully. Or maybe I would have had students who dodged and avoided and stopped engaging with the song at all because it wasn't their style and did not

*They did not think it was that cool.

speak to them. Either way, I would not have helped them love this song. In fact, I might have gotten in the way of them liking it.

This is all to say that when we teach craft, we should probably feel an urgency about having students study craft in a variety of texts, not just one. Sure, we can launch our study with a well-known story or novel. But at some point, students will need to find the texts that contain songs that sing to them, or else we will be forcing everyone to listen to Mozart when they want to listen to Kendrick Lamar. Perhaps you will start with Mozart and then have students pick a musician that they want to study. Or perhaps you will have students pick a few artists from the start and then teach Mozart across the unit, allowing students each day to apply what you have shown them in Quintet in A for Clarinet and Strings or Symphony no. 41 on pieces they have chosen to study. Either way, it will be in the transfer of what you have shown them to the music they want to listen to that will create the alchemy of love and learning.

BEFORE YOU START READING

In this section, we'll discuss the following strategies:

1. Develop Cheat Sheets

When we give students the opportunity and support to get organized and prepared before they begin their craft study, we allow for transfer of past teaching and a clear sense of the work to come.

2. Try Your Hand

Practicing the craft moves we are about to analyze helps us feel familiar with them and allows us to appreciate how difficult it is to accomplish great writing.

The balance of preparation and practice can be a tricky one to strike. How much to explain to my son about riding bikes before we set off on the road? The answer of course ideally depends on my son, but now imagine I have twenty-five six-year-olds learning to ride a bike. How much do I talk before we try to get some traction going?

When we study authors' craft, a little bit of prep can go a long way. What are those things called again? How does that move work? What does it feel like to be in the mindset of noticing how an author writes, not just what they are saying? Without this prep, going into a text like a blank slate looking for craft moves to record can be disorienting.

I lost my phone in a swamp once. It took me two hours to find it. I knew exactly what I was looking for. I could visualize my phone perfectly, could even picture it nestled in a wide swampy leaf. In those two hours, because I was looking for something in particular, I noticed so many other things, because I was looking closely. I saw frogs and weird beetles and all the shades of green and how the underside of a wide swampy leaf was actually a little ecosystem of its own, a neighborhood. The combination of a focus and accountability and freedom of time allowed me to see so much more than what I started to look for, even though that direction helped me stay on the task.

And so the study of craft is the study of the precise *and* the elusive. To get ready we must figure out a balance of choice and openness with focus and direction. When we are able to, when we can guide our students to find the phone in the swamp, we help them develop a new sense of things, a new ear for the symphony in the texts we read.

1. DEVELOP CHEAT SHEETS

THINKING ABOUT THE STRATEGY

When I was in third grade, my teacher taught a lesson that I never forgot. It was springtime in Utica, New York, the thaw after a long winter, the endless gray slush finally melting. Yellow dandelions spotted green grass. Everything was lovely again. My teacher, whose name I forget, put on a Joni Mitchell record and played us "Both Sides Now." As we listened, she told us that the clouds in the song were not really clouds. They meant something else. She asked us what word we would put in place of clouds.

And . . . I got it. The song was about how clouds are but also about how life is. Clouds equal life. When my third-grade teacher used the word metaphor, it clicked into my brain, and from that point on, I understood what a metaphor was and how to use one.

I tell this story because when we study the craft of writing, the techniques that authors use, we need to know some things. There is content to familiarize ourselves with, to memorize even. It is difficult to develop any automaticity in analyzing how an author writes if we always have to pause and struggle to find what the thing is called when the sounds in words are similar.

This means that when I begin a craft study, I sit down with colleagues and decide which techniques we are going to introduce or emphasize in this unit. Maybe four or five grade-appropriate techniques that we believe would help students get a lot out of their reading. And then we think about how to teach students those techniques directly.

But we also want to support what students already know from years past. This is always a tricky spot in my teaching because invariably when I ask any students, "What craft techniques do you remember learning last year?" the answer seems to be, "Why, none at all, thank you for asking." This is partly because asking people to recall the names for things on the spot is a terrible way to assess what people know. Instead, people tend to need reminders of what they remember, especially when they are trying something new or difficult.

When we send our students into a novel study hoping that they will notice and consider the way the text is written and the author's style, it will help if they have a tool to help them remember what they know. Teach students to make a cheat sheet of techniques that they will look for and consider as they read. Give them a few options for how these cheat sheets can go—just the names of the techniques, names and definitions, names and icons or images. Whatever will help them remember the most easily.

It will also help to set up some kind of work structure before we start reading the book, and the more that students can choose for themselves how they will work, the better. For example: What medium works best for their cheat sheets?

A physical bookmark? A digital file they can have open while they read? A letter-sized piece of paper on the desk? Thinking about this ahead of time helps us get a sense of what the work will be—we are going to use this thing every day.

Next, offer up a vision for what the work will look like. How often will students be expected to look for and note a craft technique in the text? Where will they write these notes down? Sticky notes? A notebook? How will they organize their notes?

I don't know what the right answers are for you, but I will share how I prefer to set kids up to do this work. I let students know that they can choose a different system, but they might first try this: Stop after every chapter or section in the text. Look for between two and four moves from your cheat sheet across the chapter or section. Write them down in a notebook with the page number. Do whatever work you should be doing on those moves. (This will become clearer as we move through the unit.) Rinse and repeat.

This kind of forecast of what they will be doing helps students figure out the little things that will help them work more easily and successfully.

1. DEVELOP CHEAT SHEETS

TEACHING THE STRATEGY

Lesson Flow

When we give students the opportunity and support to get organized and prepared before they begin their craft study, we allow for transfer of past teaching and a clear sense of the work to come.

One way to teach this lesson:

1. Introduce the usefulness of a cheat sheet with a story of a time when you used (or didn't use) one in your life (recipe, packing list, etc.). Let students know that today they will be setting themselves up for the work they will do in the unit.
2. Offer students cheat sheet options—bookmarks, half sheets, digital texts—and have them talk to a partner about which would be easiest to refer to often. Then discuss options for the content of the cheat sheets: Just the names of the techniques? Examples? Definitions? Icons? Ask them to discuss which version would work best for them.
3. Ask students to make a cheat sheet that includes the four or five new techniques you have taught as well as at least three or four techniques they remember learning in the past. Share cheat sheets.
4. Ask students to discuss how they think they will work best when thinking about craft: Where will they write notes? How often will they stop to write?
5. Have kids try out their cheat sheets on a short passage from a text (*The House on Mango Street*, by Sandra Cisneros, is a good resource). Ask students to read the passage and see how many techniques from their cheat sheet they can find there.

What Might This Look Like?

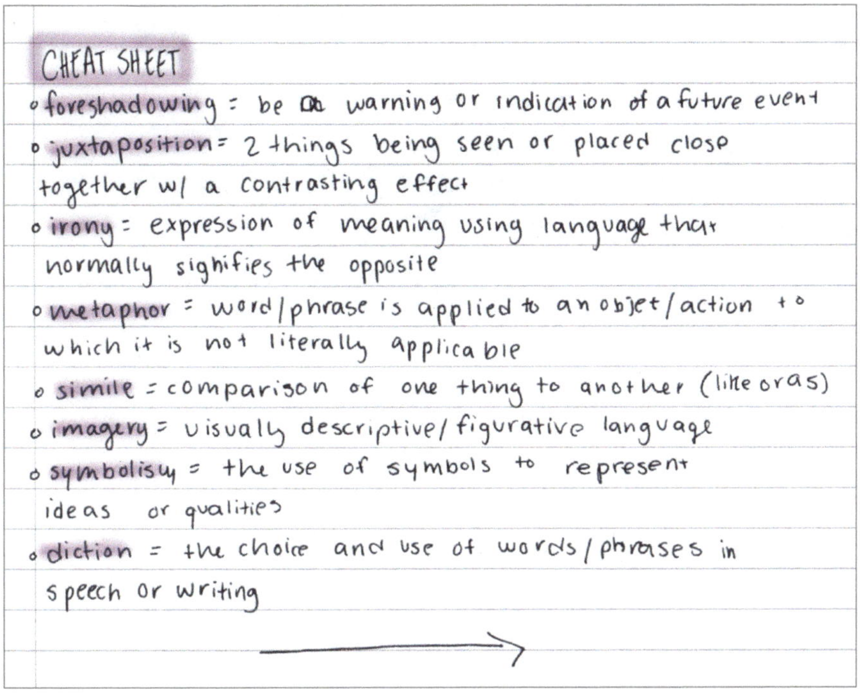

CHEAT SHEET

- foreshadowing = be a warning or indication of a future event
- juxtaposition = 2 things being seen or placed close together w/ a contrasting effect
- irony = expression of meaning using language that normally signifies the opposite
- metaphor = word/phrase is applied to an object/action to which it is not literally applicable
- simile = comparison of one thing to another (like or as)
- imagery = visually descriptive/figurative language
- symbolism = the use of symbols to represent ideas or qualities
- diction = the choice and use of words/phrases in speech or writing

Annika develops a cheat sheet of craft moves to look for and makes sure she knows what they mean.

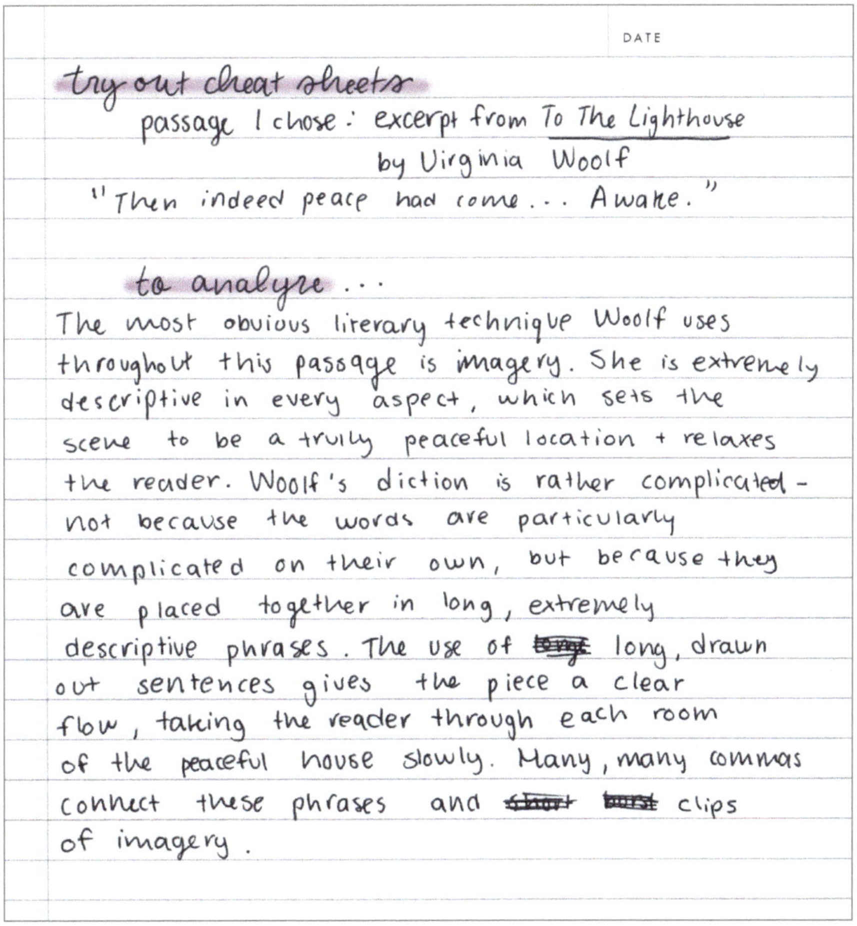

DATE

try out cheat sheets

passage I chose: excerpt from To The Lighthouse by Virginia Woolf

"Then indeed peace had come ... Awake."

to analyze ...

The most obvious literary technique Woolf uses throughout this passage is imagery. She is extremely descriptive in every aspect, which sets the scene to be a truly peaceful location + relaxes the reader. Woolf's diction is rather complicated - not because the words are particularly complicated on their own, but because they are placed together in long, extremely descriptive phrases. The use of ~~long~~ long, drawn out sentences gives the piece a clear flow, taking the reader through each room of the peaceful house slowly. Many, many commas connect these phrases and ~~short~~ ~~burst~~ clips of imagery.

Annika uses her cheat sheet to analyze a sample passage.

Providing Feedback

If your students say or demonstrate . . .	Coach them on . . .
I'm working slowly.	Using a timer to see how much they can get done if they aren't overthinking Giving a few examples to help jog their memory
I can't decide what to put on my cheat sheet: Definitions? Images? Examples?	Trying out a couple of versions in a notebook first Making two versions and seeing which one is most helpful
I finished. In like two minutes. Yawn.	Beginning to consider a sister list of reasons why authors use certain techniques

Optional Tools

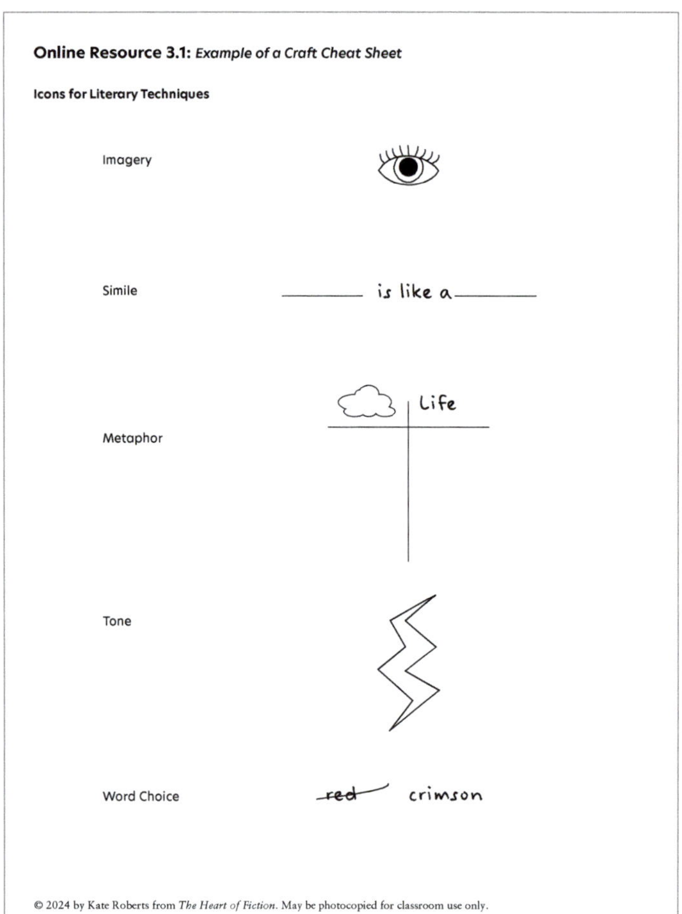
Online Resource 3.1: *Example of a Craft Cheat Sheet*

Icons for Literary Techniques

Imagery

Simile ______ is like a ______

Metaphor Life

Tone

Word Choice ~~red~~ crimson

Example of a Craft Cheat Sheet (OR 3.1)

2. TRY YOUR HAND

THINKING ABOUT THE STRATEGY

In 2005 I joined a theater group that produced campy adaptations of famous musicals. We rehearsed for two weeks and put on a two-night show. Then we did another the next month. Here's the thing: They were musicals. That meant I had to sing and dance.

Reader, I do not sing and dance.

Or, at least, I didn't before my roles in these countercultural musicals. As I committed to the fact that I would be performing these numbers in front of an actual audience in two weeks, I found myself practicing dance moves everywhere I went. Walking to school, I would try out a spin midstride. I worked hard trying to learn to do these things I did not do before. And I got *OK* at it. I did fine. Maybe even a little less than fine, but that was sort of the campy point. I hope.

I did not become a professional musical theater artist from that experience, but I can tell you that when I went to see the musical *Oklahoma* after my short dancing career was over, I had an *entirely* new appreciation for what the performers were doing. "That's really hard," I whispered to my date every two minutes, which I'm sure she was thrilled with.

Before I tried singing and dancing myself, I didn't like musicals at all. Afterward, I appreciated them so much more. I even loved a few. I didn't become a musical theater artist, but I did become someone who understood musical theater a lot more.

Before we enter into another writer's techniques, another artist's voice, it might make sense to give kids a go at trying some craft moves that they will encounter as they read. We can give our students a sketchbook of sorts, a rehearsal, so that when they do encounter these moves in the books they read, they have a greater appreciation for the work this writer is doing. "That's really hard," they might whisper to themselves as they come to a line that magically weaves sound and image and emotion with the power of language.

For this rehearsal, students will need to quickly write down a small moment from their day, week, or life. The point here is not to be too precious; it might be as simple as writing: "I woke up and looked at the clock. *Time for school!* I thought to myself as I got up to change my clothes."

Then have students take out their cheat sheets of techniques and decide which ones they would like to practice. Perhaps they choose imagery. Ask them to have a go at it on their small moment. It does not have to be good or beautiful. Just like my dancing, it just has to be . . . it. An approximation. Maybe our original piece turns into this: "I woke up to a sunbeam hot on my face. Squinting, the numbers on my alarm clock spelled out L-A-T-E. I kicked off my solar system quilt that my mom won't let me get rid of and tried to leap into my clothes."

The more techniques students can practice, the more familiar those techniques will be when they begin reading.

2. TRY YOUR HAND

TEACHING THE STRATEGY

Lesson Flow

Practicing the craft moves we are about to analyze helps us feel familiar with them and allows us to appreciate how difficult it is to accomplish great writing.

One way to teach this lesson:

1. Introduce the lesson by showing students an example of writing without craft and another of writing with craft. Use your own model writing as opposed to judging other people's work. All you need is a few lines.
2. Tell students that the best way to get to know something, like authors' craft, is to try it out yourself. Ask the class to write a few lines of a small moment—getting up in the morning, what they are doing right now, a family dinner.
3. Demonstrate how you look at the list of techniques you have gathered and choose a few to try on your own writing. Model revising a line of your small moment to include that technique. Make sure that your model fits the needs of your class (not too fancy or too simple).
4. Give students time to revise their small moments using a few of the techniques from their cheat sheets.
5. Share before and after examples with the class.

What Might This Look Like?

DATE

TRY YOUR HAND

using imagery

This particular window was the only one framed in curtains. They were pink and sheer, almost soft enough to be used as a blanket, and when the golden sun shone through them the room was filled with a bright bubble gum brilliance.

Annika tries using imagery in a snippet of her own writing.

Author's Craft Practice

Yesterday, I woke up to my dog jumping on me. I ate a microwave omlet for breakfast, and then ramen for lunch. I drove my mom to walmart and I bought a LEGO set. I built my LEGO set and showed it off. I finished my day by eating Shepard's Pie.

Yesterday, I was awoken by my dog, Carl, jumping on me like a dog jumps on a sleeping human. I microwaved an omlet for breakfast and stole my sister's ramen for lunch. Vroom Vroom! I drove my mom to walmart and I bought a LEGO set for myself. I built my $100 set in an hour or two and then showed it off. I finished my day by eating some immaculate Shepard's Pie

Charles practices his precise word choice before he gets ready to look for this technique in the books he reads.

Providing Feedback

If your students say or demonstrate . . .	Coach them on . . .
I am having trouble revising my moment.	Choosing a simple technique like descriptive language and adding three adjectives to their writing Worrying less about whether it is good or not and just practicing, like they would in an art class
I can do the descriptive stuff but not the harder things like symbolism or metaphor or tone.	Picking one hard thing; looking up examples (online or provided by you); and modeling their piece on an example
I love writing and am able to try things easily.	Revising now for different purposes: one where the story is happy and one where it is sad

Optional Tools

Online Resource 3.2: *Try Your Hand*

Technique	Original	Revised

Try Your Hand (OR 3.2)

AS THE BOOK BEGINS

In this section, we'll discuss the following strategies:

3. Get to Know the Author's Voice

Guide students to hear the rhythm and tone of the writing from the start so that they can become more comfortable with the voice of the author.

4. See What You See

Helping students see the craft in a text with ease and independence gives everyone more confidence as we begin.

5. Touch Base with the Other Stuff

When we make sure students are keeping an eye on character and theme as we delve into craft, we mirror more closely the experience of proficient reading—an experience of using multiple skills at once.

I am not the first to say that beginning a new novel is like beginning a new friendship. We spend time together, learn lessons, experience emotions. The hope of course is that this will become a close friendship. There are books out there in the world that I feel like only I understand, books that have changed my life, or at least my outlook. *The Little Prince*, by Antoine de Saint-Exupéry, for example, has accompanied me across my life. There are pages that I have gone to for solace, to help me grieve, to remember what I really believe. Every time I read, "And now here is my secret, a very simple secret: It is only with the heart that one can see rightly; what is essential is invisible to the eye" (2018, 48), something in me clicks into place. This book is my friend, truly.

I read *The Little Prince* to my son recently. He liked it OK. But it didn't hold him like it held me at that age, reading with my dad. And that is fine. All the same, he got to know this book when we first started. There was a bunch to figure out. The voice is distinctive, even hard to click into at first. It begins with the narrator describing a boa constructor eating an elephant and how he tried to draw it and was mocked by adults. My son was confused at first and asked me to reread lines. But soon he got into the flow of it, the voice, and we were off. Even though this book may not become his best friend, he still had to experience the getting-to-know-you phase. Like a work acquaintance. Getting to know a book is certainly about getting to know the characters and the ideas presented. And we encounter themes in the book right away: the importance of childlike wonder, the folly of adulthood. But we also have to get used to the craft of the text, its voice.

On the first page of my book best friend there is the line "My drawing was not a picture of a hat. It was a picture of a boa constrictor digesting an elephant" (Saint-Exupéry 2018). At first it seems like nothing special. But when you get to know the narrator, his intonations, his rhythm, it becomes *funny*. I know this because my dad showed me. I showed it to my son. Our students may not have this assistance when beginning a book, and so we have to help them get to know the craft and voice and technique of the authors right away, so that we don't waste any time when connecting to the text.

3. GET TO KNOW THE AUTHOR'S VOICE

THINKING ABOUT THE STRATEGY

I studied abroad my junior year, in England. The first night we were there, we went out to a pub, which felt very exciting because I was twenty. I struck up a conversation with some guys and sat at their table for a bit. Within one millisecond I felt desperately out of place. They seemed to be very rapidly teasing each other with pun after pun that felt both incredibly clever and terribly intimidating. I understood every other word they said because of the accent and diction they used. I sat silently and chuckled knowingly when the others laughed and then quickly made excuses about bathrooms and loos and "pardon mes" and ran away. Fast-forward nine months, and I was bartending at a local bar, working on a local farm, and dating someone incredibly clever, and very British. I could hang. I got comfortable over time with language and intonations and ways of being that at first felt so strange.

Those first few weeks in a new country felt disorienting. The language was mostly mine but everything felt topsy-turvy—words I knew didn't register right in my brain and everything felt too fast and too jumbled together. It took time to get used to it. I had to get to know how people talked and the way certain words sounded in British accents, and I had to get used to the different flow in conversation.

When we start a new book, we often feel this same way. The words are ones we know, but sometimes it takes time for it all to register. The syntax seems weird, and sentences don't quite make sense at first glance. I can't get into the flow of the book, which keeps me from connecting, engaging, enjoying. Often it isn't until the second or third chapter that I start to really get into things and lose myself. Of course this isn't always the case—sometimes I open up to the first page and I am transported immediately as if the book is singing my own heart's song. But mostly I have to give it time.

We can help students use this getting-to-know-you time well. If we don't, all too often the connection doesn't come. Many abandon a book because it's "boring," or they slog ahead if they have to without ever really clicking in.

As we start a book, it helps to make sure first that we are getting the rhythm down. What is the pattern in the sentences? What intonations are suggested? How can I hear this in my head? Which parts feel tough for me that I am going to have to reconcile or accept? If we don't get to this place of hearing the lines in our mind as we read, we will miss so much. So many jokes and ideas and beautiful descriptions will pass us by if we don't stop and learn how to hear this author's voice.

In *The Namesake*, for example, on page 1 we get insight into Ashima. She is cooking a recipe from home: "Even now that there is barely space inside her, it is the one thing she craves. Tasting from a cupped palm, she frowns; as usual, there's something missing" (Lahiri 2004). This is our introduction to the character. Both of these sentences have a split in the middle: they introduce one idea, then another. As I read, I can feel the rhythm. Da da da da da, dum dum dum. (Please don't be intimidated by my elevated academic language here; I'm a professional ☺.) And as I settle into this rhythm, I see it: the final beats highlight the real issue for her. Look again: in the first sentence the final beats say, "it is the one thing she craves." In the second sentence the final beats are "there's something missing."

It is the one thing she craves; there's something missing. I can feel that. When I get to know the rhythm, when I can feel the beats, I pick up on moments that stop me in my tracks. I hear the things that happen underneath the words. This, to me, is the magic of reading: a different sense developed, a new way to feel.

3. GET TO KNOW THE AUTHOR'S VOICE

TEACHING THE STRATEGY

Lesson Flow

Guide students to hear the rhythm and tone of the writing from the start so that they can become more comfortable with the voice of the author.

One way to teach this lesson:

1. Introduce the lesson with two versions of the same song (for example, "Blank Space," by Taylor Swift and by Ryan Adams). Discuss the differences: tone, rhythm, instruments. Explain how, in a text, the voice of the author is developed through the craft and rhythm the author adopts.
2. Offer the students a few opening paragraphs from famous novels. Demonstrate how you practice reading a few aloud, paying attention to the rhythm and tone of voice that the author seems to be using.
3. Ask students to partner up and take turns trying on a few passages with each other.
4. Coach into their fluency. Help them use punctuation; offer options for the tone: funny, sarcastic, professorial, poetic.
5. Give students time to read and get into their books.
6. Ask students to pause and try the same partner activity but with their book.
7. Have a few students read aloud a passage with a specific tone in mind, and have the class guess which tone the student is using.

What Might This Look Like?

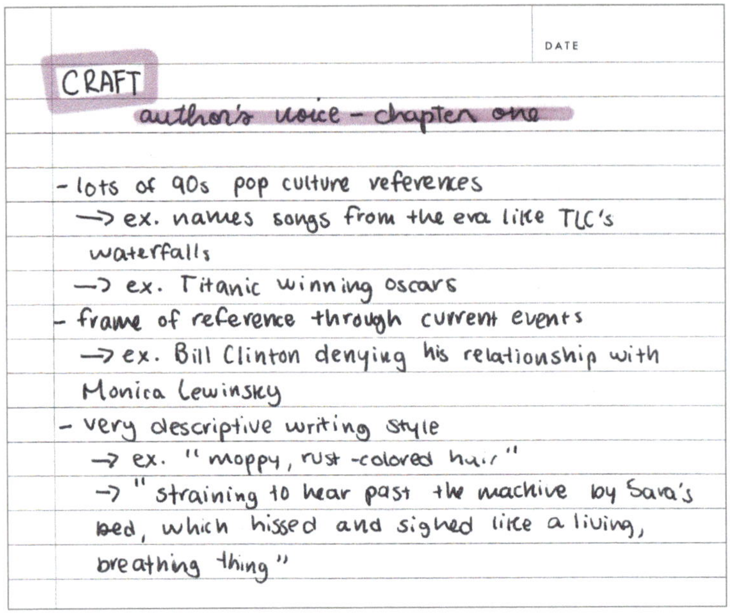

DATE

CRAFT

author's voice – chapter one

- lots of 90s pop culture references
  - → ex. names songs from the era like TLC's waterfalls
  - → ex. Titanic winning oscars
- frame of reference through current events
  - → ex. Bill Clinton denying his relationship with Monica Lewinsky
- very descriptive writing style
  - → ex. "moppy, rust-colored hair"
  - → "straining to hear past the machine by Sara's bed, which hissed and sighed like a living, breathing thing"

Annika describes what she notices about the way the author is writing.

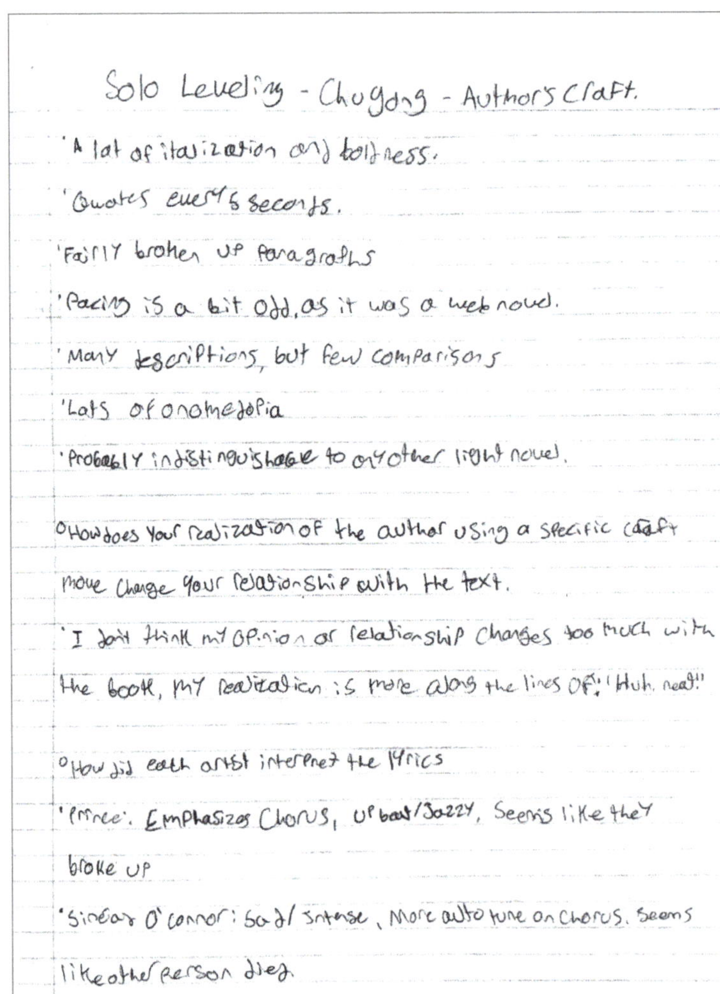

Solo Leveling - Chugong - Author's Craft.

- A lot of italization and boldness.
- Quotes every 5 seconds.
- Fairly broken up paragraphs
- Pacing is a bit odd, as it was a web novel.
- Many descriptions, but few comparisons
- Lots of onomatopia
- Probably indistinguishable to any other light novel.

° How does your realization of the author using a specific craft move change your relationship with the text.

- I don't think my opinion or relationship changes too much with the book, my realization is more along the lines of: "Huh. neat!"

° How did each artist interpret the lyrics

- Prince: Emphasizes Chorus, upbeat/Jazzy, Seems like they broke up
- Sinead O'connor: Sad/Intense, More auto tune on Chorus. Seems like other person died.

Charles gets familiar with a new author's voice.

Providing Feedback

If your students say or demonstrate . . .	Coach them on . . .
When I read, I sound kind of monotone, or I read one word at a time or haltingly.	Practicing saying the same phrase a few different ways (funny, sad, angry) Scooping more words into phrases by isolating a line
I read OK, but if the sentence is long I have trouble keeping the flow.	Looking across a page and breaking down the types of sentences the author uses Practicing the rhythm of the author first to get comfortable
My reading has flow and intonation.	Looking for the ways that the author highlights and emphasizes parts through their rhythm or tone

Optional Tools

Online Resource 3.3: *Reading with Voice*

For each, try reading a line from your book in that voice. Then, see if you can name a character from pop culture that fits the description.

The Friend: Casual, lots of slang, sounds like a kid or someone trying to chat with you.

Example: ______________________________

The Professor: Serious. Lecturing. Telling you about important things.

Example: ______________________________

The Comedian: Sarcastic, exaggerates. Always sneaking a quick joke in.

Example: ______________________________

The Poet: Soft and lyrical, always sounds like they are looking out a window wistfully.

Example: ______________________________

Reading with Voice (OR 3.3)

4. SEE WHAT YOU SEE

THINKING ABOUT THE STRATEGY

Like most couples, my wife and I have had a few times when we weren't connecting, when little issues turned bigger than they needed to be and our communication wasn't clear and compassionate. The thing about times like this is that all of a sudden everything gets kind of colored by the tension, gets painted by the hurt hearts. Everyday moments are put under the microscope. We see what we are looking for, after all, and when we are hurt, we often look for more hurt, unfortunately.

I got advice from a friend that has helped me ever since: she told me to make a gratitude list every day of the things about my wife that I loved and liked and enjoyed. Soon, the good things flowed—her thoughtfulness, the way she calls San Pellegrino "San Pan" even though it makes no sense, her expression when she wants to show me something, how she is so good at running things, the sound of her voice when she is talking on the phone with a friend, and on and on and on. It became easy. The good stuff is everywhere.

When we study the craft, the techniques, the voice of an author, we often have to decide to look for things that otherwise wash over us. We need to learn to see things that are hard to see, because the other stuff—in this case, plot and characterization—is in the way. It's not that we don't want students to notice those things, of course, but that we want to add a layer of vision to their sense of the text. Just like in my marriage: I don't not see the tough stuff when I make my lists of things I love about my wife; I just see the whole picture. In texts, we can always see more, but it takes practice.

Teach your students to train their eyes to see the way an author writes. One way you might do this is to project a passage from a text and simply ask the class to name what they notice about the way the author is writing. Write down what they say, in their language. This may not be the time to ask students to know the terms for things. Let kids name things as they see them at first. Then ask them to apply this same vision to their own reading.

Another way to tackle this skill is to offer a menu of techniques that your class might be on the lookout for and then ask them to find as many examples as they can while they read. This is a similar approach but offers students language and examples to work with. It may seem at first like this is the way to go, because it offers you more control over what they see. Be careful, however, not to be so controlling over what students see that they begin to view the whole enterprise as a scavenger hunt for the teacher. We want students to develop an ability to see craft. This ability is like a muscle, like the way your eyesight adjusts to a Magic Eye puzzle to reveal a hidden image behind pixels. Too much control is like having them stare at such a puzzle with the command "See a fish!" Try as they might, consciously trying to see the fish will not work. Instead they need to relax and see beyond. The *beyond* in texts is often the way the author is writing. And while sometimes we can break down this style into literary terms, all too often it is more elusive than that.

This is a good time to practice both abilities: the ability to find a technique someone mentions as well as the ability to let the text show you what it is. The balance will be up to you and your students. In general, I think that teaching is full of these moments: moments when I have to balance control and freedom, guidance and independence. I hope to be able to talk about why I chose the balance I did, and I probably always feel a little unsettled in my choice. When I am all into freedom and independence, I worry about rigor and accountability. When I am in control-and-guidance mode, I'm anxious about how much the kids are really learning versus just performing for me. In the examples of my thinking from *Aristotle and Dante* and *The Namesake* (see Figures 3.1 and 3.2), I combine a sense of terminology with a freedom to notice things I don't quite have the name for.

Looking for craft is a perfect example of a place where we can apply the balance that helps us stay grounded in powerful practice.

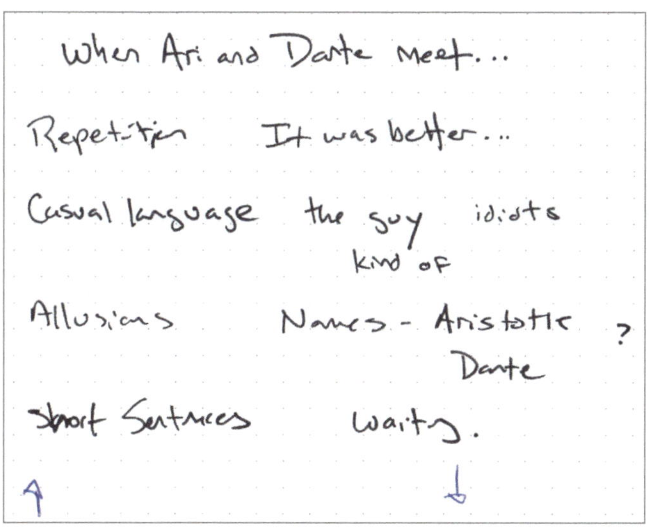

FIGURE 3.1: *Notes on the craft I noticed in an important scene in* Aristotle and Dante.

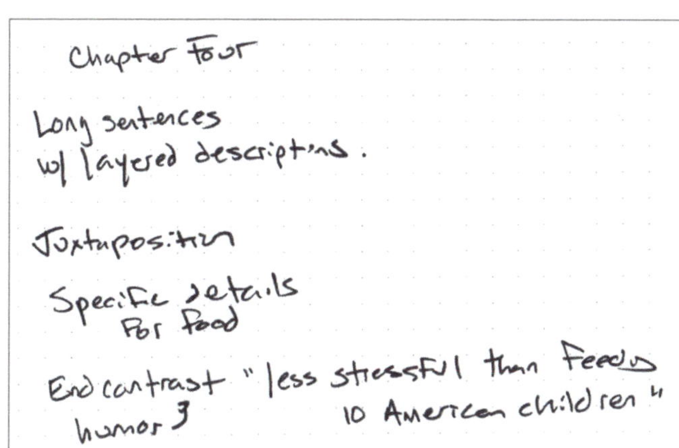

FIGURE 3.2: *An entry pulling out the craft in a text*

4. SEE WHAT YOU SEE

TEACHING THE STRATEGY

Lesson Flow

Helping students see the craft in a text with ease and independence gives everyone more confidence as we begin.

One way to teach this lesson:

1. Introduce the lesson with a story about a time when you had to be helped to see the bigger picture (when your parents annoyed you so much, for example) *or* do a Magic Eye puzzle, pointing out that often we have to train our eye to see a piece of art fully.
2. Project a passage from a text that is rife with level-appropriate craft.
3. Demonstrate how as you read, you notice lines, language, and rhythms that feel deliberate. Show how you make a list (with tallies for repeated techniques) of what you see, using formal or casual language.
4. Ask students to work with a partner and do the same for the next part of the text. Discuss as a class and make a group list.
5. Show students a list of the techniques you have taught them to look for. Demonstrate how you can read while looking for specific techniques as well. Ask them to do the same with their partners. Discuss.
6. Have students read and set up expectations for the rest of the unit: Each time they read in class or at home they should find examples of two to four techniques and do whatever work they have learned on them (right now that simply means identifying them).

What Might This Look Like?

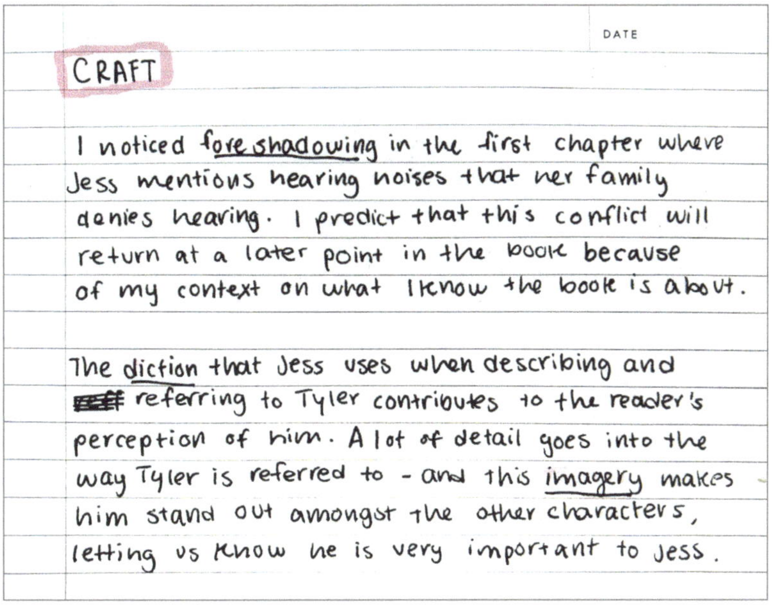
DATE

CRAFT

I noticed foreshadowing in the first chapter where Jess mentions hearing noises that her family denies hearing. I predict that this conflict will return at a later point in the book because of my context on what I know the book is about.

The diction that Jess uses when describing and referring to Tyler contributes to the reader's perception of him. A lot of detail goes into the way Tyler is referred to - and this imagery makes him stand out amongst the other characters, letting us know he is very important to Jess.

Annika uses her cheat sheet to look for specific techniques.

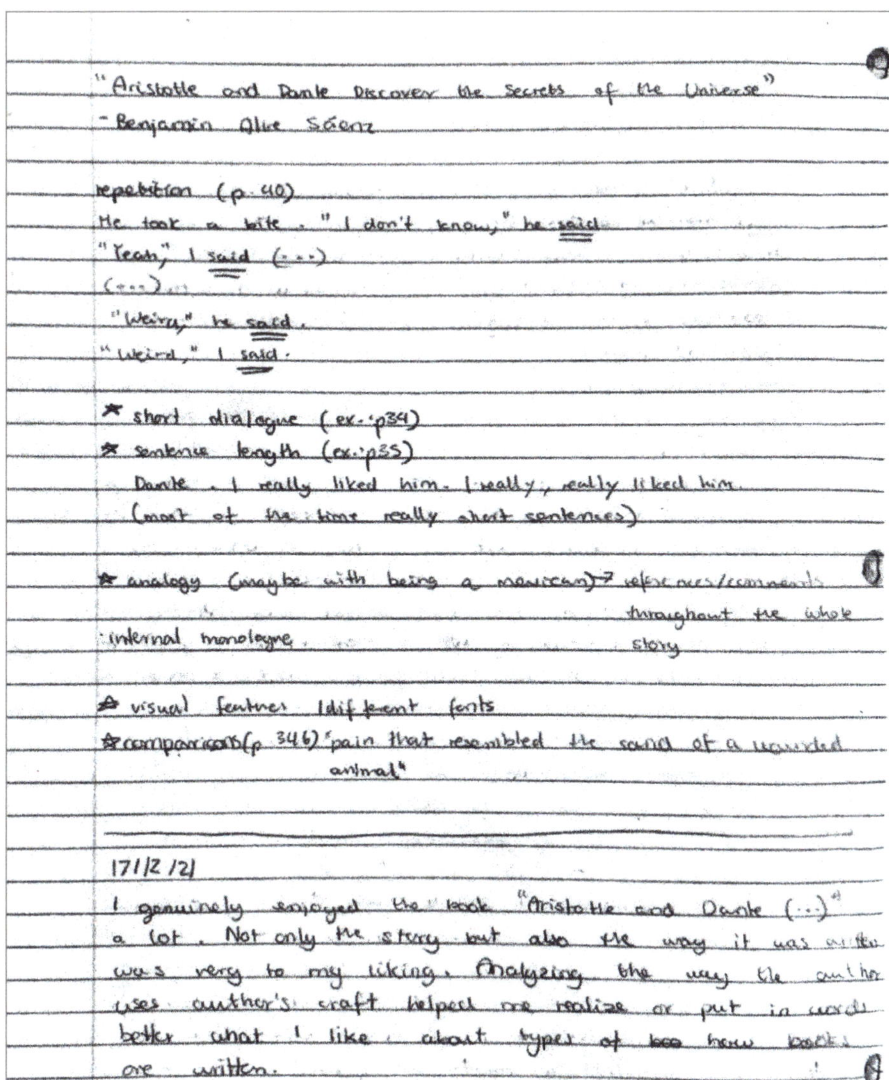
"Aristotle and Dante Discover the Secrets of the Universe"
- Benjamin Alire Sáenz

repetition (p. 40)
He took a bite. "I don't know," he said
"Yeah," I said (...)
(...)
"Weird," he said.
"Weird," I said.

★ short dialogue (ex.: p34)
★ sentence length (ex.: p35)
Dante. I really liked him. I really, really liked him.
(most of the time really short sentences)

★ analogy (maybe with being a mexican) → references/comments throughout the whole story
internal monologue

★ visual features / different fonts
★ comparisons (p 346) "pain that resembled the sound of a wounded animal"

17/12/21
I genuinely enjoyed the book "Aristotle and Dante (...)" a lot. Not only the story but also the way it was written was very to my liking. Analyzing the way the author uses author's craft helped me realize or put in words better what I like about types of how books are written.

Nayeli's notes on the techniques she noticed at the beginning of the text.

Providing Feedback

If your students say or demonstrate . . .	Coach them on . . .
I can't find anything.	Looking for word choice—the words that feel chosen by the author—or descriptive language
I can find the one thing I always find.	Picking out the phrases or lines that they like or that sound good, then trying to describe why Using a menu of more options and pushing themselves to branch out
I see everything there is to see.	Checking in on terminology and using the academic words for things Looking for patterns from the start and evaluating which techniques are most effective (emotionally impactful)

Optional Tools

Online Resource 3.4: *See What You See*

Line or phrase	What it's called/I call it

See What You See (OR 3.4)

5. TOUCH BASE WITH THE OTHER STUFF

THINKING ABOUT THE STRATEGY

When I was forty-three we bought our first home. I love our house like it's a member of the family. It's not perfect, but it's totally perfect for us. Small enough that we are on top of each other and full of character. There's a yard. We are close enough to town to walk. It's on a busy road so lots of people walk by to say hi. I knew I loved this house immediately. It was the first one we looked at. So, if we metaphorically connect this to the work of reading, I loved our house from the first moment I saw it because of its craft. The voice of the house—the feel of it—spoke to me.

Luckily, my wife knew that there are other really important things to check on when you buy a home. Like the furnace and the roof. After all, the look and feel of the house are important, but its main function is to shelter us and keep us warm without breaking the bank. So, we got an inspector, of course, and made sure the foundation was solid and that all the things worked.

When we study the craft of a text, it's important to remember the foundation and all the things that work. We should make sure that we know the character well, that we understand their struggles and motivations, and that we are getting a sense of the themes that are being developed in the text.

We need to do this because when we are busy looking for craft, we can miss the furnace of character and the foundation of theme. And if we do, it will be hard to think about why the craft matters later on, because usually craft matters because of what it helps us know and feel about the characters or because it helps set some stones down for a theme.

In *Aristotle and Dante*, for example, I start to see how insistent Ari is on separating himself and how that is connecting with the theme of pushing people away (see Figure 3.3).

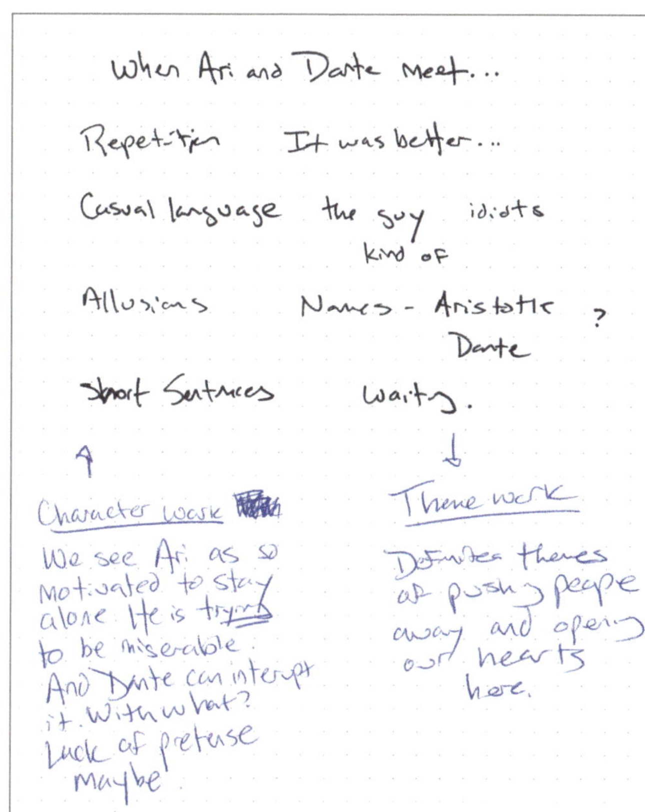

FIGURE 3.3: ***Loosely connecting character and theme to craft***

And in *The Namesake*, while I am noticing the descriptive language and detail, it is important that I hold on to the sense that the detail describing Bengali culture is so much more complete and vibrant than the detail describing American culture and that this must connect to Gogol's ambiguous feelings toward his cultures (see Figure 3.4).

Remind students that just because we are looking at one part of the text doesn't mean we can forget about all of the others. As we move forward in our studies, it will be more and more important that we begin to put these skills together to find the connections between them.

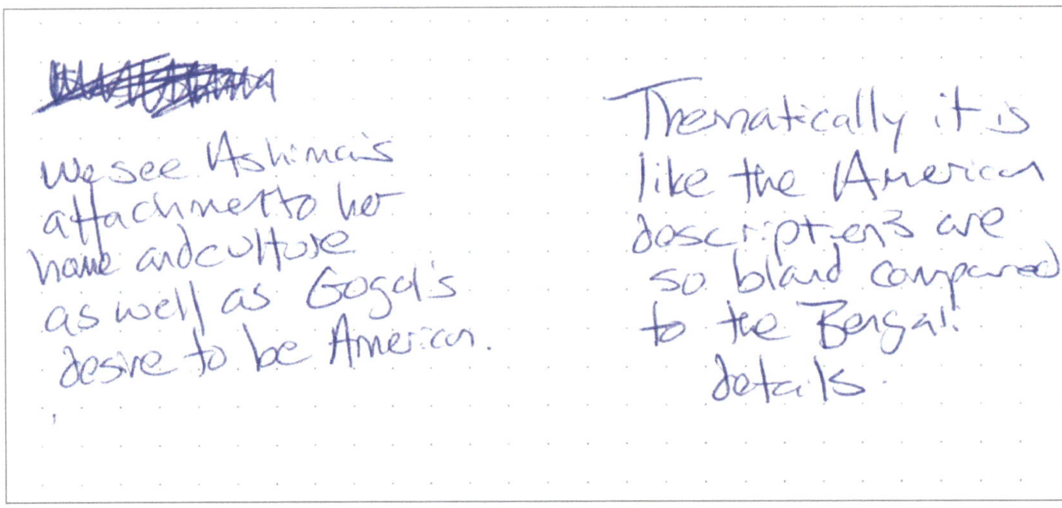

FIGURE 3.4: *Looking for connections between character and theme to the craft in* The Namesake

5. TOUCH BASE WITH THE OTHER STUFF

TEACHING THE STRATEGY

Lesson Flow

When we make sure students are keeping an eye on character and theme as we delve into craft, we mirror more closely the experience of proficient reading—an experience of using multiple skills at once.

One way to teach this lesson:

1. Introduce the lesson by reminding students of the work they have done with character and theme (or other skills you have taught them this year). Ideally show them old charts or tools that remind them visually of the work you did together.
2. Go back to the passage you used in the previous lesson ("See What You See"). Now demonstrate layering your thinking with what feels important here about the character or theme (or other work you have done in the past).
3. Ask students to go to their texts and think (or write or talk) about what else is important in the text so far, particularly along the lines of your past teaching.
4. Guide students to use tools to help them remember some of the past teaching: charts, handouts, progressions.
5. Have students plan out how often they think they should check in on these other aspects of the text formally: Once a chapter? Once a week? Have them set up their notebooks so that they have space to do this writing.

> 6
> The thing about this book is that there are these lines that she writes that are big lines. They sound different than the other. Like whe she sayn 'reputations last longer than the time it take to make them' that is just like her too, x is like that she is quiet until she has something to say that is really powerful and the way the author writes is like that too like a beat.

This student stops for a moment to think through how the craft connects to other elements of story.

Providing Feedback

If your students say or demonstrate . . .	Coach them on . . .
I can't really remember what we did before.	Using tools to help them remember Making sure they spend more time on this per chapter or section: practicing holding on to character and theme as they go
I notice that stuff, but I'm taking on easier things to think about, like how the character feels.	Reflecting on where they were in their practice of these skills before by looking at old notebook entries Working with assignments that will feel more challenging and rewarding, like considering the hidden sides or motivations or contradictions in a character
I'm able to see lots of intersecting skills in one passage.	Each time they notice craft, asking themselves: Which does the technique connect to: Character? Theme? Something else?

Optional Tools

Online Resource 3.5: *Technique Analysis: Character and Theme*

Technique and Page #	Character Connection	Theme Connection

Technique Analysis: Character and Theme (OR 3.5)

IN THE MIDDLE OF THE BOOK

In this section, we'll discuss the following skills:

6. Notice the Patterns of Craft

To help students get a sense of the author's voice, show them how to describe the patterns they see in the author's writing.

7. See the Purpose in the Craft

It's important that students get comfortable with exploring why authors use certain techniques in their writing, which means practicing this thinking every day.

8. Connect Craft to Character

Noting the craft an author uses to develop their character can help students uncover hidden connections, ideas, and surprises as they read.

When we are studying craft and the techniques an author uses to convey connection and meaning, the middle of the book is a comfortable place to be. By now we probably have a decent sense of the author's voice, of the moves they make as a writer, of the flow of the text. Hopefully we also know the characters well and are familiar with their problems, the push and pull of their relationships and dreams. If all is well, issues are turning into themes before our eyes and we are clicked into the plot.

To analyze technique in the middle of the book is to pay attention to purpose, repetition, and connection. It's about noticing not just what but how often and why.

It's like any journey we take. Boarding the train, stepping onto the plane, packing the car and getting on the road—everything feels slightly novel and a bit exciting. At the end of our trip we can see what it all was; we wrap things up in meaning and get ready to say goodbye. The middle of the trip is different. We are in it. If it's good, we are enjoying ourselves without so much thought. If it is difficult, we are just trying to get through it, man. The meaning we make is in the moment. "There she goes again," we think as our family member does the thing she does.

The middle of the book, when we look at craft, is the place where we infer. We begin to guess at the purpose behind the technique. We don't know the ultimate point the author might be making, but we can see the breadcrumbs of meaning they are leaving behind. Our inferences might prove true, or we might need to revise them, but they are the best thoughts we can have based on our understanding of the text and the world.

Inferring is very difficult to teach. We know the phrase "read between the lines," and we know how to phrase questions that ask students to infer ("So why do you think the author chose that word?"). But when our students struggle to perform these tasks, we falter a bit. How exactly do you become better at filling in gaps, particularly when discussing something as personal and elusive as craft? These lessons will not solve the problem entirely, but they may help.

6. NOTICE THE PATTERNS OF CRAFT

THINKING ABOUT THE STRATEGY

Recently I've been noticing how much there is of my mother in me. We are very different. There is intense love between us and sometimes a gap as well. So, I didn't see the similarities for a long time. But now, in middle age, they are becoming clear. I have my mother's earnestness. When my mom is connected and engaged, she is all in. She will tell you exactly what she thinks, and she will listen hard. She cares about things deeply but also has a realism and a wry wit that ground her. I have these things too, I think. I also have her laugh. My mom laughs easily and often. She laughs at her own jokes, as I do. She laughs at the world, at how ridiculous things are. She laughs at herself and how ridiculous she is. I do this too.

It wasn't until recently that I really realized how deeply I take after her. Isn't that funny? It is only now that I can feel in my heart how deeply we are related, in profound and positive ways. Because while these things—earnestness and an easy laugh—may seem small, they are not. These parts of me, these ways I am in the world, are a huge force in my life and have been a huge part of the things that have gone well for me. My earnestness allows me to really listen: to my partner, to teachers. My easy laugh can help lighten the mood, help point out the absurdity of life, help things feel more fun. If I had only one of these, I would be either too serious or too flip. The combination, it turns out, is one of my favorite things about myself. My greatest gift comes from my mom.

It took me a long time to see this because it's a subtle thing. I needed to see it over time to see the pattern. Until I started looking for it, it was invisible. Now, I see it all of the time.

When we study the craft of an author, it can feel like this. I have been getting to know my voice for the beginning of my life; now in the middle I can see the patterns that are emerging that I couldn't see before. In books, at the beginning we are getting to know the voice of the author, but by the middle we should be able to see the ways they tend to write, the moves they make consistently, and of course the exceptions as well.

Teach students to think about the techniques they see authors using over and over again. Teach them to consider when the author uses that move, if there is a common topic or event that brings that technique out of them. Teach them to start unpacking the effect the author's voice has on us by describing the emotional tenor of the moment.

In *The Namesake*, for example, by the middle of the book I can see that the descriptive language, particularly around food and homes and things, is not just something Lahiri does once or twice. It is a consistent drumbeat. And she does not use it just when describing Bengali culture. She uses it to describe Gogol's environments. At his school, with his girlfriends, at home. Lists of foods eaten.

Descriptions of cloth and furniture and books read and music listened to. It's like the senses are on overload. I may not yet know why she is doing this (though in a following lesson I will begin to guess). But I can see the pattern: we situate ourselves with Gogol by describing the senses in very specific detail.

By noticing the patterns in the craft, we can start to hone our understanding of that technique. We get to know it well, so well that we will be able to see it in other texts, across time. The other night, for example, both of my boys saw the moon and stopped in their tracks and exalted at the sight in pure, earnest joy. They do this a lot, almost as much as they laugh.

Thanks, Mom.

6. NOTICE THE PATTERNS OF CRAFT

TEACHING THE STRATEGY

Lesson Flow

To help students get a sense of the author's voice, show them how to describe the patterns they see in the author's writing.

One way to teach this lesson:

1. Introduce the lesson by giving an example of a time someone sounded unlike themselves—a friend who suddenly acted awkward, for example. Point out that we can recognize this because we have a sense of the way a person typically sounds; we know their voice. Authors are the same: we can notice the way they write to help us get to know them.
2. Show two scenes or paragraphs from a book your class knows. Make sure they have similar styles or utilize similar techniques. Ask the class to look for patterns across the two chunks of text. Make a list, and point out that you now have a theory as to the way this author writes.
3. Then, show a third scene and ask students to look for the pattern.
4. Show students that they can get a running jump on the patterns an author is using by looking through their notes about craft and looking for repetition. Then explain that as they read from now on, they should be on the lookout for patterns.
5. Have students read and look for patterns as you confer.
6. Ask students to share out the patterns they see, practicing language like "[Author] uses ________ when ________."

What Might This Look Like?

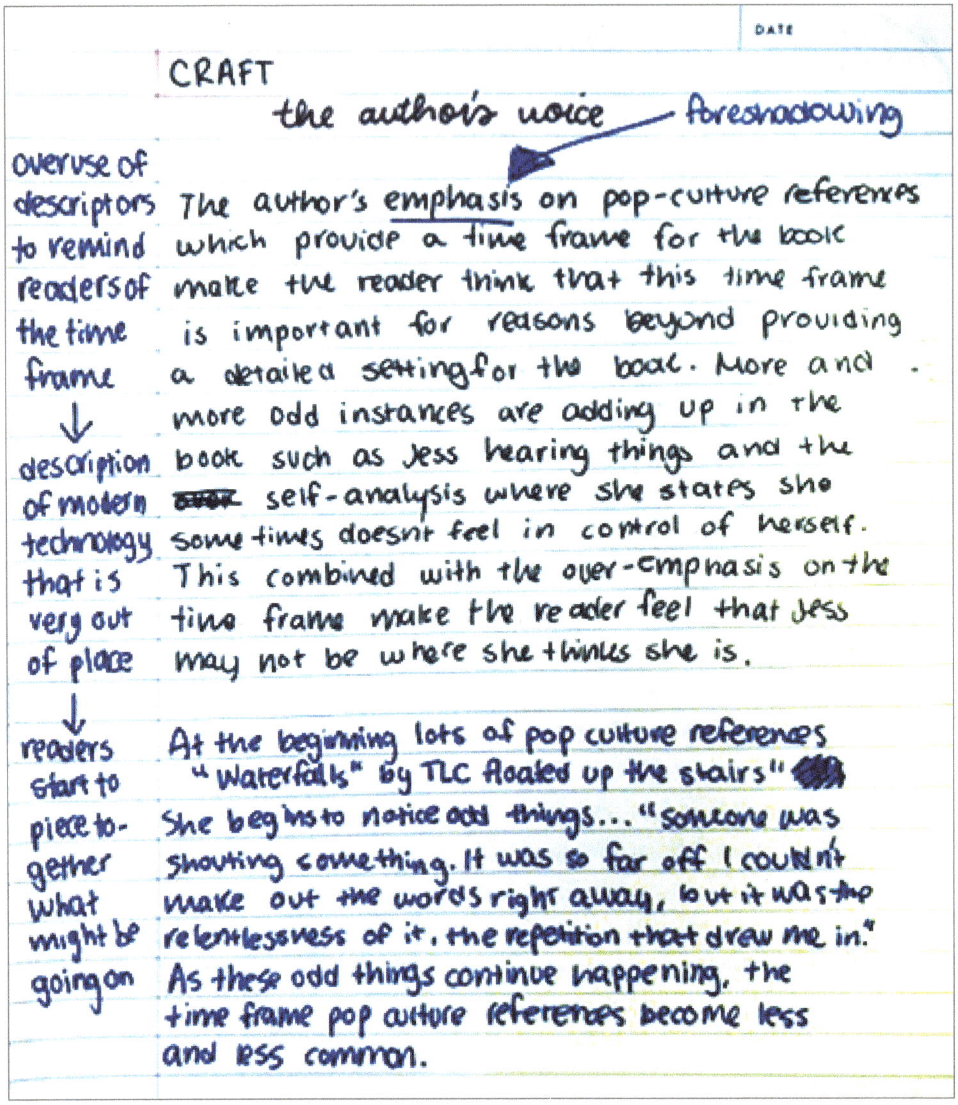

DATE

CRAFT

the author's voice — foreshadowing

overuse of descriptors to remind readers of the time frame
↓
description of modern technology that is very out of place
↓
readers start to piece together what might be going on

The author's emphasis on pop-culture references which provide a time frame for the book make the reader think that this time frame is important for reasons beyond providing a detailed setting for the book. More and more odd instances are adding up in the book such as Jess hearing things and the self-analysis where she states she sometimes doesn't feel in control of herself. This combined with the over-emphasis on the time frame make the reader feel that Jess may not be where she thinks she is.

At the beginning lots of pop culture references "Waterfalls" by TLC floated up the stairs" She begins to notice odd things... "Someone was shouting something. It was so far off I couldn't make out the words right away, but it was the relentlessness of it, the repetition that drew me in." As these odd things continue happening, the time frame pop culture references become less and less common.

Annika captures the craft she sees coming up again and again in the text.

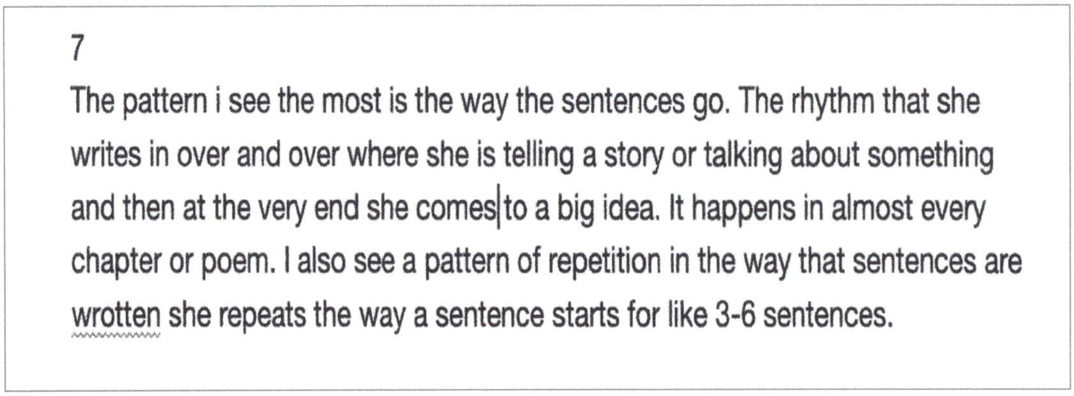

7

The pattern i see the most is the way the sentences go. The rhythm that she writes in over and over where she is telling a story or talking about something and then at the very end she comes to a big idea. It happens in almost every chapter or poem. I also see a pattern of repetition in the way that sentences are written she repeats the way a sentence starts for like 3-6 sentences.

Miles notices patterns of craft in a text.

Providing Feedback

If your students say or demonstrate . . .	Coach them on . . .
I am having trouble seeing any patterns.	Noticing things that are more in plain sight: length of sentences, descriptive language Looking at how chapters start and end and noticing if there is anything similar about them
I can see one thing that is repeated but can't really say when it happens	Looking at the beginnings and endings of things Paying attention to what the topic is—a description of a place or a character, perhaps—and trying to name it: "the technique when the topic of ______ comes up"
I can see a bunch of stuff being repeated and can start to notice when the author writes like that.	Starting to consider why the author might choose that technique at that moment: What effect does it have on them? What does it make them think about the topic?

Optional Tools

Online Resource 3.6: ***Noticing Patterns of Craft***

Technique	Tally	When it is used
Descriptive language and imagery	23x	Transition to a new place, when he is with family or girlfriends

Noticing the Patterns of Craft (OR 3.6)

6. SEE THE PURPOSE IN THE CRAFT

THINKING ABOUT THE STRATEGY

Unfortunately for my kids, I'm learning how to parent as I go. Case in point: the other day my youngest literally did the opposite of what I asked of him about twenty or fifty or a million times in a row. I became exasperated and asked him, crossly, "Why are you doing this?" It was one of those moments that put me on my heels, because he looked at me with total honesty and said plaintively, "I don't know!"

Of course he doesn't know. He's a child. Most adults have trouble pinpointing why exactly they did a thing they did, but here I am expecting my five-year-old to analyze his motives while emotionally charged.

Now move to our classrooms. We have taught students to notice some things that an author does while writing that makes their writing, well, theirs. They have even started to uncover patterns in the way the author writes. Naturally, our next question is often the same as I posed to my kid: "Now why did the author write like that?" And what we get back is often a similar expression of confusion and frustration.

But let's take a look at something I tried with my son yesterday. We had a similar moment: me asking, him not listening. But instead of asking him, "Why did you do that?" I gave him choices. I said, "So did you not listen because you didn't want to do what I asked, or did you really not hear me because you were too absorbed in what you were doing, or were you feeling angry and defiant?" And you know what? With those choices, he could see it all more clearly. So much more that he was able to come up with *his own reason*. He said, "Well, I can hear you, but in my mind I think I'll just finish this quick and then do it, and then I forget." Brilliant. We can work with that.

This is what many of our students need when they are starting to consider the reason why an author uses a technique. They need choices. They need a menu to work from. They need someone to say, "Well, did the author do that to reveal character, to develop an idea for a theme, or to set a tone?" This support allows students to grab on to something when navigating the abstraction of *purpose*.

So, when teaching the purpose of craft, offer students some choices first—some generic reasons, or purposes, to write one way or another. Your list of choices can be long or short. But give kids time to get really comfortable with reading a text and saying, "Oh, I see that Jhumpa Lahiri is using multiple points of view to develop a theme." This allows students to grow more confident. And often, they are right.

The next step to purpose, then, is to help students become more text-specific in their answers. For example, if I say Jhumpa Lahiri uses multiple points of view to develop the theme, then I need to then be able to say which theme these points of view develop and maybe even a little bit more about how they do that. As I develop my abilities, and my confidence, I will start to get comfortable saying, "Jhumpa Lahiri uses multiple points of view to develop the theme of connection and how the ways that family and culture connect us are huge forces bigger than what we think we want. Gogol and his family are in separate worlds, but because we are inside their minds, we feel the true connection between them."

But this level of analysis takes time to develop. When I move too quickly, when I push kids to get into how the craft achieves the purpose, the thinking gets jumbled and confused and then that feeling of "this isn't for me" comes up again in students.

Instead, we want to take each step on this journey as a whole phase of development to get comfortable with and to celebrate. Pay attention to how long you think your students need to use their menus for purpose. Stay there awhile, until it feels easy. Then urge them to simply get specific about what the techniques show about character, which theme, and so on. Save the how for the rest of their days with you—and in school.

7. SEE THE PURPOSE IN THE CRAFT

TEACHING THE STRATEGY

Lesson Flow

It's important that students get comfortable with exploring why authors use certain techniques in their writing, which means practicing this thinking every day.

One way to teach this lesson:

1. Introduce the lesson by talking about a time when someone misunderstood you. Explain that misunderstandings happen when we read, too: we don't *really* know why an author writes like they do.
2. If you like, share that William Golding refused to publicly make any comment on interpretations of *Lord of the Flies*, saying instead that the only interpretation that should matter to the reader is their own. Suggest that there is no right answer when we ask, "Why did the author do that?"
3. Show students a chart with your general purposes written out. (See "Optional Tools, OR 3.7" for a list.)
4. Revisit a familiar passage and consider which purpose best fits that moment.
5. Have students try identifying purpose on another technique with their partners.
6. Ask students to go back to their patterns and ascribe purpose to the ways the author tends to write.

What Might This Look Like?

DATE

CRAFT

writing in Little Women

Louisa May Alcott uses lots of imagery in her writing. The scenes are very vivid to the reader because of how much description is used to set up the scenes and characters. Her sentences are long, and filled with adjectives as imagery. The prose is complex because of all the imagery, but very concise and thus understandable to the reader.

In the scene, the author uses the names of the sisters to take us around the room/setting. As they are named, another part of the scene is described while relating to them. Lots of imagery is used here as well. Alcott also contrasts the sisters against each other by stating that Meg was at ease and then describing how uncomfortable Jo is by placing her in a different setting at the same party. Thus, she characterizes Meg as someone comfortable in her feminity + role at the party, while Jo is the opposite.

In my book, the author characterizes Jess as different from those surrounding her by constantly making others dismiss Jess when she asks questions. There is also more imagery and description surrounding details only Jess notices, drawing our attention to it.

Annika shares her connections between craft and purpose from a whole-class text,* Little Women, *and then begins to find similar techniques in her independent book.

The author uses repetition to develop a tone

The author uses strong lines to develop the character's true beliefs

Also i think that the poem structure is there because it feels more emotional

A student uses sentence frames to name a general purpose for the techniques in a text.

Providing Feedback

If your students say or demonstrate . . .	Coach them on . . .
I am having trouble choosing a purpose.	Going with their gut Reviewing what they know about character, theme, tone, etc.
I can choose a purpose, but I usually choose the same one.	Looking for examples of other purposes and banning themselves from the one they are comfortable with Reviewing what they know about character, theme, tone, etc.
I can easily choose a purpose that matches the technique.	Starting to practice getting specific by explaining exactly what theme, what aspect of the character, or what tone this technique expresses Practicing freewriting about how a technique achieves its purpose

Optional Tools

Online Resource 3.7: ***Purpose in the Craft***

Technique: ____

The author uses this technique in order to:

- Reveal something about the character?
- Create a mood or develop a tone?
- Introduce an idea?
- Hint at a flashback?
- Hint at foreshadowing?

Purpose in the Craft (OR 3.7)

8. CONNECT CRAFT TO CHARACTER

THINKING ABOUT THE STRATEGY

I have always had the same pair of shoes, essentially. A big black pair of boots. They have evolved of course, from Doc Martens to my current work-appropriate boots. And yet still I always wear the same essential thing on my feet. It is a technique in my style. It was a subconscious process. I didn't decide exactly. I just went with what felt right.

I could end here. It's not like it is that important that it deserves tremendous thought. People aren't staying up at night wondering, *But why?!*

And yet there is more there. Something attracts me to these boots. There is something about me, about my character, that shows up in that choice.

When I dig beneath the surface, I see that I wear big black boots because, when I came out as gay in the nineties, that is what I wore at the start of my journey to accept myself. They made me feel like me. They helped me feel like I might fall in love or, even more miraculous, have someone fall in love with me. They helped me fit somewhere. And they represented a part of me that felt very much like *me*: a desire for a little bit of rebellion, for freedom, for a kind of open skepticism that is still a big part of my identity. So, I wore big black boots and I hitchhiked in them and moved to New York City and adventured through my twenties, all in beetle-black boots. Over time, I began to choose more conventional routes in my life. Teaching. Then coaching. I started to travel, wrote a book, began presenting sometimes in hotel conference rooms with chandeliers.

And I still wore my boots. Because even though my life has changed and I am a mom who works in schools, I want to hold on to that twenty-three-year-old bartender too. So, I hold on to my boots whenever I can.

When we analyze the craft of the author, when we really dig into why the author writes like that, it helps to consider what we learn or feel or believe about the characters. How are the two connected? Take, for example, my notebook entry about *Aristotle and Dante* in Figure 3.5, where I attempt to connect the diction of Ari with what we know about his inner conflict.

Or consider my notes about *The Namesake* in Figure 3.6, where I explore the connection between all of the setting description and Gogol's motivation to become American.

We can teach students to always keep an eye on the character when we study craft, looking for what connections there may be.

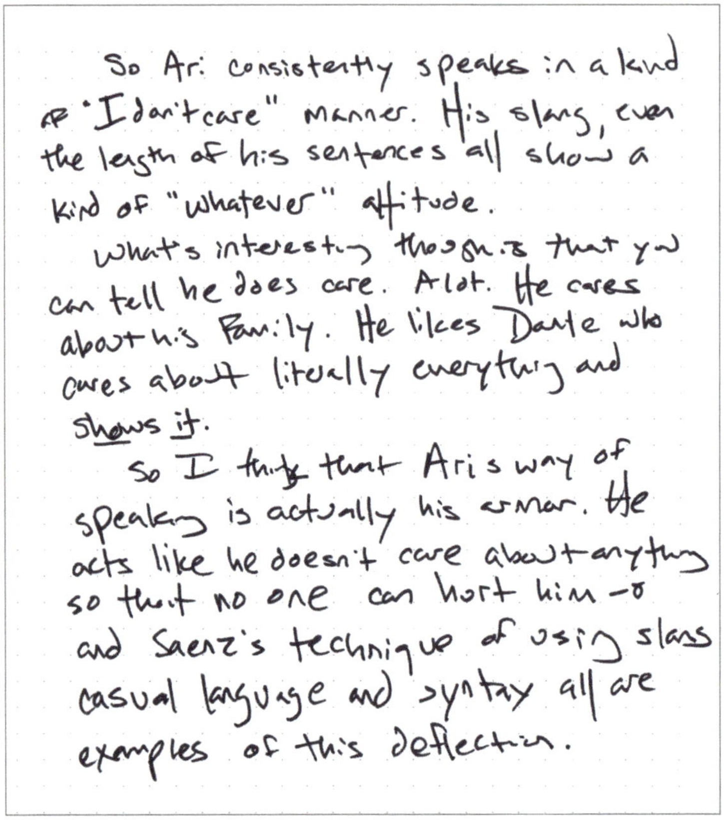

So Ari consistently speaks in a kind of "I don't care" manner. His slang, even the length of his sentences all show a kind of "whatever" attitude.

What's interesting though is that you can tell he does care. A lot. He cares about his family. He likes Dante who cares about literally everything and shows it.

So I think that Ari's way of speaking is actually his armor. He acts like he doesn't care about anything so that no one can hurt him → and Saenz's technique of using slang casual language and syntax all are examples of this deflection.

FIGURE 3.5: *Working on defining the purpose and effects of craft on how we see the character*

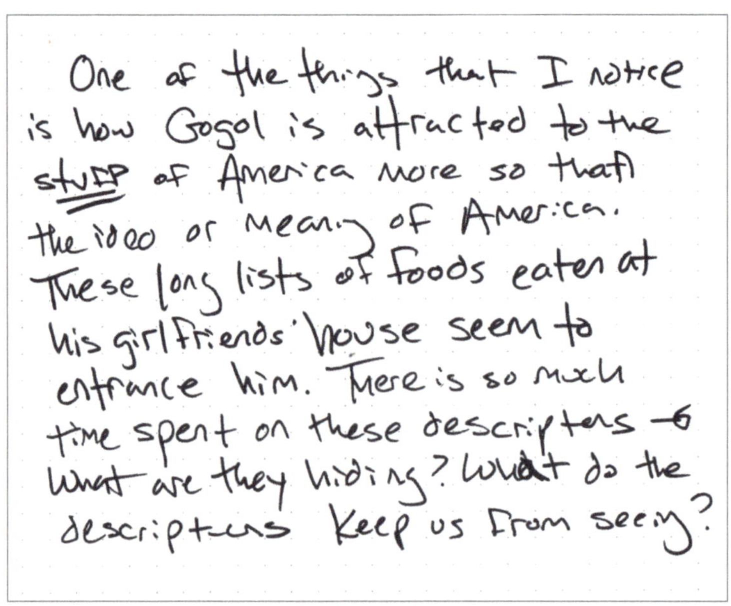

One of the things that I notice is how Gogol is attracted to the stuff of America more so than the idea or meaning of America. These long lists of foods eaten at his girlfriends' house seem to entrance him. There is so much time spent on these descriptions → What are they hiding? What do the descriptions keep us from seeing?

FIGURE 3.6: *Finding the relationship between an author's technique and the character development that emerges from it*

8. CONNECT CRAFT TO CHARACTER

TEACHING THE STRATEGY

Lesson Flow

Noting the craft an author uses to develop their character can help students uncover hidden connections, ideas, and surprises as they read.

One way to teach this lesson:

1. Introduce the lesson with something about your personal style that actually embodies an important part of your identity. Point out that one of the strongest connections to the craft of the text is the characterization the author is going for—that the author's craft decisions relating to characters give clues about the characters just as your style choices give clues about you.
2. Demonstrate by showing a scene from a text the students know. Point out a technique the author is using, and show students how you look for connections to the character by asking: Does it show a trait? A belief? A motivation? A change or shift? A relationship?
3. Have students try this on another part of the text. Share out ideas.
4. Ask students to choose an aspect of the author's style that they think might be connected to a character and to write out their rough-draft thoughts connecting the two (you might want to share an entry you wrote as a model).
5. Have students read and look for further connections as they do.

What Might This Look Like?

DATE

craft and characterization

The author's continual use of specific pop culture references throughout the book are vital to the plot of Jess's life being a TV show. They characterize her as a typical teen girl living her life, and are an important aspect of building up her extremely average (from the outside) life in an average town as an average American girl. The almost exessive nature of these references highlights how vital the setting of the book is to Jess. However, as the book shifts when Jess discovers the truth about her life, the references do as well by slowing down. This contrast makes the reader second-guess the setting on a whole new level - what year is it really? This contrast of lots of pop culture references at the start to fewer once the plot shifts/twists also indicates a change in Jess herself away from being a normal teenage girl.

Annika notices how when the craft or technique of a text shifts, often it is because of shifts happening with the character.

The character x is really motivTED TO become more herself and who she really is. And the way the author writes is like that too because in some ways who x is is hidden until these big sentences come out. Or the rhythm makes you kind of go along with everything until one line stops you and you notice her true self.

her relationships too because when twin tells her to go away she has a big line about the ballon and ti shows how they love each other and are there for each other but also twin needs to be his own self and not always the one protected by x.

A student explores different sides to the characterization that are developed through the craft of the text.

Providing Feedback

If your students say or demonstrate . . .	Coach them on . . .
I am not sure how this connects to the character.	Using a sentence frame to help: ________ [craft technique] shows or emphasizes that ________ [character] is ________ .
I can make some concrete, almost literal connections.	Considering other, more inferential connections between craft and character, like a hidden aspect of their character, the feeling of a relationship, or a motivation for their actions
I am able to connect the craft of the text to the character.	Looking for how the craft works across time in the book and seeing if it matches the development of the character

Optional Tools

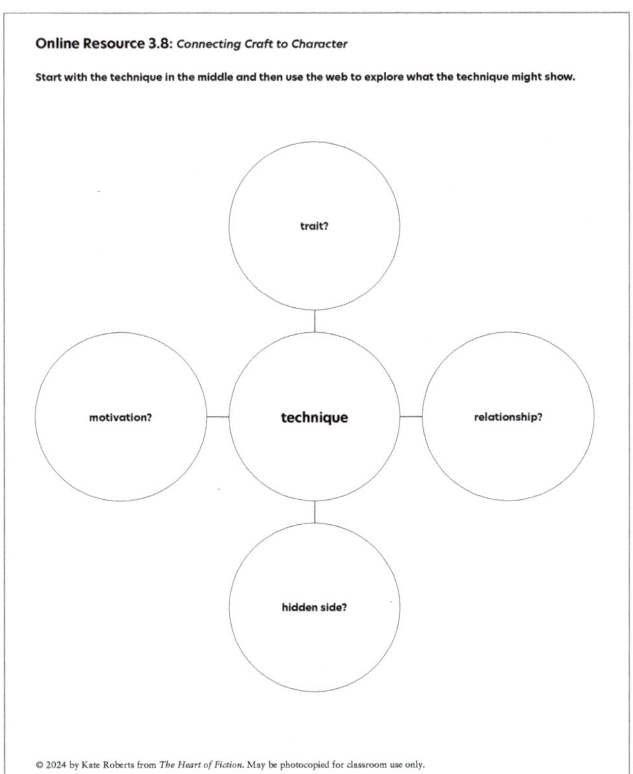

Connecting Craft to Character (OR 3.8)

AT THE END OF THE BOOK

In this section, we'll discuss the following skills:

9. Refine the Links Between Craft and Purpose

Guide students toward specificity in their thinking about craft and its purpose.

10. Create Craft Theses

Help students see the techniques an author uses as serving a larger purpose in the text as a whole.

11. Track How Craft Develops Theme

Challenge students to look for the ways that craft and theme connect.

By the end of a novel, the bulk of your work in studying the craft of the text is done. You have a sense of the author's style, you understand why they may be writing like that, you are making connections to the craft across the text and to different elements of the story, like character.

Now things are coming to a close, and if you are engaged with the book, you probably will not want to spend a ton of time thinking about literary technique and syntax. If the book is going well for you, you will want to find out what happens.

This is why you have a choice to make here in the final push: you could either teach your students to finish the book reasonably quickly and then double back and do some analysis on what they have read or continue to teach students to slow down and pick up analysis as they move through the final chapters.

If you choose to teach kids to read and then double back, make sure that they mark places that feel important—either because of the techniques the author uses or because of the scene itself—as they go. This will make the analysis work to come feel much less tedious. If they are jotting as they go, it might help to ask students to make quick predictions each time they stop: What do they think this is leading to? What does the craft suggest? A happy ending? Tragedy? This will help make the work they are doing as they read feel like it is building anticipation instead of interrupting the flow of reading.

In any case, as we get to the end of the book, we get glimpses now into the author's plan (or, at the very least, the happy accident). We get to see if the moves the author made had real purpose or if they were simply beautiful ornaments to the story told. And when we find that there is meaning behind the metaphors, we get the satisfaction of a mystery solved, a eureka moment that makes us feel quite clever and fully immersed in the text.

9. REFINE THE LINKS BETWEEN CRAFT AND PURPOSE

THINKING ABOUT THE STRATEGY

There is power in the specifics of things, which is a large part of an author's craft. Style equals, in part, the details you choose. For example, in 2010 I got married. I could tell you that it was a beautiful day. But I could also tell you about the look in my wife's eyes—present, warm, connected. I could tell you about how blue the sky was and how I haven't seen a sky that deep and clear since that day. It was warm, just warm enough that if there wasn't a breeze you would get hot. But there was a breeze, cool like a forest stream. As I stood, I looked out at the crowd, and for just a moment, they were fuzzy, out of focus, as if the energy of their presence and our history was fogging my view of them. When Maggie came toward me, everything blurred out again, and all I could see was her face, beautiful—my person.

I cannot really capture it in words. But I can try. And if others studied this text later on, I hope they would not just say, "The imagery shows that she loves her wife." This is true, but it is also incomplete—so vague as to be almost insulting to the message I would be trying to convey.

Being able to pinpoint a technique and a purpose is great. It's great to say, "Hey, there is some imagery and I think it is developing a theme." But to be able to discuss this, to explain and break down and analyze—this begins to feel like the work of the English major. This is the work that feels out of reach for students who do not plan to study literature for their whole lives.

And yet, when you look across media, many people are doing this work who are not avid readers of ancient texts. Social media platforms are rife with everyday people doing deep analysis on TV shows and movies and comic books and, yes, books. Like @lissajostewart on TikTok, who published deep dives into the characters of the Chronicles of Narnia. Or @straw_hat_goofy, who embraces superhero movies and animated films as if they were Russian novels. When I watch this content, I am filled with joy, because it shows how much fun analysis can be.

When we teach students to be as specific as possible, we show them how to have this kind of fun. For example, in the scene from *The Namesake* in Figure 3.7 (Lahiri 2004, 93), either I can say that Lahiri uses lists of descriptions or I can get more precise and say that here Lahiri uses multiple lists of proper nouns like "Colin, Jason, and Marc" and "Dylan and Clapton and The Who." I can stay general and note that the details help develop the setting, or I can be specific and say that these proper nouns cue us to feel the white suburbanity of Gogol's American life. I can say that this has the effect of developing a theme, or I can name the theme it develops—perhaps something like "Lahiri uses lists of proper nouns like *Colin* and *The Who* to develop Gogol's surroundings as being white and suburban, in contrast to the setting details of his Bengali home. This enforces the idea that the American dream is often a dream of whiteness." Without specifics, we stay stuck in the lane of "Lahiri uses descriptions to develop both the setting and the theme."

> Gogol does not date anyone in high school. He suffers quiet crushes, which he admits to no one, on this girl or that girl with whom he is already friends. He does not attend dances or parties. He and his group of friends, Colin and Jason and Marc, prefer to listen to records together, to Dylan and Clapton and The Who, and read Nietzsche in their spare time. His parents do not find it strange that their son doesn't date, does not rent a tuxedo for his junior prom. They have never been on a date in their lives and therefore they see no reason to encourage Gogol, certainly not at his age. Instead, they urge him to join the math team and maintain his A average. His father presses him to pursue engineering, perhaps at MIT. Assured by his grades and his apparent indifference to girls, his parents don't suspect Gogol of being, in his own fumbling way, an American teenager.

FIGURE 3.7: *A scene from* The Namesake

9. REFINE THE LINKS BETWEEN CRAFT AND PURPOSE

TEACHING THE STRATEGY

Lesson Flow

Guide students toward specificity in their thinking about craft and its purpose.

One way to teach this lesson:

1. Introduce the lesson by showing students two examples of a craft analysis. One should be general and the other detailed. (Feel free to use the examples from *The Namesake* in the previous pages.) Point out the difference: one focuses on the details and the other focuses on the categories.
2. Demonstrate taking one of your annotations that analyzes the purpose of craft and making it more specific, for example, naming the exact example of the craft, naming exactly what it offers about the character or tone or theme.
3. Give students another general annotation from a class text to work on making more detailed with their partners.
4. Share out examples; write a class version together.
5. Ask students to spend some time going back to a few of the techniques they have analyzed and making them more specific.
6. As students read on, ask them to continue this work, at least twice a chapter.

What Might This Look Like?

DATE

CRAFT

linking craft and purpose

1. Imagery

→ The author uses imagery to draw the reader's attention to important characters, events, or details that help develop the theme and our perspective on what is important and relavent to Jess, the main character. When small, seemingly insignificant events are described in detail w/ imagery, the readers know to pay more attention to that section as it may be relavent later.

help us feel connected to Jess + her story

2. foreshadowing

→ The author's use of foreshadowing helps the book stay engaging throughout. As a reader, picking up on a small detail that becomes relavent later that you may have predicted feels good. Readers also feel connected with Jess's story and perspective when she puts pieces of information together to solve/discover an issue/question that has been foreshadowed. By writing with lots of foreshadowing, the author creates a thrilling story that keeps the reader analyzing and asking questions the entire time.

Annika works to connect technique and purpose.

Ther author uses repetition to develop a tone of feeling out of control but trying to keep going. The repetition feels like an out of control car

The author uses strong lines to develop x's true self because they pop in ut of nowhere when usually x is just trying to get by

Miles practices quickly linking craft and purpose as he reads.

Providing Feedback

If your students say or demonstrate . . .	Coach them on . . .
I am having trouble being specific.	Focusing first on the craft by giving an example and discussing what is happening in the moment
I can be specific about the craft, but I'm having trouble focusing my purpose analysis.	Freewriting about the thing they think the craft is doing (e.g., freewriting about the character in the moment of the text they are focusing on)
I am able to analyze both the craft and purpose with detail.	Starting to gather other examples of either the craft or the purpose (e.g., looking at how many times the author uses imagery to reveal character)

Optional Tools

Online Resource 3.9: ***Naming a Purpose for Technique***

Technique	Category of purpose	Text specific example of purpose
Descriptive language in setting	Creates a mood	Creates a dreamlike, unreal mood through the use of soft colors and long sentences

Naming a Purpose for Technique (OR 3.9)

10. CREATE CRAFT THESES

THINKING ABOUT THE STRATEGY

My mom likes to poke fun. She likes to razz people. It has taken me a long time to realize that she does it in order to connect, to show how well she knows me, and that she does not mean to be critical. She means it as an expression of love. I'll say something about myself and she will come back sarcastic with "No, really? You?" and it can feel like she is making fun of me, but in reality she is saying, "I know you, I know you are like this, and I accept it."

This theory, this thesis, took me a long time to develop. We don't have quite that long when we are teaching a class.

Crafting theories about the technique in a text is tough, but if students have done the work in this chapter, it will be much easier. Consider where a student who has followed the path of these lessons is: they have a collection of techniques they have found in the text, they have identified patterns, they have explored the purpose within the choices an author makes with their language. Now they just have to put it together, to see the larger pattern across the novel or story, to see the common craft or common purpose these moves hold.

The easiest way to do this is to go back to our notes. To group the techniques we see repeated together and examine their potential common purpose. Or, going in the other direction, to consider a grand purpose we see in the author's writing and then connect a few different techniques that strive to achieve that goal.

But we can also lean here on another source of power in our classrooms: talk. Having students work together to draft a thesis around the literary techniques they see in a text allows them to support each other in low-stakes ways: I can draft ideas with blank spots and perhaps my partner can fill them in. I can be wrong and be challenged to think more accurately. I can search for a word or example or next move to make in my analysis and either be helped out by my partner or at the least have an audience to dial up the need to find the word or idea I am looking for.

Of course, we can use talk across the work we do with students and most likely we should use it consistently in our teaching. In the previous lessons across each section of this book, I have tried to include examples of times when partners could work together. But let's talk about talk a bit now.

Having students work together can expose two major pitfalls that I hope to avoid. The first is not giving students enough guidance, not channeling them in ways that will be productive. For example, if my students have not read the same book as their partner, they won't really be able to help them discuss the actual craft in that specific book. If they are new to analyzing craft in general, they may not be able to exactly coach them in the skill either. Instead, it might be more productive if students use this talk opportunity to hold each other accountable to the teaching in the room. For instance, instead of expecting students to help their partner answer the question of what craft pattern they see as most significant in the book, it might be more helpful if they coach their partner to look through their notes and see what keeps coming up—a strategy I've taught them, that hopefully is recorded on some sort of tool that kids can access. Partners can use the tools in the room, past teaching, and their own process to help each other think the next thought.

The other pitfall is that we control the talk too much: we hand them the graphic organizer to fill out together. We give them a thousand talk prompts or a questionnaire to follow. This extreme stifles conversation. It's too easy, even if the questions or prompts are hard, because it doesn't require any social exchange or openness of thought.

Instead, encourage partners to use what they have—the charts in the room, their notes on the strategies you have taught, and their own experience—coach each other and guide each other toward the craft thesis that feels just out of reach.

10. CREATE CRAFT THESES

TEACHING THE STRATEGY

Lesson Flow

Help students see the techniques an author uses as serving a larger purpose in the text as a whole.

One way to teach this lesson:

1. Introduce the lesson with an example of powerful writing about craft. Point out that one way people talk about and think about texts is by working to name big, overarching things an author does.
2. Show students the sentence frames that they will be loosely using to form their theses:

   ____________ uses ____________ to ____________ .
   [author] [technique] [purpose]

   ____________ creates ____________ by ____________ .
   [author] [purpose] [technique]

3. Demonstrate how you can fill in one easily because you have been thinking about it. Then demonstrate how you look through your notes on a text to look for other possibilities.
4. Have students work with partners to develop their own craft theses. Ask partners to consider how many examples they can find in the text (of the craft or the purpose), their understanding of the technique and how it works, and the complexity of their purpose.
5. Share some of the class's craft theses.
6. Ask students to plan out a craft essay (that they may or may not write). How would they argue their point? What evidence would they use?

What Might This Look Like?

DATE

craft thesis statement

- The author Anna Carey uses imagery to emphasize important scenes and people, create a vivid setting that engages the reader, and evoke feelings in the reader surrounding the main character and her situation.

- The author Anna Carey creates an engaging story that requires analysis and gives the reader an opportunity to hypothesize about what will happen next through foreshadowing.

- The author uses Juxtaposition between the first and second halves of the story to emphasize the difference in the societies, make it clear and shocking to the readers how much has changed in Jess's life (making us empathize with her), and offer a chance to do some reflection on the commentary surrounding technology and its place in society.

Annika crafts a rough thesis statement that strives to capture her connections between craft and purpose across the text.

Elizabet Acevedo uses repetition, strong lines and the structure of poetry to show us how X changes from a person hiding her true self to being the person she is.

A quick example of a working craft thesis

Providing Feedback

If your students say or demonstrate . . .	Coach them on . . .
I am having a hard time finding the technique or purpose that runs across the whole book.	Tallying up their notes: how many times did they see the author use ____? Going with their gut—taking the first thing that jumps into their mind and then checking to see if it's true
I can fill out the sentence frame but can't really discuss my thinking.	Looking for multiple examples from the text to discuss Making sure they understand the literary technique they are discussing and how it shows up in the text
I am able to name a craft thesis and discuss it.	Trying to explain not just what purpose the craft embodies but also how that technique achieves that purpose

Optional Tools

Online Resource 3.10: *Sentence Frames for Craft Theses*

These sentence frames can help students try out different ways to create a cohesive analysis of the craft in a text. Try a few different frames to see which one "clicks."

General: Technique → Purpose

________ (author) uses ________ (technique) to ________ (purpose).

Three Techniques → One Purpose

________ (author) uses ________ (technique), ________ (technique) ,

and ________ (technique) to ________ (purpose).

General: Purpose → Technique

________ (author) creates ________ (purpose) by ________ (technique).

Three Techniques → One Purpose

________ (author) uses ________ (technique), ________ (technique) ,

and ________ (technique) to ________ (purpose).

Three purposes → One technique

________ (author) uses ________ (technique), to ________ (purpose)

________ (purpose), and ________ (purpose).

Sentence Frames for Craft Theses (OR 3.10)

11. TRACK HOW CRAFT DEVELOPS THEME

THINKING ABOUT THE STRATEGY

If I am being honest, I kind of feel like you all are probably done now. Your kids have worked hard; they have figured out patterns and purpose in an author's use of literary techniques that they can discuss. If it were me, I would celebrate. I'd ask kids to reflect on how the messages and moves of the text connected to them, how much or how little they related to the text, how much they learned or need to learn.

And yet we might as well try to take that last fancy step, right?

In my work in classrooms, I see a desire for one more move. We crave a kind of analysis that discusses exactly how the literary techniques of a text develop the ideas in the story. There is in me as an ELA teacher an intangible desire to create a mini English major out of every kid in my class, and I see this same desire in many of the English teachers I work with.

So while I would recommend fighting this urge and taking the time to revel and reflect on our experience, I know that some among us (and, OK, even me, too, when I am particularly tempted) will want to take their students to that next level. In this lesson, we'll look at ways to do that.

But what is it exactly we want students to do? In *The Namesake*, it might look like taking my sense of the way Lahiri uses descriptive language to convey the physical comforts of culture and how the American dream is so much about materialism and then taking a theme in *The Namesake*, like "The American dream is a mirage," and trying to fit the two together: "By juxtaposing rich descriptions of food, clothing, and décor, Lahiri shows us that at its core, the American dream is just a desire for different (or more) stuff. Gogol rejects the materials of his family's culture but craves the new lists of meals and clothing and apartments of his birthplace; but by the end we see that these material things do not bring happiness, peace, or even belonging. The dream is a mirage."

To do this, we have to teach our students how to lay their analysis of the craft in a text on top of their understanding of theme. This does not come naturally, as many of us aren't quite sure what should connect the two. We can consider the relationship of craft and theme by looking at what aspects of the technique connect to which parts of the theme. In my example, I see that the way Lahiri's setting descriptions are elaborated upon with great, rich detail but don't wind up mattering all that much matches the part of the theme that asks, *What matters?* Aspect of craft equals long lists of setting descriptions. Aspect of theme equals the materialism of the American dream. Connection: the descriptions emphasize *things*. This turns out not to mean that much, compared with connection and love.

Or perhaps it is not the aspects of the craft and theme that will connect, but instead that how they work in the text matches how the theme works in life. For instance, in *Aristotle and Dante* I could say that Sáenz's use of casual "whatever" language for Ari has a journey in the novel—first it pushes people away, then it becomes what people like about him, and finally it becomes a flirtation that he can abandon. This matches the way the theme of Ari learning to let people in by being himself works—first he pushes people away, then he is himself but people like him, and finally he learns to push past his defenses without losing them entirely. The way the technique functions matches the way the theme is developed.

When we help students do this synthesis work, this labor of finding connections between complex ideas, we offer students the opportunity for epiphany. In my experience with doing this lesson with students, there are always groups of kids who at some point in the lesson look up as if struck by genius—they see it now! The way the author uses dashes is completely the way that they show us how change works in life—suddenly, with no warning.

While not all students will have these light-bulb experiences, offering these lessons as workouts to students each year increases the possibility that they will. After all, we don't want to offer our students only lessons we already know they will be successful with. We want to be sure to challenge, with support.

11. TRACK HOW CRAFT DEVELOPS THEME

TEACHING THE STRATEGY

Lesson Flow

This lesson challenges students to look for the ways that craft and theme connect.

One way to teach this lesson:

1. Introduce this lesson by discussing riddles. Show a few. Discuss how solving riddles requires people to synthesize, problem-solve, and develop greater persistence in thinking.
2. Share with students that today they will be trying to solve this literary riddle: How do the techniques an author uses connect to the development of a theme they are trying to convey?
3. Demonstrate some examples of this thinking (like my examples from the previous page or from essays on pop culture). Be sure to show at least one that is a good attempt but doesn't quite connect the threads.
4. Teach that when we are trying to connect craft to theme, it helps to consider what kind of connection they might have: Is there an aspect of the technique that matches an aspect of the theme? Or does the way the craft is used across the text match the way the idea is developed?
5. Ask students to practice writing to connect their thinking, perhaps using prompts or sentence frames.
6. Have students discuss their thinking with partners or groups, with a focus on trying to name what partners did well.

What Might This Look Like?

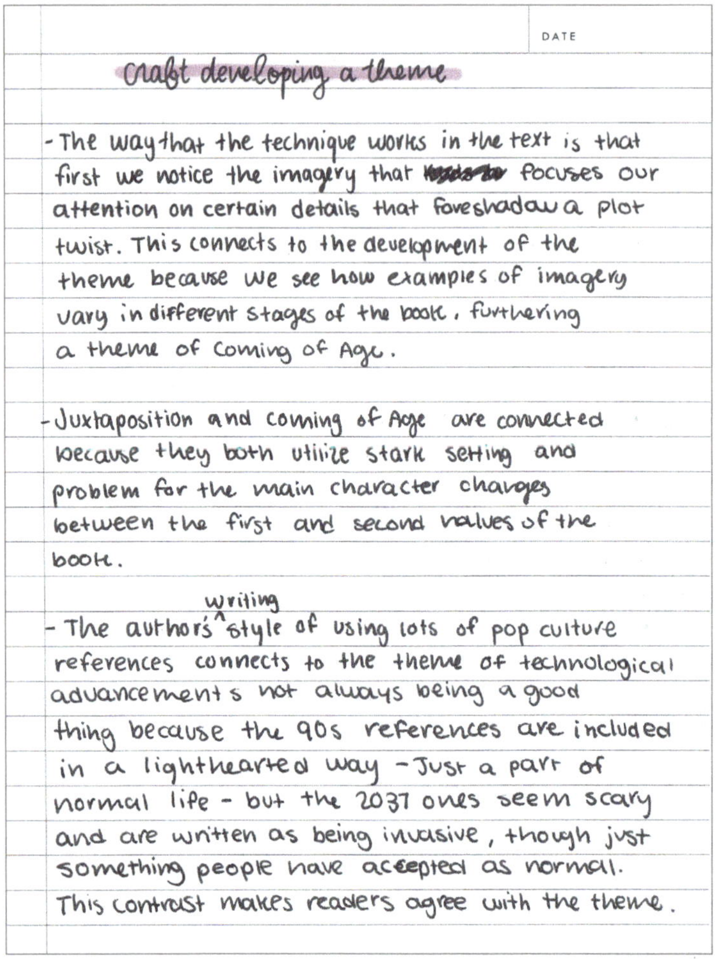

DATE

craft developing a theme

- The way that the technique works in the text is that first we notice the imagery that focuses our attention on certain details that foreshadow a plot twist. This connects to the development of the theme because we see how examples of imagery vary in different stages of the book, furthering a theme of Coming of Age.

- Juxtaposition and coming of Age are connected because they both utilize stark setting and problem for the main character changes between the first and second values of the book.

- The author's writing style of using lots of pop culture references connects to the theme of technological advancements not always being a good thing because the 90s references are included in a lighthearted way - Just a part of normal life - but the 2037 ones seem scary and are written as being invasive, though just something people have accepted as normal. This contrast makes readers agree with the theme.

Annika articulates how she thinks the craft in the text develops the themes.

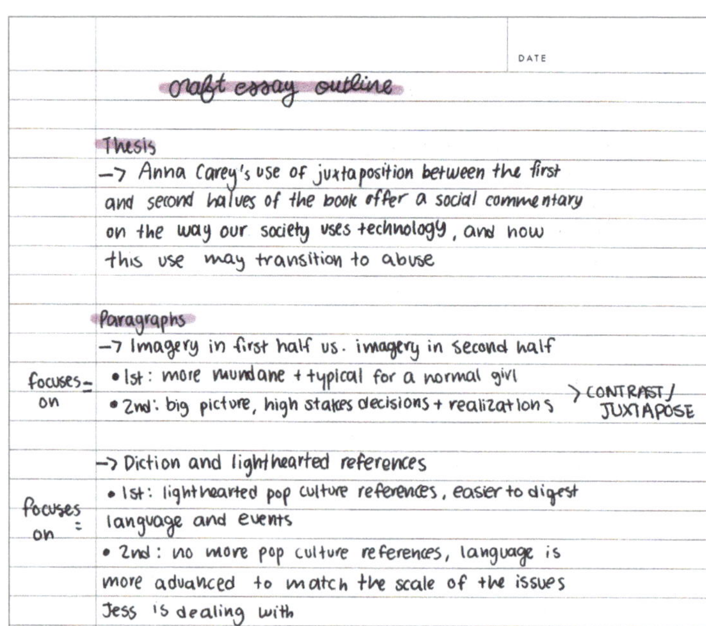

DATE

craft essay outline

Thesis

→ Anna Carey's use of juxtaposition between the first and second halves of the book offer a social commentary on the way our society uses technology, and how this use may transition to abuse

Paragraphs

→ Imagery in first half vs. imagery in second half

focuses on:
- 1st: more mundane + typical for a normal girl
- 2nd: big picture, high stakes decisions + realizations → CONTRAST/JUXTAPOSE

→ Diction and lighthearted references

focuses on:
- 1st: lighthearted pop culture references, easier to digest language and events
- 2nd: no more pop culture references, language is more advanced to match the scale of the issues Jess is dealing with

Annika outlines a possible essay for a craft thesis.

Providing Feedback

If your students say or demonstrate . . .	Coach them on . . .
I can't even get started with this!	Just focusing on what kind of connection there might be: Is there anything in common between the theme and craft? Or is there something similar about the way they work across the text?
I mean, I think I figured out the way they connect, but I am having trouble elaborating.	Trying to get the basics down: The way ________ is like the way ________ is because they both ________ . Freewriting to connect, using some thought prompts to help them: This is significant because ________ . The reason for this is ________ . On the other hand, this connects to ________ .
I am able to have a go at this.	Practicing on a few other techniques in the text and seeing if they can start to make these connections more easily now

Optional Tools

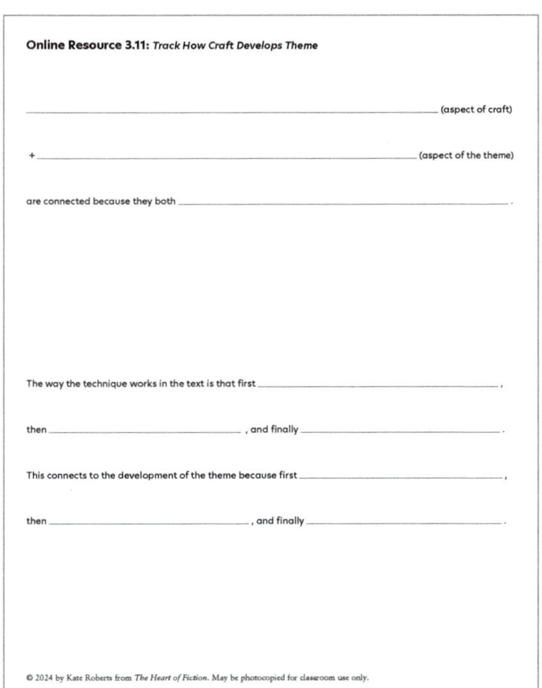

Online Resource 3.11: *Track How Craft Develops Theme*

________________________ (aspect of craft)

+ ________________________ (aspect of the theme)

are connected because they both ________________________ .

The way the technique works in the text is that first ________________________ ,

then ________________ , and finally ________________ .

This connects to the development of the theme because first ________________________ ,

then ________________ , and finally ________________ .

© 2024 by Kate Roberts from *The Heart of Fiction*. May be photocopied for classroom use only.

Track How Craft Develops Theme (OR 3.11)

What to Do When the Unit Is Done

As we get to the end of a unit on studying the ways that authors use their craft to evoke, reveal, and develop the humanity of their stories, something interesting happens: the work is kind of done.

Consider that when we study characterization, we may still have real work to do once the book is over—putting everything together, connecting the dots. When we study theme, some hard work happens once the book is done: we can begin forming the interpretation of the whole text. But with craft, we have done so much work already that by the time the book is done, we might even find ourselves in a loop—the techniques we see are recursive. The author keeps doing similar things with their writing, and we keep noticing. "Oh, there goes that Hawthorne again with his long, luxurious sentences!" [*nerdy chuckle*].

In a way, when the novel is done, we get to flex our intellectual muscles a bit. If we have followed the path of this book, students will have a series of techniques they see the author using for various purposes or effects. They will have identified some patterns, either in techniques used or purposes strived for, and they will have connected these moves and moments to larger ideas in the novel, particularly toward character or theme.

They have done the work. Now let them show off a bit.

Write an Essay

To be sure, if your students haven't written a literary essay in some time, this would not be the first one they should warm up with. Craft essays aren't easy to write, in the sense that the techniques an author uses are hard to make arguments around.

While your class will be ready to propose the moves and madness within the techniques found in the text, they may have a tougher time explaining how these writerly moves create the effects they do. This is English major stuff. That being said, proposing to your class that they try to write difficult analysis is not bad; in fact, it should be celebrated.

Celebrated. That's the word that matters here. If we ask students to write craft analyses, and we are aware of the parts of that work that are truly difficult, even for us, then it stands to reason that we should celebrate whatever effort our students put into the work. While it will be quite easy for them to propose a selection of techniques that serve a singular purpose, or conversely a purpose that is reached through a variety of techniques, it's likely that they will not have the experience and ability yet to truly unpack how exactly that simile creates an eerie effect. Applaud their efforts as you coach them toward coherence.

The other aspect of this work to celebrate, however, isn't what is maybe a little out of reach for your students but instead what is going to come very easily for them. Because at this point it should not be hard for students to form an argument around the author's craft. The trick is to decide if their thesis will center on the technique that has many purposes or the purpose that is achieved through many techniques. Students can go through their notes, creating an outline of sorts based on one of these structures, and by the end of a class period the majority of your kids will feel very proud of themselves. This is certainly something to celebrate, as it comes as the result of the hard work they have done across this text.

So, have them write some fancy craft essays at the end of a craft unit. Absolutely. But only if you are ready to celebrate what comes easy as the result of the work they have done and to celebrate the effort they make on the thing that they might not be fully ready for.

Synthesized Infographics

As mentioned earlier, by now your class has done a whole lot of work around noticing craft and inferring purpose. They have tracked patterns and considered connections. If an essay feels like it will take the wind out of your sails, perhaps students can strive to capture the web of technique and purpose across a text in a more visual, twenty-first-century way.

Asking students to create infographics that capture their thinking about the craft in the text allows them to synthesize what they have learned and to consider how best to teach what they have learned. It can also help infuse creativity and other modes of expression in our classrooms. While some may create tables and charts with thoughtful formatting, others will create infographics that are an expression of their analysis while also being a clever example of craft themselves, like the example in Figure 3.8.

Synthesizing infographics allows us to tie up all the loose threads of our thinking while giving us an opportunity to show our talents.

"Inspired by" Pieces

Another way we can come to a landing after the work in this reading unit is to offer up the sincerest form of flattery: imitation.

When I was in college, I loved the author Jeanette Winterson. I read all of her books, and when I wrote stories, I tried to write like her. I was not that good at it. But I tried. And in the process, I learned something about syntax and the power of rhythm in writing and how to open up a portal from your heart to the language you use. It was formative, even if my stories were just not that good.

When we come to the end of a craft study in reading, we can step back and try to write like the author. The easiest way to get this going is to ask students to choose a moment from their lives in the last year—ten minutes of their life—and write that story down to the best of their ability. Then, we can guide them to go back into that first draft and begin to layer in the moves that they saw their authors use. They can add as many layers as they like, they can rewrite every line, or they can adopt only the moves that spoke to them. In any case, as they hand in their craft vignettes, they should offer the first draft and the last, along with a quick reflection on what techniques they adopted and why.

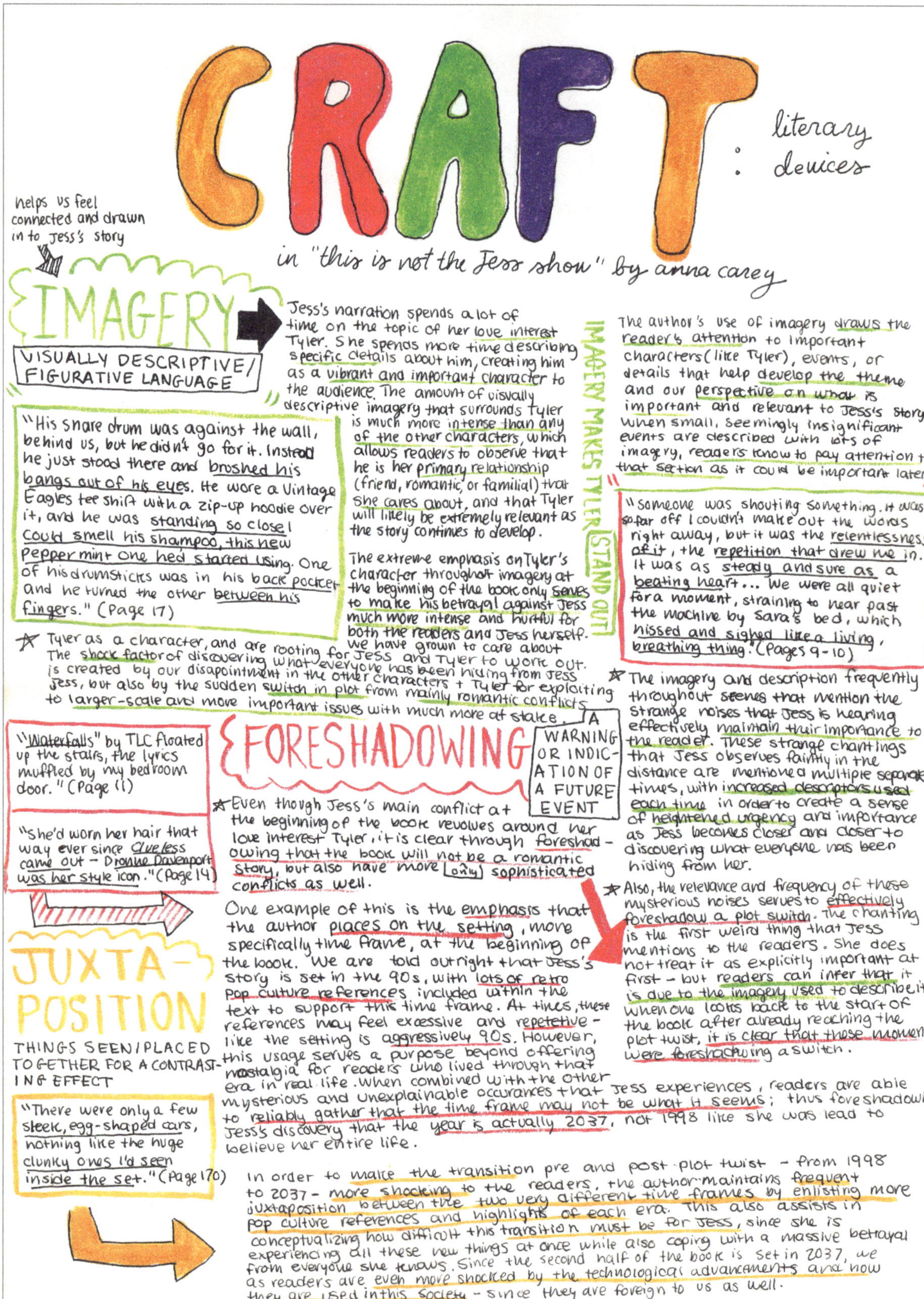

FIGURE 3.8: *Annika captures her thinking on craft visually.*

At the End of the Day

My wife has started gardening. She is working hard at it. More often than not she comes into the house glowing from sweat and work and soil. This spring, her efforts are starting to come together. Our yard is full of surprises.

To be honest, this happened last year too, but I wasn't really paying attention. Maggie tried to show me stuff that she was growing and I just kind of lightly noticed. "Oh, cool," I'd say and then move on to make dinner. But this year I have been paying more attention not just to what comes out of the ground but to what goes into it. The timing, the amount of sunlight, the care. I've been paying attention. And now I can see so much more. I see that weird purple flower that was maybe not going to make it because of the infernal rabbits, and because I know what went into that weird purple flower, I am authentically excited to see it bloom.

When we know the techniques of a thing we appreciate it more. It may not make sense at first to your students why you are pushing them to notice the rhythm and words and devices an author uses. It may feel removed from what they care about at first when they read: plot and character and maybe theme. But the glory of a craft study is that it teaches you to see things. Entire new palettes of color can emerge from a text just because we have become attuned to the work that went in. We start to . . . appreciate things more.

As John Green has said, "To fall in love with the world is not to overlook suffering. For me anyway, to fall in love with the world is merely to look up at the night sky and feel your mind swim before the beauty and the distance" (2020). Yet we cannot do this if we don't know what we are looking at. To teach students to appreciate the way a text is woven together with ideas and language is to teach them to fall in love with another piece of the world. As English teachers, or English language arts teachers, we cannot force this love, and we can't teach our students to love everything. But when we offer them the windows into craft, we give them one more thing to appreciate deeply. We give them one more way to adore.

Endnote

My sons are learning how to swim this summer. In their class, the instructor is helping them first get used to the feeling of water on their faces. Neither of my boys liked the feeling when they began. But they are working on it and doing really well. They can't swim yet. Not yet, though they are exactly where they need to be.

Putting your face in the water does not equal swimming. Strategies do not equal teaching.

Strategies are important. Like getting our faces in the water, they give us and our students something clear to practice with the hopes that engaging, interesting work will follow. Good ones demystify our teaching and create light-bulb moments for students. Great ones are responsive and change to fit the needs of the people using them. My sons are learning to put their faces in the water, and the strategies they are using, like wiping with a washcloth after each submersion, are making that work feel energizing and achievable even if it is difficult. Neither of my kids wanted to take a swimming class, but the strategies help them feel some success, and they are becoming more engaged with each dunk.

The washcloth thing is a big deal. It makes my boys feel comfortable with trying something that feels out of their depth. But the real work is in the other stuff: the attitude of the teacher (warm, funny, confident), the repetition of practice (every day for half an hour), the consistent sense of what comes next (floating, it turns out), the experience of it all (fun, fulfilling).

Perhaps it isn't the most business-savvy idea to minimize the importance of the book you just wrote in the last few pages. Nevertheless, when it comes to fostering all students to become more powerful and independent readers, watchers, listeners, thinkers, and citizens, strategies are the washcloth you use to dry your face as you are learning to get it wet. Important. Necessary. Impactful. But they aren't swimming. They aren't reading. They are just a part of it.

And yet they are such an important part. My youngest now begs for a bath each night so he can spend at least four thousand hours going underwater. He loves it. Two weeks ago, water on his face felt impossible and intolerable. Then he got some good strategies nestled in great learning conditions, and now he is a fish.

Certainly we can think about reading in similar ways? We can consider how the conditions of our classrooms nurture independence and growth, we can count on some clear, concrete strategies to support our students, and we can center purposeful practice and the creativity of analysis. We can teach.

This book is the washcloth, the ways to support kids in learning the skills they need to unlock texts more powerfully and independently. Let's learn how to teach these skills masterfully together, so that we can focus our energies on the stuff that matters most: the ideas we have, the connections we form, the sense of self we develop as we work on something and improve. Every single student in every single classroom deserves these things, and when skills stand in the way, when we can't quite get our faces wet, the power and joy of reading will always elude us. This book offers ways to get our faces in the water, ways to ensure our students feel ready and confident to take the next step.

Have fun, read well, and good luck.

Works Cited

Bishop, Rudine Sims. 1990. "Mirrors, Windows, and Sliding Glass Doors." *Perspectives: Choosing and Using Books for the Classroom* 6 (3): 3.

Bomer, Katherine. 2016. *The Journey Is Everything: Teaching Essays That Students Want to Write for People Who Want to Read Them*. Portsmouth, NH: Heinemann.

Calkins, Lucy, and TCRWP colleagues. 2017. *Units of Study for Teaching Reading, Grades 6–8*. Portsmouth, NH: Heinemann.

Cisneros, Sandra. 2004. *The House on Mango Street*. London: Bloomsbury.

Coates, Ta-Nehisi. 2015. *Between the World and Me*. New York: Spiegel and Grau.

Coppola, Shawna. 2019. *Writing, Redefined: Broadening Our Ideas of What It Means to Compose*. Portsmouth, NH: Stenhouse.

Cruz, M. Colleen. 2004. *Independent Writing: One Teacher—Thirty-two Needs, Topics, and Plans*. Portsmouth, NH: Heinemann.

Ebarvia, Tricia, Lorena Germán, Kim Parker, and Julia Torres. n.d. "What Is #Disrupt Texts?" #Disrupt Texts. https://disrupttexts.org/lets-get-to-work/.

Feigelson, Dan. 2014. *Reading Projects Reimagined: Student-Driven Conferences to Deepen Critical Thinking*. Portsmouth, NH: Heinemann.

Gonzales, Jennifer. 2018. "Frickin' Packets." *Cult of Pedagogy* (blog), March 26. https://www.cultofpedagogy.com/busysheets/.

Green, John. 2020. "The Anthropocene Reviewed, Reviewed." *The Anthropocene Reviewed*, August 27. Podcast, 24:39. Produced by WNYC Studios. https://www.wnycstudios.org/podcasts/anthropocene-reviewed/episodes/anthropocene-reviewed-john-green.

Hall, Michael. 2015. *Red*. New York: HarperCollins. https://www.michaelhallstudio.com/books/bk_red.html.

Hellman, Lillian. 1953. *The Children's Hour*. New York: Dramatists Play Service.

Hirsch, E. D. 2020. *How to Educate a Citizen*. New York: HarperCollins.

Johnson, Aeriale. 2020. "Teaching Compassion—Not Empathy—and Critical Reading." *School Library Journal*, August 24. https://www.slj.com/story/Teaching-Compassion-Not-Empathy-and-Critical-Reading-Opinion-literacy-libraries.

Kaku, Michio. 2011. "Michio Kaku: The Universe Is a Symphony of Vibrating Strings." May 30. YouTube video, 4:06. https://www.youtube.com/watch?v=fW6JFKgbAF43.

Kittle, Penny, and Kelly Gallagher. 2018. *180 Days: Two Teachers and the Quest to Engage and Empower Adolescents*. Portsmouth, NH: Heinemann.

Lahiri, Jhumpa. 20 04. *The Namesake*. Boston: Mariner Books.

Lee, Harper. 2006. *To Kill a Mockingbird*. New York: Harper Perennial Modern Classics.

Marcetti, Allison, and Rebekah O'Dell. 2018. *Beyond Literary Analysis: Teaching Students to Write with Passion and Authority About Any Text*. Portsmouth, NH: Heinemann.

Miller, Donalyn. 2015. "Pinterest Is Not Pedagogy." *Texas Library Journal* 91 (3): 101.

Morrison, Toni. 2007. *Beloved*. New York: Vintage Classics.

Roberts, Maggie Beattie, and Kristen Robbins Warren. 2016. "Thinking While Reading: The Beautiful Mess of Helping Adolescents Discover and Celebrate How Their Minds Work." *Voices from the Middle* 24 (2): 56–63.

Sáenz, Benjamin Alire. 2012. *Aristotle and Dante Discover the Secrets of the Universe*. New York: Simon & Schuster Books for Young Readers.

Saint-Exupéry, Antoine de. 2018. *The Little Prince*. Translated by Irene Testot-Ferry. Ware, UK: Wordsworth Editions.

Santman, Donna. 2007. "Interpretation and Critical Thinking." Talk given at the Teachers College Reading and Writing Project, Calendar Day, New York City.

For Product Safety Concerns and Information,
please contact our EU representative GPSR@taylorandfrancis.com
Taylor & Francis Verlag GmbH, Kaufingerstraße 24,
80331 München, Germany

Printed by Integrated Books International,
United States of America